THE
PEOPLING
L⊙NDON

FIFTEEN THOUSAND YEARS OF SETTLEMENT FROM OVERSEAS

Map of London's Boroughs

ENFIELD

BARNET

HARROW

HARINGEY

WALTHAM FOREST

REDBRIDGE

HAVERING

HILLINGDON

BRENT

CAMDEN

ISLINGTON

HACKNEY

BARKING & DAGENHAM

EALING

Kilburn

WESTMINSTER

Notting Hill

HAMMERSMITH & FULHAM

KENSINGTON & CHELSEA

Soho

St Giles

Clerkenwell

Spitalfields

TOWER HAMLETS

CITY

Whitechapel

Limehouse

NEWHAM

SOUTHWARK

GREENWICH

BEXLEY

Southall

Earl's Court

HOUNSLOW

RICHMOND UPON THAMES

WANDSWORTH

LAMBETH

Brixton

LEWISHAM

MERTON

KINGSTON UPON THAMES

SUTTON

CROYDON

BROMLEY

SCALE

0 1 2 3 4 5

MILES

THE
PEOPLING
L⊙NDON

FIFTEEN THOUSAND YEARS OF SETTLEMENT FROM OVERSEAS

Edited by Nick Merriman • Foreword by Colin Holmes

museum of LONDON

First published in Great Britain in 1993 by
The Museum of London
150 London Wall, London, EC2Y 5HN

Reprinted 1994

Distributed to the booktrade throughout the world by Reaktion Books Ltd,
1–5 Midford Place, Tottenham Court Road, London, W1P 9HH UK

British Library Cataloguing-in-Publication Data
A CIP catalogue record for this book is available from the British Library.

ISBN 0 904818 59 4

Set in Gill Sans and Albertus

Colour origination by World Print, Hong Kong

Printed and bound in Great Britain by
BPC Hazell Books Ltd
A member of
The British Printing Company Ltd

Contents

continued

PART III

Acknowledgements

The Peopling of London project was designed from the outset to benefit from the advice and experience of as wide a range of people and institutions as possible. We thank them all.

Grateful thanks are extended to the following benefactors: The Baring Foundation, Carlton Television, The Worshipful Company of Barbers, The Haberdashers' Company, The Worshipful Company of Grocers, The Worshipful Company of Woolmen, The Worshipful Company of Insurers, The Worshipful Company of Ironmongers, The Worshipful Company of Marketors, The Worshipful Company of Musicians, The Worshipful Company of Spectacle Makers, The Worshipful Company of Weavers and The Guild of Air Pilots and Navigators for sponsoring elements of the project, and to the following who lent material to *The Peopling of London* exhibition and provided valuable additional advice: John Arno; Bank of England; Black Cultural Archives, Brixton; Brian Farrow; British Library; British Museum; Col. Capadose; Julien Courtauld; Dutch Church Council; Executors of the Estate of the Late Countess Beauchamp; Finsbury Local History Library; Guildhall Library; India Office Library; Jewish Museum; Mrs E. Kimmins; Mrs K. Koziell; London Museum of Jewish Life; Mary Maguire; Jesús Martínez; Jack Miller; National Maritime Museum; National Museum of Labour History; National Portrait Gallery; Mrs P. O'Connell; Mr J. Pes; Tony Pilson; Public Record Office; Pyrford plc; Mrs E. Rosen; Royal Albert Memorial Museum, Exeter; Royal Pavilion Art Gallery and Museums, Brighton; St John's College, Cambridge; Suzanne Samson; Elma Sampson; Science Museum; Ian Smith; Southwark Library; Tower Hamlets Local History Library; Mrs Anna Tzelnicker; Victoria & Albert Museum; Wandsworth Local History Library.

The principal organisers of the project were Nick Merriman, Nichola Johnson, Sophia Pegers and Rozina Visram. However, almost everyone at the Museum of London has been involved in some way or another, and thanks go to them all, and to colleagues at MoLAS.

Thanks go to staff at other museums and institutions for their help: Rickie Burman, London Museum of Jewish Life; Edgar Samuel and Jennifer Marin, Jewish Museum; Finbarr Whooley, Grange Museum of Community History; Sue MacAlpine and Sarah Levitt, Gunnersbury Park Museum; Christine Johnstone, then of Hackney Museum; Rachel Hasted, then of Bruce Castle Museum; Angela Fussell, Croydon Museum; David Mander and staff, Hackney Archive Department; Richard Bowden and staff, Marylebone Library; Margaret Swarbrick, Victoria Library; Nichola Smith and staff, Southwark Local Studies Library; Richard A. Shaw, Wandsworth Local History Library; John A. Newman and staff, Minet Library, Lambeth; Howard Bloch and staff, Newham Local Studies Library; Chris Lloyd and Harry Watton, Tower Hamlets Local Studies and Archives; Jane Kimber and staff, Haringey Archives, Bruce Castle Museum; the staff of Lewisham Local Studies Library; Julian Watson, Greenwich Local History Library (Woodlands); David Withey, Vada Hunt and staff, Finsbury Local History Library; Andrea Cameron and staff, Hounslow Library; Caroline Hammond and staff, Chiswick Library; Malcolm Holmes, Camden Local Studies Library; Richard Knight, Holborn Local Studies Library; Marion Gooding and staff, Ealing Local Studies Library; Sam Walker and staff, Black Cultural Archives; the staff of the Greater London Record Office; the staff of the British Library at Bloomsbury and Colindale; Hildegard Mahoney, Photographer's Gallery; John Kirkham, Dr Barnardo's Photographic Department; David Webb, Bishopsgate Institute Library; Ralph Hyde, Sharon Tuff, Jo Wisdom and the staff of the Guildhall Library; the staff of the Royal Commonwealth Society Library; Tim Thomas and Penelope Tuson at the India Office Library; the staff of the Public Record Office; the staff of the Polish Cultural Centre; Abdul Hamid, Arab League Library; the staff of the Notting Dale Urban Studies Centre; Mr Ip, Westminster Reference Library.

The following individuals have also given a great deal of help: Ziggy Alexander, Audrey Dewjee, Peter Fryer, Jagdish Gundara, Chris Power, Ron Ramdin, Jeff Green, David Dabydeen, Terri Colpi, William Fishman, Reece Augustino, George Eugeniou, Mary Hickman, Alan O'Day, Ruth Silverstone, Amarjeet Chandan, Udyan Prasad, Jatinder Verma, Manick Govinda, Robert Perks, Abraham Lue, Mel Wright, Doc Rowe, the late Paddy Fahey, Haris Pellapaisiotis, Ravi Govindia, Tassaduq Ahmed, Parviz Zabihi, Zia Siraj, Bhadra Patel, Richard Allen, Rachel Warner, Annie Harris, Maggie Hewitt, Mary Fitzpatrick, Christine Hagan, Sylvia Collicott, Cass Breen, Seamus Taylor, Leslie and Connie Ho, Anna Tzelnicker and Philip Bernstein, Giuseppe and Marinetta Giacon, Shridhar Hari Gholap, Patricia Pons, Ernest Marke, Connie Mark, Derek Keene, Marika Sherwood, Hermione Harris, Stephen Bourne, Mrs Gwen Davies, Keith Cardwell, Ronald Goldstein, Philip Sions, Chris Parker, Sehri Saklatvala, John Charalambous.

Foreword

London has been an important centre for the settlement of immigrants and refugees throughout the period of recorded history. Immigrants, as well as migrants, have been pushed and pulled into the city by the magnet of economic forces. Refugees, for their part, have also been attracted to the city where they have secured a temporary or permanent shelter from the well-founded fears of persecution which haunted and pursued them in other countries. In practice, however, economic and political influences cannot be disentangled quite so easily; after all, society is an inter-connected totality. As a result, it is not always possible to draw a sharp demarcation line to separate immigrant from refugee. In all cases, however, we need to recognise the weight of interactive forces, in basic terms the influence of both push and pull pressures which led to movement across frontiers.

At specific times certain areas of London have revealed the influence of immigration at its strongest. Today, one might think of Brixton, but if this essay were being written in the late nineteenth century the areas of Whitechapel and Stepney would come to mind. Indeed, the East End has functioned as a point of immigration and initial settlement for many different groups at different times. The building which stands at the edge of Fournier Street and Brick Lane functions today as a mosque for the local Muslim population. In an earlier age it served as a synagogue for the ultra-Orthodox among the Jews who arrived in increasing numbers from Russian Poland during the late nineteenth century and up to the First World War. Even earlier, the building had been used as a church by the descendants of the Huguenots, the French Protestants who came to London in the sixteenth and seventeenth centuries to escape from the rigours of Catholic persecution in an absolutist state. That one building, therefore, symbolises the continuity of immigration. Not that the East End alone is a reminder of this process; in the West End, in Soho, a similar trend can be detected. The contemporary bustle of workers with, for example, Chinese, French, Cypriot or Italian roots, is an echo of Soho's earlier history.

A continual pattern of arrival can therefore be witnessed, and in some cases it has been mapped and recorded. Anglo-Jewish history needs to draw upon the experiences of Jews in London. Indeed, some scholars believe that this concentration has developed excessive proportions, obscuring as it sometimes does the Jewish communities in other major cities such as Leeds, Manchester and Glasgow. But if the Jews in the capital have been relatively well served by historians, the same cannot be said of other groups. Where is the history of the Spanish in London? There is little to bite upon, even by way of a foundation. And, in other cases, such as the Germans, on whom information is more plentiful, it tends to be scattered, and the synthesising hand which draws together these threads and knits them into a coherent historical whole has not been much in evidence. A wider implication follows from these observations on neglect. With the historical importance of London as a centre for immigrants and refugees, one might expect to find a history of that process, a study which melds together the diverse histories of the groups who have arrived from other lands. In fact, no such history exists. It is a shocking and surprising gap. At the same time its yawning absence underlines the fact that for many practising historians the history of immigration is a marginal territory to be visited perhaps in passing but which hardly warrants an exhaustive visit.

In its attempt to fill this gap *The Peopling of London* should be welcomed. Through its various contributions we become better informed about the range of groups who have come to Britain. We are reminded that, there is a long history of immigration into Britain; it has not been a post-war phenomenon. We are made more knowledgeable about various forms of racism which immigrants and refugees have encountered. We are also made aware of the varied contributions, economic, social and political, which these groups have made to the capital; such detail acts as a reminder of the wider role they have performed in the building of the nation.

In presenting such information, every effort is made to draw upon a wide range of evidence. Historians who restrict themselves exclusively to the printed source sell themselves short. We need to listen. And in *The Peopling of London* we can hear the voices of the newcomers. We need also to look around and witness the visual symbols of immigration. There is so much to see: hence, as the first essay shows, a walk along Blackstock Road in Finsbury Park reveals in a hundred-yard stretch 'an Irish pub, Indian newsagents, food shops and restaurant, a Greek-Cypriot delicatessen, a halal butcher, a variety of West Indian businesses, a West African restaurant with taxi service above, a Chinese take-away, a Lebanese flower shop, a Jewish-run ironmongers, an Italian restaurant and a Spanish-run off-licence'. All historians of immigration should use their boots.

The Peopling of London makes a contribution, to the history of immigration and, more generally, to the history of London. As a result, it is likely to be noticed in academic circles, but it is aimed at a wider audience and, in particular, it hopes to strike a chord within the communities whose experiences it helps to preserve. This identification will be further strengthened, by the exhibition which accompanies the book until mid-1994. Taken in tandem, the book and the exhibition might act as catalysts which stimulate an even more probing analysis of immigration into London, which asks why people uprooted themselves to come to the city, how they fared after their arrival, how they helped to influence the city through their continuing presence, and also how they were themselves changed in that process.

Professor Colin Holmes

Preface

This book, and the exhibition which it complements, are the first major public manifestations of a larger, long-running Museum of London project, aimed at reflecting the history of ethnic diversity in the capital. Several factors have prompted the Museum to undertake the project. One is the realisation that conventional histories, including the Museum's existing permanent galleries, do not reflect the important role played by settlers from overseas in the development of London. The result of this omission is that large numbers of Londoners do not see their own history in the Museum of London — an imbalance we hope we can begin to redress by mounting the exhibition and publishing this book. Another motive for producing both exhibition and book is to counter the assumption that London has experienced extensive immigration only since the end of the Second World War. It seems timely for the Museum to demonstrate that the city has had a cosmopolitan population from its inception; and that diversity is a natural and important element of London life rather than a recent 'problem'.

The project has seen the Museum reaching out to Londoners on a scale not previously attempted. In representing the history of different communities, we wanted to involve members of those communities themselves as much as possible. Extensive consultations were therefore held with community members and academics specialising in the history of different groups. As so much community history has not been written down, but resides in people's heads, over a hundred hours of tape recordings of personal testimony were made. One of the major ways in which interviewees were located was through the *Museum on the Move* campaign. A mobile trailer toured markets, community centres, supermarket car parks, and other venues that the Museum does not normally reach, with a display about *The Peopling of London* project, asking people to help by providing information. This exercise also led to many people lending personal memorabilia, such as passports and photographs, to the exhibition, which complemented material produced by an extensive review of the Museum's existing collections and a campaign of contemporary collecting and photography.

The opening of the exhibition on 16 November 1993 was the culmination of this first phase. It sets out an overview of the story of *The Peopling of London* as it is understood so far. It has been supplemented by a full programme of public events such as lectures, films, musical performances, storytelling and reminiscence workshops, designed to amplify some of the exhibition's themes. A particular feature has been 'focus weeks', where the Museum has opened its doors for particular communities to represent their history and culture in their own terms. A full programme for schools has been run, and a special *Peopling of London* resource pack produced for schools, with sponsorship from Carlton Television.

This book forms another major element in *The Peopling of London* project. We hope it will provide further information for those interested in the history of specific groups, and stand in its own right as a resource book for teachers, students and interested members of the public. Much of the information presented here has been drawn together for the first time from widely scattered material. In the hope of encouraging people to undertake further work on this important subject themselves, we have indicated some of the basic sources in an extensive bibliography and a guide to libraries, archives and museums in London that can provide further material.

The Peopling of London project does not stop here. The programme of contemporary collecting and oral history recording continues, and the *Museum on the Move* has become a permanent feature of the Museum's outreach programme. Longer-term projects include the incorporation in the Museum's permanent galleries of the previously neglected presence and contribution of overseas settlers to London's development, the development of a new gallery devoted to London since 1945 and the development of a space in which to mount displays on and by different community groups.

Reaching out to involve members of the public more closely in the Museum's work, and in the production of their own histories, is an exciting and challenging task. Mistakes are bound to be made on the way, since the book and the exhibition must inevitably be very provisional statements. Nevertheless, the Museum of London sees it as a vital part of the work of a modern museum. As well as being about objects, museums must also be about people, for it is people who make history.

Max Hebditch
Director of the Museum of London

PART I

The World in a City

Nick Merriman and Rozina Visram

Visitors to London in the 1990s are struck by the breadth of its cultural diversity. Today, Londoners come from all over the world, speak nearly 200 languages other than English[1] and practise all of the world's major religions. The 1991 census has shown that many London residents were either born overseas, or born in London but identify themselves as belonging to ethnic groups tracing their origins overseas (see Appendix 2: Table 1). Cultural diversity is, however, not new in London's history, and it is certainly not just a post-war phenomenon. Although a large proportion of London's population has always been drawn from the surrounding regions, there has also been a significant presence of settlers from overseas since the city's earliest development. London itself was founded by people from overseas and the Roman town was cosmopolitan from the outset. Since then, immigration from overseas has been a persistent theme in the city's history. As the contributions in this volume show, London's growth and development owes much to the skills and contributions of groups of people from near and afar. For the first millennium of its history, the city was fundamentally shaped by settlers from the Germanic lands, Scandinavia and Normandy. There were Irish and Jewish people in London from at least the twelfth century. Flemish, German, Italian and Spanish merchants settled in London from medieval times. The mid-sixteenth century saw Dutch, German and French Protestants living in the city, as well as many Black slave-servants.[2] The expansion of Britain's trade and the establishment of colonies in the seventeenth and eighteenth centuries brought new people to London. For instance, in 1709 an advertisement in the *Tatler* offered an 'Indian Boy' to be disposed of,[3] while there are references to the Chinese in Stepney by 1782.[4] The first arrivals from the American and Australasian continents — both native inhabitants — came to London in 1616 and 1792 respectively.

At the beginning of the nineteenth century, William Wordsworth noted that in the streets of London he could:

See among less distinguishable shapes,
The Italian, with his frame of images
Upon his head; with basket at his waist
The Jew; the stately and slow-moving Turk,
With freight of slippers piled beneath his arm!

...

The Swede, the Russian; from the genial south
The Frenchman and the Spaniard; from remote
America, the Hunter-Indian; Moors,
Malays, Lascars, the Tartar and Chinese,
And Negro ladies in white muslin gowns...[5]

while in 1867, *The Times* commented:

There is hardly such a thing as a pure Englishman in this island. In place of
the rather vulgarised and very inaccurate phrase, Anglo-Saxon, our national
denomination, to be strictly correct, would be a composite of a dozen
national titles.[6]

By the nineteenth century, then, London was already a cosmopolitan world city
with a history of cultural diversity stretching back to the Romans. Twentieth-
century immigration into London has simply continued this trend, and improved
communications have drawn populations from wider afield. In this introductory
chapter, we attempt to put the historical threads linking London's diverse
communities into context by looking at motives for migration, patterns of settlement and at the substantial contributions made by these communities to London.
We shall conclude by looking at the reactions of Londoners to newcomers over
the centuries, at the antipathy encountered by immigrants, and at how they have
responded. In the subsequent chapters of this volume we first examine the history
of those communities no longer 'visible' today, and then present a series of
personal views of the histories of communities still retaining their distinct identity.

Motivations for Settlement from Overseas

What has drawn people to London from overseas? To begin with, they came
principally as invaders seeking land, livelihood, wealth and power. Long before
London was founded, the Middle Thames Valley was a place for prehistoric settlers
to hunt and later, to farm. For the Romans, Britain was another source of slaves,
raw materials and luxuries for its vast empire, and London was developed
principally as a port to channel these goods southwards. To the Anglo-Saxons,
settlement of the area offered a chance to acquire farming land and develop a place
to trade, while to the Vikings, raids on London were part of an extensive campaign
of settlement and plunder. By invading England, William of Normandy managed to
control a territory many times the size of his native land.

Since then, immigration into London has been of a peaceful nature, its patterns
shaped by two fundamental factors: the geographic position of the immigrants'
country of origin and its historical ties with Britain. Southern England's physical
proximity to Scandinavia, Germany, the Low Countries and northern France has
inevitably drawn them into economic, political and cultural relationships which have

Tombstone of the Roman
soldier Lucius Pompeius
Licetus, who came from
Arretium (now Arezzo)
in Italy

4

led to movements of population. In periods when transport by boat was often easier than travel by land, in many ways they formed a single economic region, and it was from these countries that many of London's earliest overseas settlers were drawn. The presence of large numbers of craftworkers from the Low Countries in medieval London is just one example of how geographical proximity and long-term political and cultural relationships conjoined at specific times with demands for skills not readily available in London.[7] A climate for further cultural exchange was created by European-wide political alliances, particularly through the intermarriage of royal households. A glance at the history of the British monarchy shows the extent of these links. William I, William III and George I came from Normandy, Holland and Hanover respectively to claim the throne. Many monarchs married spouses from Europe: for example Henry II married Eleanor of Aquitaine, Mary Tudor married Philip II of Spain, Charles I married Henrietta Maria of France and Queen Victoria married Prince Albert of Saxe-Coburg-Gotha. All brought with them something of the culture of the continental courts, and encouraged overseas artists, craftworkers and financiers to take up residence in London.

Further afield, the historical relationship that developed between Britain and certain parts of the globe through trade, conquest and colonisation, explains the presence of people from those areas in London from the sixteenth century. British rule over the Indian subcontinent, part of the Caribbean archipelago, Hong Kong, Australia, New Zealand, Canada, parts of Africa, and Cyprus, conferred British citizenship upon their inhabitants. Later, as members of the Commonwealth, they were able freely to enter Britain until 1962. The consequences of the colonial relationship that Britain has had with these countries is simply summed up by a phrase often used by Black commentators: 'We are here because you were there.'

The motivations prompting people to leave their homelands in search of a new life in London have been complex, requiring an analysis of the economic, political and religious climate of their country of origin, as well as of the conditions and opportunities offered by London, and its reputation — at least in more recent times — as a liberal and cultural capital. On an individual level, the desire for adventure and a sense of freedom has prompted many to put down their roots in London.

Some people, however, have come to London involuntarily, brought as slaves or servants, from the Roman period onwards. In the seventeenth and eighteenth centuries many 'sugar barons' from the West Indies or 'nabobs' from India brought their slave-servants with them when returning to London. Samuel Pepys records, for example, that the Earl of Sandwich returned from abroad in 1662 with 'a little Turke and a negro' for his daughters, and 'many birds and other pretty noveltys'.[8]

Often adorned in extravagant finery, these servants acted as status symbols for their owners, and appear in aristocratic portraits of the period. Frequently they were sold once their owners no longer required them, as newspaper advertisements of the time demonstrate. Nor did involuntary immigration finish with the ending of slavery. British families returning from India also brought their servants

Proclamation for the relief of French Protestants, 1687. Many Huguenot refugees arrived in London destitute. Several successful appeals were made for funds to assist them

and ayahs, just as Filipino 'maids' today may have little choice about their migration to London and have frequently been made destitute once abandoned or mistreated by their employers.[9]

With only marginally more choice have been those who have settled in London after fleeing religious and political persecution, or even war, at home. The first such refugees were Protestants escaping persecution in the Low Countries, Germany and France in the mid-sixteenth century and again in the late seventeenth century, when large numbers of French Huguenots sought asylum in England.[10]

Smaller groups of French royalists found a temporary home in London following the revolution of 1789. Necessity drove many to more plebeian occupations to make ends meet. The Marquis de Montazet, for example, earned his living by cleaning windows, and Chevalier Anselme became a waiter; Chateaubriand, however, nearly starved.[11] On the other side of the same coin, London was also home to political revolutionaries unwelcome in their own countries, such as Giuseppe Mazzini, Sun Yat Sen and Karl Marx. Expelled from Prussia after the failure of the 1848 revolution, Marx lived first in Paris and then in London with his family from 1849 until his death in 1883. Studying in the British Museum Reading Room, he produced the bulk of his prodigious literary output during this period, including the monumental *Das Kapital*. He is buried in Highgate cemetery.

Seekers after freedom and liberty did not come only from Europe. After the American War of Independence, several thousand 'Empire Loyalists', including several hundred Blacks, escaped to London after the British withdrew.[12] Before the abolition of slavery in America, a number of Black slaves sought freedom in London. The plight and manner of escape of William and Ellen Craft in 1851 excited much interest at the time: Ellen had disguised herself as a White man, while William posed as 'his' slave.[13] They made their home in Hammersmith from 1857.

Jewish refugees have found a haven in London in two major periods, first between 1881 and 1914 following pogroms in Russian Poland and Rumania, and again in the late 1930s in the face of Nazi persecution in Germany and Central Europe.[14] Among the latter was the psychoanalyst Sigmund Freud, whose house in

Hampstead is now a museum. More recent, post-war, refugees have included Hungarians arriving in the aftermath of the 1956 uprising, British-passport-holding East African Asians forced out by policies of Africanisation, those escaping the regimes in Chile, Argentina and Iran, and people fleeing war, famine, persecution and social dislocation in the former Yugoslavia, Vietnam, Somalia and the Kurdish areas of Turkey, Iran and Iraq.

However, the overriding motivation for migration to London from abroad over the centuries has been economic, the result of a combination of factors 'pushing' people to emigrate from their countries of birth acting together with complementary factors 'pulling' them to London. Religious and political persecution, as noted above, has been one major factor impelling people to emigrate, while in the nineteenth and twentieth centuries the great expansion of London drew labour and capital from countries with limited opportunities for economic advancement among their growing populations. Thus, from the early nineteenth century, economic conditions prompted rural people from northern and central Italy to travel seasonally to London. Here they pursued occupations such as selling hot chestnuts and religious plaster figures or by performing street music.[15] The Irish were similarly propelled to London over a long period by the underdevelopment of the Irish economy, with major periods of migration being stimulated by the additional factors of heightened poverty and starvation.

Partition of India, following the end of British rule in 1947, created economic and social dislocation. Pressure on land drove many to London, where the post-war boom provided the chance of a new start. In the West Indies, there was large-scale unemployment after the Second World War, and the restrictions on immigration to the USA imposed by the McCarran-Walter Act of 1952 prompted thousands to turn towards Britain.

The principal complementary factors 'pulling' people to London over many hundreds of years have been the opportunity of employment and, frequently, the existence of schemes actively seeking much-needed labour and skill from abroad. The earliest example of such encouragement is the welcome extended to Flemish weavers by Edward III in order to use their skills to develop the cloth industry. Throughout the sixteenth and seventeenth centuries, foreign expertise was imported into Britain, where it was in advance of that available locally, stimulating the further development of crafts and industries from glass-making to dyeing.[16] Cromwell's willingness to allow Jews to resettle and openly practise their religion, in 1656, was in large measure prompted by his desire to use Jewish mercantile capital and commercial connections to promote English trade.[17] In the later nineteenth century, German Jewish financiers were drawn to London by Britain's more advanced industrial economy, while thousands of German clerks were attracted by higher wages and better working conditions, as well as to avoid military conscription.[18] Americans were drawn by business opportunities and close cultural ties.[19]

In more recent times, different overseas groups have been encouraged to settle in London to fill the need for wage labour in the reconstruction of British industry and infrastructure after the Second World War. First were the Poles, the majority of whom did not wish to return to a Communist country,[20] followed shortly afterwards by 'displaced persons' housed in camps all over Europe, and Italians recruited to work in industry and hospitals.[21] The scheme was seen, in the words of the Ministry of Labour, 'partly as an act of charity and partly to suit ourselves'. Levels of immigration from Ireland, predominantly among young unskilled and semi-skilled workers, were particularly high, reaching levels not seen since the nineteenth century. The 1951 census, for example, shows 237,257 Irish-born people living in London. They worked in the construction industry, the National Health Service and London Transport, attracted to the last two by recruitment drives in Ireland. With the need for labour still remaining acute, Britain turned to its other traditional source, its colonies and ex-colonies. In 1956 London Transport sent recruiting teams to Barbados and in 1966 to Trinidad and Jamaica. The British Hotels and Restaurants Association and various regional hospital boards followed suit, the latter encouraged by the then Health Minister, Enoch Powell, later to become a virulent campaigner against immigration.[22] There was a certain amount of active recruitment from the Indian subcontinent as well, as one manager explained: 'After the war there was ... a shortage of workers ... we tried employing continentals and refugees, but it didn't work out ... In 1950 [we] employed Indian workers.'[23] It is fair to say that, historically, whenever the economy has demanded it, immigrants have been encouraged and welcomed by those in power, even if, subsequently, different responses have come to the fore.

Patterns of Settlement

The journalist George Sims, writing in 1902, first coined the phrases 'China Town' and 'Little Italy' to describe the Chinese district around Limehouse in the East End, and the area of Italian settlement in Clerkenwell. However, it is worth remembering that, unlike other cities in Europe in previous centuries, or the USA and South Africa this century, there have never been laws defining areas of residence in London. The overall result has been that London does not have any areas that are *exclusively* occupied by immigrant groups. Instead, the availability of cheap housing, employment, ease of transport and the presence of compatriots have been some of the major determining factors in initial settlement patterns. Over the centuries, several parts of London have become associated with immigrant communities. Some bear few visible signs today of the groups that once lived there; others still play host to a variety of old-established groups and more recent incomers; while yet other areas develop into new community focal points as people move away from the inner city. The following is a brief examination of the influences of overseas groups that can be seen in some of these places today.

The area of London within the city walls has been fundamentally shaped by overseas settlers, although relatively little of their impact is now immediately visible. The walls themselves, and some of the principal roads, such as Aldersgate Street and Wood Street, were laid out by the Romans. A number of churches, including

The Royal Exchange, by Wenceslaus Hollar, 1668. The building provided a meeting place for London merchants and overseas traders

St Paul's, were founded by overseas clergy or benefactors from Anglo-Saxon times onwards.

From the medieval period, the city was host in particular to communities of 'aliens' involved in finance and trade. Some are commemorated by street names — Old Jewry and Lombard Street — while the influence of more recent settlers is seen in the names of city financial firms such as Minet, Cazenove and Rothschild. The Jewish community of the Readmission, which produced many of these financiers, is also commemorated by Jewry Street in the east of the city and by the Spanish and Portuguese Synagogue in Bevis Marks which has been in continuous use since its foundation in 1701. Even longer continuous use can be claimed by the Dutch Church, which still occupies the same site in Austin Friars that was granted to the community in 1550. Similar sites, located in 'liberties' in the precincts of former monasteries destroyed in the Dissolution such as Blackfriars and St Martin's, were particularly attractive to overseas settlers because they were able to practise their crafts there free from the jurisdiction of the city authorities.

Immigrant communities also tended to develop outside the city walls for the same reason: they were less subject to the interference of the guilds there, and accommodation tended to be cheaper. Once small enclaves had been established, they tended to become self-perpetuating through a process of chain migration as new arrivals settled near people they knew or with whom they had common bonds of language and culture. Southwark, London's first suburb, has long been associated with immigrant communities practising a variety of industrial occupations. Weavers Lane is a reminder of the Flemish weavers who lived in the area from the fourteenth century, while the adjacent Potters Fields indicates where Dutch potters brought new ceramic technologies to the South Bank in the late sixteenth century. Pottery production was just one of a wide range of industries practised in the sixteenth and seventeenth centuries by overseas workers in Southwark, which also included copper-smithing, glass-making, dyeing, and the manufacture of leather goods. In the late eighteenth century, the Irish began to settle in the area, working principally as casual labourers and domestic servants. The Irish population grew through the nineteenth century, firmly establishing a community whose presence can still be seen today in St George's Cathedral and in the many cultural organisations, pubs and clubs in Southwark.

The western suburb, particularly Soho, still retains a reputation for cosmopolitanism that stretches back to the Protestant refugees of the sixteenth century. Since then, it has had a particular association with French communities, a link enhanced by successive subsequent groups of refugees from the persecutions following the Revocation of the Edict of Nantes in 1685, from the revolution of 1789, and from the Commune of 1870. The French Protestant Church in Soho Square and the Catholic Notre Dame de France in Leicester Place are reminders of this presence, as are the numerous French restaurants and the French House pub.

Greek Street is a reminder that there was once a small Greek community in the area, served by an Orthodox church built in 1677 in St Giles. St Giles was also particularly associated with the Irish community from the seventeenth century. Today no trace remains of the notorious 'rookeries' they inhabited, although St Patrick's Church in nearby Soho Square, founded in 1792, is the oldest Catholic mission in England dedicated to the saint. Italians moved to Soho in the late nineteenth century and developed the particular association of the area with food and catering, still seen today in the numerous Italian cafés and restaurants and the long-established delicatessens on Old Compton Street. In the 1920s and 1930s, Cypriots found employment in the area, often in Italian-run businesses. Following the persecution and internment of many Italians during the Second World War, some Cypriots bought these businesses cheaply and opened their own cafés and restaurants around Charlotte Street. After the war the Chinese also established restaurants, supermarkets and herbal medicine shops, bringing a uniquely Oriental presence to the area (see colour plate 6). Today, with the more recent addition of Thai and Middle Eastern restaurants, and thronged with tourists, Soho retains a highly cosmopolitan atmosphere.

The eastern suburb of the city, too, has a long association with immigrant communities, beginning again with medieval Flemish weavers, expanding with Dutch and Walloon refugees in the mid-sixteenth century and greatly increasing with the Huguenot settlers of the late seventeenth century and Irish workers in the eighteenth. Some of the fine houses built by the Huguenot master weavers can still be seen around Spital Square and Fournier Street, although the humbler dwellings of the bulk of the population, the journeymen weavers and their families (both French and Irish) have long been demolished.

Nearby Whitechapel was one of the centres of the non-Jewish German population in the late eighteenth and nineteenth centuries. St George's Lutheran Church, built by them in 1763, still survives today in Little Alie Street.

Whitechapel was also home to the next major group of incomers, the eastern European Jews. The area is still home to around 4000 Jews, served by a few Jewish shops, bakers and restaurants — and of course synagogues — while the streets bear witness to a much larger presence in the past (see colour plate 6). The Heritage Centre in Princelet Street, for example, was once one of about 116 synagogues serving 120,000 Jews in the area. Brady Street Cemetery is the final resting place of many of them, including Nathan Meyer Rothschild, while the Old Sephardi Cemetery on the Mile End Road, founded in 1657, is the oldest surviving Jewish cemetery in the country.

Today the area is dominated by the Bengalis, whose ancestors first came as lascar sailors.[24] They have replaced the Jewish community as the leaders in the local garment industry, and like them have also developed a distinctive presence of their own with restaurants, shops and mosques, the largest of which is the East London Mosque on Whitechapel High Street, built in 1984.

The most telling symbol of the changing communities to which Spitalfields has played host is the Jamme Masjid on the corner of Fournier Street and Brick Lane (see colour plate 2). This building started life as a Huguenot church in 1744, fifty years later it became a Wesleyan chapel, then from 1898 to 1975 it housed the Spitalfields Great Synagogue, until it was sold and given a new lease of life by the Bengali community.

The docklands area also has associations with immigrant communities, due to a combination of location, job opportunities and availability of accommodation. For many years the area has hosted communities of sailors from China, India, Malaysia, Yemen, Somalia and West Africa. Of these a small Chinese presence still remains in Limehouse,[25] and former inhabitants are commemorated by the Chinese graves in the East London Cemetery in Plaistow. The Somali community in Tower Hamlets

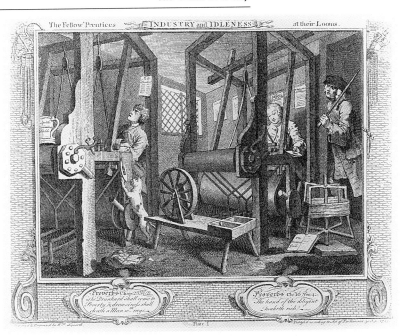

The Fellow 'Prentices at their Looms, by William Hogarth, 1747. The print shows a typical workshop in Spitalfields where many Huguenot weavers had settled

11

has been augmented in recent years by the arrival of refugees.[26] The presence of Norwegian, Swedish and Finnish seamen in the docks initially on the north side of the river, is today marked on the other side of the river in Rotherhithe, by their respective churches in Albion Street and Lower Road.

The strong South Asian presence in Southall (mainly of Sikhs from the Punjab) arose through a demand for labour for the expanding industries of west London. Tradition has it that the personnel officer of Woolf's rubber factory in the area, who had served as a police officer in the Punjab, recruited many Punjabis in the 1950s. From this small start, the Punjabi population grew through a process of chain migration, and Heathrow Airport provided jobs for women when families were reunited in the 1960s and 1970s. Today, temples, Indian businesses, sari shops, jewellers, food stores, record shops, restaurants, and cinemas showing Indian films, give Southall a strong Punjabi character.

Again the initial settlement patterns of the first post-war Jamaican settlers in the late 1940s arose from the search for employment. They were initially housed in Clapham, in former air-raid shelters. From here they were directed to the local labour exchanges and found accommodation in and around Brixton.[27] From such circumstances has developed today's notable Jamaican presence in the area. Settlers from the other Caribbean islands, separated by differences in dialect and culture, formed their own distinctive communities: Trinidadians and Barbadians in Notting Hill, Guyanese in Tottenham and Wood Green, and Monserratians in Finsbury Park.[28]

Many communities, having established a foothold in the London economy through working long hours in unsatisfactory conditions, have tended to move out of the initial area of settlement as business has prospered, leaving the way clear for the next group of newcomers to make their mark. This mobility has meant that many of today's communities have moved some distance from their original settlements, either establishing themselves in new centres, or spreading fairly evenly throughout the city.

The classic example of such migration within the capital has been that of the Jews. From the East End, there has been a move northwards in an arc stretching from Ilford in the east to Hendon in the west, as businesses have expanded and a move to the suburbs was prompted by a desire for improved housing and educational opportunities. Two areas particularly associated by the general public with the contemporary Jewish community are Stamford Hill, with its distinctive Hasidic community, and Golders Green, with its substantial middle-class Jewish population, Jewish cemetery and its large number of shops catering for a Jewish clientele.

Just as there is still a Jewish presence in the East End, a small but distinctive Italian community still exists around the historic 'Little Italy' in Clerkenwell, with its Italian church, cafés, delicatessens and community centre. However, Italians now live in all London boroughs, having followed opportunities to develop businesses and find better accommodation. The symbolism of the initial place of settlement is clearly important: a similar pattern has also been followed by the Greek-Cypriots.

Camden, with its Greek Orthodox Church of All Saints, opened in 1948, is still a focus for the community. However, the majority of Cypriots now reside in Hackney, Palmers Green, Islington and particularly in Haringey, whose Green Lanes area has a dense concentration of Cypriot shops and houses (see colour plate 6).[29] The Stoke Newington end of Green Lanes has a specifically Turkish-Cypriot enclave served by its own mosque on Stoke Newington Road. The Polish community, formerly concentrated around the wartime headquarters in Kensington, has similarly moved out to adjoining boroughs.

The spread of the Irish community throughout London from the initial concentration in St Giles is largely a reflection of the demands for labour linked to the expansion of London's industrial economy. By the nineteenth century, as well as being established in Southwark, the Irish had settled in Whitechapel, Finsbury, Marylebone, Wapping and Bermondsey, and then in Woolwich, Lewisham, Lambeth and Camden. Today, Kilburn has a particularly strong association with the Irish, which developed in the post-war period because of the high concentration of light industry and construction companies in the area. The Irish presence there, easily visible in its Catholic churches, Gaelic sports associations, pubs and clubs hosting Irish music, and the proliferation of Irish newspapers on sale, is such that the area has been nicknamed 'County Kilburn'.[30]

Although some areas of London are strongly associated with certain communities, there are no parts exclusively dominated by a single ethnic group. Indeed, the experience of most Londoners — in inner London at least — is one of a great diversity of communities at the local level. By way of example, we mention Blackstock Road in Finsbury Park, the local high street of one of the authors. Here, in a hundred yard stretch can be seen an Irish pub, Indian newsagents, food shops and restaurant, a Greek-Cypriot delicatessen, a halal butcher, a variety of West Indian businesses, a West African restaurant with taxi service above, a Chinese take-away, a Lebanese flower shop, a Jewish-run ironmongers, an Italian restaurant and a Spanish-run off-licence. It is this rich mix of cultures rubbing alongside one another that characterises contemporary London, and adds so much to its vitality.

The Contribution to London

To the vast contributions of immigrants through the centuries of London's development, we shall confine ourselves to but two, the economic and the cultural. However, in passing we must also note that in the field of religion and politics immigrants have had a highly significant influence, as several contributions to this volume demonstrate. The revival and continued flourishing of the Roman Catholic Church in London, for example, is in no small measure due to the presence of Irish, Italian and Polish communities professing that faith. In politics, the influence of immigrants has been seen in Chartism, the anti-slavery campaign, the trade unions and numerous other movements.[31]

In the absence of comprehensive statistics, it is very difficult to evaluate the precise impact of the economic contribution of overseas populations from the city's earliest development to the present. However, capital investment in industries and other businesses, the supply of much-needed labour, as well as the variety and number of economic activities undertaken by immigrant groups, are some visible measures of their contribution.

From the medieval period, the role of immigrants in finance is well known. In the seventeenth century, it was predominantly a group of Dutch, Huguenot and Jewish financiers, meeting around Jonathan's Coffee House in Change Alley — later to become the Stock Exchange — who developed the systems that were eventually to make the City of London the world's financial capital. When the Bank of England was founded in 1694, seven out of the twenty-four founder directors were Huguenot or Walloon. Sir John Houblon, the first governor, was also a Walloon. When the stability of the country was threatened by the Jacobite rebellion in 1745, over a third of the five hundred or so signatories to a loyal address presented to the King by city merchants, had Dutch, Huguenot or Sephardi names.

> With their extensive and influential international connections, their financial expertise and willingness to take risks, they contributed significantly to the creation of London as the world's monetary centre. What the seventeenth-century immigrants did for technology, the eighteenth-century immigrants did for public finance and the techniques of investment and speculation.[32]

During the Napoleonic Wars this role was continued by the Goldsmid brothers, Benjamin and Abraham, followed by Nathan Meyer Rothschild, who helped the

These medals were worn by sworn brokers on the Royal Exchange. The Jewish Lindo family were brokers continuously from the 17th to late 19th centuries

government raise the huge sums needed for the war, and came to dominate England's international money dealings.[33] In the late nineteenth century, German financiers such as the Schroeder family, Edgar Speyer and Ernest Cassel added their weight to the London scene.

It is in the fields of industry and commerce that immigrant groups have made their greatest impact. The vital contribution of overseas artisans to the development of crafts and industries in medieval and post-medieval times has frequently been described, and is covered in the next chapter. The Courtaulds are a particular example of a successful immigrant family who began as gold- and silversmiths and later moved into textiles, developing the internationally known firm of today. Many other famous household names were first set up by nineteenth-century overseas settlers, such as Louis Steigenberger, whose Hackney paint firm became Berger Paints (see colour plate 12). Other Germans brought expertise and labour in mechanical and electrical engineering, the manufacture of precision instruments, and chemical production through such firms as Siemens Brothers, and Siebe Gorman. Originally developed outside London, but later having a substantial presence in the city, were ICI, which arose from a firm founded by the German Ludwig Mond, and the retailers Burton and Marks & Spencer. In London itself, Gordon Selfridge instituted the American-style department store in 1909. The tradition of South Asian business activity also goes back to the nineteenth century, with Cama and Company, the first Parsi firm. Ignatius Sancho, with his grocery shop in eighteenth-century Westminster, is perhaps the pioneer Black entrepreneur. In the twentieth century the proliferation of the 'ethnic' business economy, especially in the food sector, is one of the most distinctive features of London's economic life. Many of the traditional corner shops and small newsagents would almost certainly have disappeared from London's streets if they had not mostly been taken over by South Asian families prepared to put in the hard work and long hours necessary to make them profitable (see colour plate 4).

However, it would be wrong to concentrate exclusively on stories of successful entrepreneurs. The great majority of immigrants have not been so distinguished, yet have contributed greatly to London's economic prosperity by their labour. The Irish played a notable role here in the heyday of the industrial revolution and Britain's maritime expansion. They provided an army of reserve labour which dug canals, and built the docks and railways (see colour plate 13). Later, 'McAlpine's Fusiliers' and employees of firms such as Murphy's and McNicholas laid roads, cleared slums and built many of London's housing developments. The embellishment of buildings with mosaics and the laying of asphalt were particular specialisms of some Italian firms. In the docks, the Irish were predominant among the labour force, particularly as stevedores.[34] Mention must also be made of the sailors of many nations who transported manufactured goods to the corners of the Empire and contributed 'to swell the tide of wealth poured upon our shores'.[35] During the Second World War, Chinese, African and South Asian sailors helped keep lines of communication open, enabling vital food supplies to reach London.

During the Second World War, immigrant labour kept industries going in London, while after the end of the war, as we have seen, people from Europe, the Caribbean and the Indian subcontinent were brought in as replacement labour to rebuild London's infrastructure and supply the needs of industry. These post-war settlers have kept many essential services running, such as the hospitals and transport systems. More recently, they have been joined by migrant workers from Spain, Morocco, Latin America and other 'Third World' countries who provide the essential service behind the scenes in hotels, restaurants and hospitals. In the medical field, overseas settlers have also made a marked contribution as doctors. The many Jewish, Asian and Black doctors working in the health service today are part of a long tradition of immigrant involvement in the field that can probably be traced back as far as the medieval period or even earlier.

One of the most immediately obvious ways in which London's cultural life has been transformed by the presence of overseas communities is in the area of food, from the humble oxtail soup introduced by the Huguenots to the now popular Indian snack, samosas. The Cockney slang 'nosh' itself derives from a Yiddish word meaning a tasty titbit. The effect of all this has been a revolution in the eating habits of Londoners.

The pioneers in the popularisation of Continental catering styles were the Italians, beginning in the nineteenth century with the introduction of ice-cream and coffee and chocolate shops. The influential Swiss-Italian Carlo Gatti seems to have introduced ice-cream to London for the first time in 1850 and went on to establish a new type of Continental-style café in London, aimed at families, with plush red seats, mirrors on the wall and orchestral music.[36] He represents one of a long line of Italian catering entrepreneurs that today finds its expression, for example, in the Forte business empire, which itself began in 1935 when Charles Forte set up in business at the Meadow Milk Bar in Regent Street. Another major enterprise with overseas beginnings started when César Ritz moved from Germany to manage the Savoy Hotel before opening his own hotel, the Ritz on Piccadilly, in 1906, where the cuisine was supervised by Auguste Escoffier.

However, it has been the post-war period, with the boom in eating out as a leisure activity, which has witnessed the greatest influence of overseas cuisine. The coffee-bar boom and the *trattorie* popularised by Mario Cassandro and Francesco Lugattola in the 1960s brought the now-familiar Anglo-Italian dishes of pizza, spaghetti, ravioli and lasagne to a wide clientele. Among the Chinese the initiative began in the East End with the entrepreneur Charlie Cheung before moving west to Soho[37] and then out into the suburbs, with the result that Chinese food, or at least its Westernised version, is now a familiar part of Londoners' diets. Chinese caterers have also taken over a large number of fish and chip shops. An even greater influence has been exercised by the development of Indian restaurants. From a handful, such as the Veeraswamy in Regent Street, in the pre-war period, Indian restaurants now form a part of every London high street, and curry is as accepted a form of food as fish and chips. Something of the role formerly played by fish and chip shops has also been taken over by Cypriot establishments purveying take-away kebabs and köfte. In Cypriot restaurants, these, and other dishes such as moussaka, kleftiko, taramosalata, hummous and tsatsiki, have been popularised since the 1940s and are now found all over London.

At the more exclusive end of the market, Italian, Greek, Jewish, French and Polish delicatessens have long been a source of fine specialist foods, while Jewish bakeries such as Grodzinski's have helped to bring beigels and other specialities to a wider audience.

Another major contribution has been in the broad field of the arts (see colour plate 3). Painting in particular has been deeply influenced by the talents of European court painters such as Lucas Hornebolte and Hans Holbein, as the next chapter shows. In the latter half of the sixteenth century, some of the most influential portrait painters were Guillim Scrots, Gerlach Flicke, and the De Critz and Gheeraerts families. The majority of the influential painters of the seventeenth century were either foreign-born, or born in London of foreign parents. Alongside such figures as Anthony van Dyck and Peter Lely we can mention Daniel Mytens, who received a grant of a house in St Martin's Lane in 1624 from James I, and was made 'king's painter' under Charles I, and Jan Wyck, who was married at the Dutch Church in Austin Friars and died at Mortlake in 1700. Topographical drawing and painting was similarly dominated by foreign artists, such as Claude de Jongh, who produced one of the earliest views of London Bridge, and Wenceslaus Hollar, particularly known for his views of the City after the Great Fire, who is buried at St Margaret's Church, Westminster. Westminster was also home to two later topographical artists, Leonard Knyff and Johannes Kip. In the eighteenth century overseas-born artists were also prominent. Johann Zoffany, born in Regensburg, became a master of the theatrical portrait and the conversation piece after beginning painting clock-faces shortly after he settled in London in a garret in Drury Lane in 1758. In the later part of the eighteenth century, the work of Angelica Kauffman was popularised through the engravings of Francesco Bartolozzi.

In the succeeding century the names of the Swiss-born painter Henry Fuseli, the Dutch-born Lawrence Alma-Tadema and Dante Gabriel Rossetti, son of an Italian political exile, particularly stand out. This period also sees American painters settling in London, such as J. A. M. Whistler, whose studio in Tite Street, Chelsea, was later taken over by John Singer Sargent. Straddling the nineteenth and twentieth centuries is Walter Sickert (1860–1942). A member of the Camden Town Group and famous for his scenes of theatrical and domestic life in London, he was born in Munich, the son of a Danish artist and his Anglo-Irish wife.

In this century, second- and third-generation members of immigrant families such as Mark Gertler, David Bomberg and Lucian Freud have depicted London, alongside a new generation of Black and Asian artists such as the late Aubrey Williams, who have been creating a distinctive Black British art.

In sculpture, too, artists born overseas or with roots abroad, have made their contribution, from Pietro Torrigiano, who was employed by Henry VII on the building of his future tomb, to Eduardo Paolozzi, who is particularly well-known for his mosaic work which decorates Tottenham Court Road Underground station.

Over the centuries, London has recognised the talents of many overseas writers now accepted into the canon of English literature. A good number of these, such as Jonathan Swift, Oliver Goldsmith, Richard Brinsley Sheridan, Oscar Wilde, W. B. Yeats and George Bernard Shaw, were born in Ireland but spent significant periods of their lives settled in London. The American-born poet T. S. Eliot also lived in London, working as a teacher at Highgate Junior School, and then as a clerk at Lloyd's Bank between 1917 and 1925 while he worked on his poems such as *The Wasteland*, encouraged by fellow exile Ezra Pound. Before the Second World War, another influential member of the poetry circle was J. M. Tambimuttu, an Indian from Sri Lanka, founder-editor of *Poetry London*. They have been joined by a generation of post-war writers who reflect the cosmopolitanism of the London literary tradition. Among the many names we might select Simi Bedford, Merle Collins, Kazuo Ishiguro, Hanif Kureishi, Doris Lessing, Timothy Mo, Caryl Philips, Salman Rushdie, Samuel Selvon and Arnold Wesker, as representative of this diversity. Publishing has also had its fair share of immigrants, including Krishna Menon, who began the Penguin/Pelican imprint with Allen Lane, Paul Hamlyn, a child refugee from Nazism, Carmen Callil of Virago Books (and until recently Managing and Publishing Director of Chatto and Windus), and Naim Atallah, Palestinian owner of Quartet Books.

In the performing arts, the immigrant contribution in London has been equally visible. In music, pre-eminent in the eighteenth century was George Frederick Handel, who settled permanently in London in 1716 until his death in 1759. His influence led to a succession of foreign composers and performers coming to London, some for a short while, other making London their home for a certain period. Among the former we may count Joseph Haydn, who came to London for eighteen months between 1791 and 1792 after a commission to write and conduct several new scores at a series of concerts; among the latter are Johan Christian Bach ('the English Bach'), who became composer to the King's Theatre in London in 1762, and lived in England for twenty years. A good proportion of musical instrument-makers in London in this period were also from overseas, such as the Italian, Clementi, who ran an early music business making pianofortes andcomposing music for the new instrument. Among later classical composers withimmigrant ancestry were Gustav Holst, born in England of Latvian parents, who lived in London from 1893 and died there in 1934, and the Black composer Samuel Coleridge-Taylor, who was born in Holborn in 1875 and lived most of his life in Croydon.

An emphasis on the classical should not lead us to overlook the immigrant contribution to the popular-musical tradition, upheld in the nineteenth century by German street bands, Italian hurdy-gurdy and barrel-organ players, and Black, Indian and Irish street singers.[38] In the field of popular music, London has led the way in

Bust of the composer George Frederick Handel who lived in London for 43 years until his death in 1759

the post-war period, absorbing influences from the USA, Africa and Asia, and synthesising them into new forms as in the past with jazz and 'negro' spirituals. The Black community has for long produced some of the most innovative developments, from the Trinidadian steel bands of the 1950s to the ragga sounds of today. Young Black musicians in London have at various times been ahead of those in the Caribbean in developing reggae, particularly in the 1980s when London produced performers such as Aswad, Smiley Culture, and the dub poet Linton Kwesi Johnson. More recently, the mantle has been assumed by innovators in soul music such as Soul II Soul. Young Indian musicians have fused disco and traditional Indian music into a unique *bhangra* dance music popular in clubs. Today, London is host to a kaleidoscope of musical styles collectively grouped under the term 'world music'. These can be as diverse as salsa and lambada from Latin America, soca from Trinidad, juju music from Nigeria, high-life from Ghana, soukous from Zaire, traditional Chinese music, and Irish folk music.

The stage is another area where settlers from overseas have excelled in London. David Garrick, grandson of Huguenot refugees, was in the forefront of this tradition, which was continued in later years by Laurence Olivier, also a descendant of Huguenots. The visiting American actor Ira Aldridge blazed a trail as a Black tragedian in the first half of the nineteenth century, to be followed almost a century later by Paul Robeson, who lived in London between 1928 and 1939. Other London-based actors, both on stage and screen, who have overseas ancestry include Peter Ustinov, Dirk Bogarde, John Gielgud, David Yip, Rula Lenska, Peter Finch, Zia Moyeddin and Roshan Seth. Less well-known perhaps has been their contribution behind the camera, through people such as the Hungarians Alexander, Vincent and Zoltan Korda, and Emeric Pressburger, who were instrumental in shaping the London film industry. New talent is supplied by many 'ethnic' film companies today, such as the Black Audio Film Collective.

London has also seen a vibrant Jewish entertainment tradition from the performers in the Yiddish theatre, to impresarios such as Bernard Delfont and Lew Grade, who have branched out into all forms of popular entertainment. Jewish comedians, from Bud Flanagan (real name Chaim Weintraub) to Marty Feldman, have also been particularly successful. We should not forget, either, Britain's most famous clown, the London-born Italian Joey Grimaldi, who is today commemorated by Grimaldi Park on the site of his burial place in Pentonville Road.

Finally, a major contribution has been made by London's overseas communities to England's sporting achievement. In the late eighteenth and early nineteenth centuries, boxing was one way for poor immigrants to climb the ladder to rapid success. The Sephardi Jew, Daniel Mendoza, was one of the most famous pugilists in the 1780s and 1790s, and his mantle was taken on by another Jew, Sam Elias (Dutch Sam) in the early nineteenth century alongside Irish boxers, such as Peter Corcoran and Michael Ryan and 'Sir' Dan Donnelly. The Black fighters Bill Richmond, his son 'Young Richmond' and Tom Molineaux, all achieved distinction on the London boxing scene at the beginning of the nineteenth century, a tradition continued by such boxers as Frank Bruno and Nigel Benn today.[39] At the end of the nineteenth century Prince Ranjitsinhji was the first Indian to play cricket for the English national team, beginning a process which has now led to over half of a recent Test team comprising people with overseas ancestry, and people of African-Caribbean and South Asian descent regularly representing the nation at athletics, soccer and a number of other sports.

And so through the ages overseas settlers have brought with them their rich and varied cultures, elements of which have been bestowed upon their adopted city for its enrichment. As we shall see, however, their reception by other Londoners has not always been equally generous.

A Liberal Tradition?

Londoners are proud of the city's — and Britain's — tradition of offering asylum to the oppressed of all nations. Samuel Smiles called it 'the world's asylum, the refuge of the persecuted of all lands ... one of the most composite populations found in the world'.[40] It has been generally felt that, in theory at least, Britain prides itself on the strength of its toleration, seeing hostility as the monopoly of others.[41] This was reflected in the 'open-door' policy on immigration operated until 1905, which allowed refugees from many lands to find a home in London. As we have seen, this also allowed prominent political exiles to settle in London. It is noteworthy too that this apparent liberalism drew people such as Jomo Kenyatta, Ras Makonen, George Padmore and C. L. R. James, who became influential figures in the dismantling of Britain's colonial rule.

Evidence also suggests that many newcomers found a better reception here than in other countries. Cecil Roth, a major historian of the Jewish presence in England, for example, declared 'there was probably no country in Europe in which the Jews received better treatment than England.'[42]

However, 'better treatment' is a relative term, and an examination of the reception accorded to immigrant communities over the last millennium shows that at most periods, the indifference of the majority of Londoners could easily be translated into overt hostility.

As early as 959, King Edgar was criticised for inviting people with 'evil foreign customs' to England.[43] The persecution of the Jews in the Middle Ages is well documented,[44] but they were not alone in suffering the hostility of the general population. The mid-thirteenth-century Waverley Chronicle states bitterly that 'numerous foreigners of various tongues have so increased over the years and are so richly endowed with rents, lands, vills and other benefits that they hold the English in contempt as inferiors'.[45] In the Peasants Revolt of 1381, industrial rivalry drove the rebels to massacre as many Flemings as they could find.[46] Concerns about employment surfaced again in 1450, when petitions complained to the King that the land was so overrun with Frenchmen, Picards, Flemings, Spaniards, Scots and Lombards 'that your lyge pepyll Englisshemen, cannot imagen nor tell whereto, nor to what occupacion, that they shall use or put their children to lern or occupye'.[47]

CONSIDERATIONS
UPON THE
Mischiefs that may arise
From Granting too much Indulgence
To FOREIGNERS.

Occasioned by the late
Election of Broadstreet Ward,
WITH
Mr. *ADDISON*'s Opinion of the *FRENCH*,
and their innate Hatred to the *ENGLISH*.
And an EXTRACT of Sir *John Knight's* SPEECH
in Parliament against F O R E I G N E R S.

Anti-French pamphlet, 1735. Among other things it complains that the French are extremely enterprising and industrious and might take over 'all the profitable Branches of Trade'

Even the Huguenots, praised by some for their 'virtue, travail, faith and patience', were deplored by others as 'the very offal of the earth', who would 'rob us of our religion too'.[48] The Irish have suffered from a long history of negative stereotyping, reflecting Ireland's historical relationship with Britain, the reduced circumstances in which Irish immigrants found themselves, and the cultural differences between the Irish and the English, particularly over religious matters. The latter came to a head during the Gordon Riots of 1780, provoked when Parliament lifted some restrictions under which Catholics had to live, which led to attacks on Irish people and property in London.

The British Union of Fascists, under the leadership of Oswald Mosley was violently anti-Semitic. The repugnance felt by most Londoners towards them was shown on 4 October 1936 when 100,000 Londoners prevented Fascists from marching through the Jewish East End

Jewish stereotyping has been a staple part of English visual arts and literature from Shylock to Fagin and beyond. The influx of Eastern European Jews in the late nineteenth century also brought extreme anti-Semitism to the fore, being described as an 'alien immigration plague' of 'semitic sewage'.[49] In the same year as this description was published, 1901, the British Brothers' League was founded as an alliance of East End workers and Tory MPs aimed at halting Jewish immigration. Public concern articulated by these developments resulted in the 1905 Aliens Act, the first of the major legislative controls on immigration. Anti-Semitism resurfaced again in the 1930s with Oswald Mosley's British Union of Fascists, when an effective public response was co-ordinated against them.

Xenophobia, racial prejudice and violence has also been the experience of many other groups in London, notably the Black, Chinese and South Asian communities.

The owner is a British Subject

Door lintel from Tolmers Square, Euston. During the First World War, some Londoners of German descent attempted to protect their homes and businesses from attack by such signs

Anti-German feeling in the First World War was encouraged by books such as these

GERMAN SPIES
IN ENGLAND
WILLIAM LE QUEUX

A Startling Exposure
THE GERMAN SPY SYSTEM

The Methods of Spies
HOW THEY HAVE BEEN OFFICIALLY PROTECTED

Astonishing Facts
NEVER BEFORE MADE PUBLIC

Outspoken Revelations
OF VITAL INTEREST TO EVERYONE

PRICE ONE SHILLING

The Chinese in Limehouse were frequently seen as an unwelcome alien presence, misunderstood by a population influenced by lurid press stories of opium-smoking, the white-slave trade, and Oriental gangsters.[50] Some of the most extreme treatment, however, was meted out on the German community in Tower Hamlets, Newham and Hackney during the First World War when they came under physical attack by a populace equating them with 'the enemy alien'.[51] London-born members of the German community were interned in both world wars, along with Italians in the Second. Anti-Black sentiment has also led to violence, notably in Canning Town in 1919 when there were race riots in many British cities, which also led to attacks on the Chinese population in Poplar.[52]

After the Second World War, responses have focused on race issues. It was the 'coloured' settlers who elicited hostile responses ranging from 'No Coloureds' signs on boarding houses, to outright violence. As early as 1949, for example, following several nights of antagonism, a thousand Whites besieged a hostel in Deptford where Blacks were staying; nine years later the Notting Hill area witnessed further acts of violence against Black people. In the 1960s, White Residents Associations in places such as Southall campaigned against immigrants moving into their areas, and in the East End a skinhead subculture developed and carried out racial attacks on Pakistani settlers. In 1967 the National Front was launched, while a year later two approaches to the perceived problem were presented by Enoch Powell in his so-called 'rivers of blood' speech, and by the Race Relations Act, which attempted to provide ethnic minorities with some measure of protection from discrimination in employment, housing and other services. The Greater London Council also introduced a wide range of initiatives to combat racism, before its abolition in 1986. Despite the good intention of such moves, the general experience of members of London's ethnic minorities can be of exclusion and marginalisation in many areas of life, and racial violence is still common.

What causes such hostile responses is too complex a question to tackle in a general introduction of this kind. Economic factors, religious and cultural differences, a history of colonial exploitation, with its pseudo-scientific racism, sexual jealousy and nationalism, are all ingredients. Among these, however, some have suggested that a persistent fundamental influence has been 'the perception of immigrants and refugees as an immediate competitive threat for society's scarce resources'.[53] The political consequences of these hostile responses have been manifest in a long history of official control of immigrant populations.

In the medieval period, aliens, that is to say 'one born in a strange country, under the obedience of a strange prince or country',[54] could travel to London without check or interference, but had to submit to certain regulations once they had arrived. Under Edward I, alien merchants in London were obliged to reside with English 'hosts', and a special tax, or subsidy, was levied on aliens from all walks of life.

From time to time, monarchs invoked acts to expel foreigners, often unsuccessfully: the Jews in 1290, Italian merchants in 1456, all Frenchmen not denizens in 1544, all 'blackmoores' in 1596 and all 'Irish beggars' in 1629. Throughout the eighteenth and early nineteenth centuries legislation existed to expel foreigners for the sake of the 'peace and tranquillity of the realm', and the sanction of deportation still exists.[55] The first limited checks on unrestricted entry into the country, however, did not begin until the French Wars of 1793–1815.[56] In 1836, the Registration of Aliens Act specified that the master of every ship coming to England from abroad had to submit a list of the aliens he was carrying, but this was not stringently enforced. As we have seen, the influx of Eastern European Jews resulted in the Aliens Act of 1905, the first piece of legislation requiring people to submit to examination before entering the country. This Act laid the basis for future legal control over immigration, and was further reinforced by the Aliens Restriction Act of 1914, passed on the first day of the First World War amid scares about German spies. The requirement of this Act, that aliens must register with the police, remains in force today. The 1919 Aliens Act, which remained in force until 1971, made entry

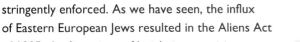

Anti-racist literature (1970s–1990s)

Anti-Nazi demonstration in Curtain Road, 20 August 1978

at the discretion of an immigration officer, restricted the employment of aliens, and gave the Home Secretary powers of deportation. In 1914 the British Nationality and Status of Aliens Act conferred the status of British subject to all inhabitants of the British Empire; the 1948 British Nationality Act reinforced this principle. However, as with the Jews at the turn of the century, concern arose over Black and Asian Commonwealth citizens who came in response to the post-war labour gap. This culminated in the Commonwealth Immigrants Act of 1962, which introduced a system of employment vouchers, in effect controlling immigration from the 'New Commonwealth'.[57]

This Act brought an end to the liberal, open-door policy on the immigration of Commonwealth citizens. The door has since closed even tighter, with a succession of legislative measures. The 1968 Act, passed in response to the immigration of Asians expelled from Kenya, restricted entry to UK passport-holders who had a parent or grandparent born in Britain.[58] The 1971 Immigration Act further divided immigrants into 'patrials' and 'non-patrials'. 'Patrials' — free from immigration controls — were people who could trace their citizenship to British parents or grandparents (ie the overwhelming majority are White), while non-patrials, who are mostly Black or Asian, no longer had an automatic right of residence in the UK. The 1981 British Nationality Act conferred the status of Overseas Citizens on non-patrial UK citizens, a status they cannot pass on to their children. In the words of a Runnymede Trust report, this denies them any legal claim to live anywhere in the world.[59]

From the foregoing it could be concluded that Britain's liberal tradition — if it exists at all — is only a relative one. Tolerance of ethnic communities has tended to be a thin veneer covering far from liberal attitudes, both at the official and popular level.

Nevertheless, there has also been a long history of struggle against hostility and prejudice, both from the communities themselves as well as sympathisers from the wider public. The struggle for emancipation from slavery is one such case. It is now recognised that slaves set themselves free by running away and establishing a flourishing free Black community, but that they used the 1772 Mansfield Judgment[60] to aid their emancipation, and were helped by philanthropists such as Granville Sharp and by Black abolitionists such as Olaudah Equiano, Ottobah Cugoano and Robert Wedderburn.[61] The removal of the religious 'disabilities' which prevented Jews from participating fully in economic and civic life was similarly gradually achieved through a combination of the efforts of the Jewish community and sympathetic Christians influenced by the general mood of religious tolerance of the nineteenth century.[62]

In the twentieth century, a number of organisations have emerged which have attempted to improve the position and opportunities of ethnic minorities in London and the rest of the country. Some have looked for support exclusively within their own community, while others, such as the League of Coloured Peoples, formed in 1931 by Harold Moody, have been deliberately multi-racial and sought a broad can-

vas of support for change. The ready availability of support among the general
population for immigrant communities under threat from extremism was perhaps
most poignantly demonstrated on 4 October 1936, when 100,000 ordinary
Londoners, both Jewish and non-Jewish, came together under the Spanish
Republican slogan 'They shall not pass', to prevent 2500 members of the British
Union of Fascists marching down Cable Street and into the Jewish East End. The
tradition of active involvement in the struggle against racial prejudice has continued
in the post-war period. In the 1960s and 1970s Black and Asian people mobilised
themselves into their own support organisations such as the Black People's Alliance
(founded 1968) as an expression of a developing pride in their identity. In 1969, the
BPA led the first Black Power March on Downing Street to protest against immigration controls.[63] In the 1970s and 1980s the emergence of an active Black voice
in the campaign against discrimination has been assisted by new broad alliances such
as the Anti-Nazi League and the Anti-Racist Alliance, which have helped mobilise a
broad spectrum of support among the general population, through campaigns such
as 'Rock Against Racism'.

Londoners All

The long history of overseas immigration into London shows that the city's inhabitants can come from a great diversity of backgrounds, and that most Londoners
of today could ultimately find ancestors who have come from overseas. Post-war
immigration is simply one part of a centuries-old historical process which has also
seen, on the other side of the coin, Britain being a net exporter of population over
the last hundred years. As with many earlier communities, the first generation of
migrants often retain close links with their country of origin and dream of an
eventual return. In practice, post-war settlers such as the Italians, the Poles, the
Cypriots and the South Asians, have put down their roots here and made London
their home. They have raised families here, they have made homes and friends, and
invested a great deal culturally, emotionally and financially in their adopted city.
Their children and grandchildren have grown up to see themselves as Londoners,
and often have little attachment to their parents' or grandparents' country of origin,
seeing it principally as a place for holidays rather than as 'home'. The younger
generations are both 'ethnic' retaining some elements of their cultural identity,
their religion, and their traditional language, but they are also Londoners,
re-forming their identities as they become part of London's general social fabric,
as generations before them have done. Their aspirations and interests, despite
the frequent structural disadvantages they encounter as British-born members of
'immigrant' groups, are the same as any others of their age. Through them, London
is slowly absorbing another element in its rich history of cultural diversity, something we can all celebrate and of which we can be proud.

Endnotes

For full details of publications, see Bibliography.

1 From a 1993 survey by the Association of London Authorities, quoted in *The Runnymede Bulletin*, no. 266, June 1993, p6.
2 The term 'slave-servant' was introduced by Professor Douglas A. Lorimer (quoted in Fryer, 1984 p203) to denote Black servants' intermediate status between chattel slavery and the domestic service of Whites.
3 *The Tatler*, no.132, 9–11 February 1709.
4 *Morning Chronicle*, 27 July 1782.
5 William Wordsworth, *The Prelude*, Book VII, lines 211–28. Penguin edition, Harmondsworth, 1983. With thanks to Alex Werner for bringing this passage to our attention.
6 Quoted in Walvin, 1984, p19.
7 See Kiernan, 1978, p28 on the role of physical proximity.
8 Robert Latham and William Matthews (eds), *The Diary of Samuel Pepys*, vol.3, G. Bell and Sons Ltd, London, 1970, p95.
9 For ayahs, see Visram, this volume. For Filipinos see, for example, the *Independent*, 12 December 1989, p3.
10 See Merriman, this volume.
11 Cunningham, 1897, pp258–9.
12 See Tames, this volume.
13 *Illustrated London News*, 19 April 1851, no. 479.
14 See Kershen, this volume.
15 See Sponza, this volume.
16 See Merriman, this volume, and Cunningham, 1897, pp177–9.
17 Roth, 1941, (rev. ed. 1978) p158.
18 Holmes, 1988, pp22–4.
19 See Tames, this volume.
20 See Sword, this volume.
21 Holmes, 1988, pp212-15. Only a proportion of the Italians worked in London.
22 Walvin, 1984, p108; Holmes, 1988, p221; Humphries & Taylor, 1986, p117.
23 Peter Wright, *The Coloured Worker in British Industry*, Oxford University Press for the Institute of Race Relations, Oxford, 1968, p42.
24 The term 'lascar' was applied initially to sailors from India, and through time became used more loosely to denote 'Oriental' or 'Asiatic' sailors, and could also encompass Arabs and Africans (Visram, 1986, p53)
25 See Shang, this volume.
26 See Hussein, this volume.
27 Lambeth Council, *Forty Winters On. Memories of Britain's Post-War Caribbean Immigrants*, Lambeth Council, London, 1988.
28 Humphries & Taylor, 1986, p125.
29 See McAuley, 1993, for further information on this community and others covered in this book.
30 David Orr, 'Co Kilburn: portrait of an Irish community in London', *Magill*, December 1988, pp32–9.
31 See Colin Holmes, 'Building the nation: the contributions of immigrants and refugees to British society', *Royal Society of Arts Journal*, November 1991, pp725–34.
32 C. Wilson, 1969, pxviii.
33 Kiernan, 1978, p48.
34 Lees, 1979, pp121, 241.
35 *Report of a Meeting for the Establishment of a 'Strangers' Home' for Asiatics, Africans, South Sea Islanders and Others, Occasionally Residing in the Metropolis*, March 1855, p19. Church Missionary Society Archives.
36 See Sponza, this volume, and Felicity Kinross, *Coffee and Ices: The Story of Carlo Gatti in London*, Felicity Kinross, London, 1991.
37 Holmes, 1988, p229.
38 For street music see Mayhew, 1861, vol. III pp178–214; J.T. Smith, 1874; Panikos Panayi, 'Germans in 19th century Britain', *History Today*, 43, pp48–53, January 1993, and Sponza, this volume.
39 John Ford, *Prizefighting: The Art of Regency Boximania*, David and Charles, Newton Abbot, 1971.
40 Samuel Smiles, *The Huguenots: Their Settlements, Churches, and Industries in England and Ireland*, London, 1867, pp99–100.
41 Survey in E. J. B. Rose et al, *Colour and Citizenship: A Report on British Race Relations*, Institute of Race Relations/Oxford University Press, London, 1969, p587.
42 Roth, (rev. ed. 1978), 1941, p203.
43 Antonia Gransden, *Historical Writing in England*, Routledge and Kegan Paul, London, 1974, p328.
44 See Merriman, this volume.
45 Gransden, op cit, p415.
46 R.B. Dobson, *The Peasants Revolt of 1381*, Macmillan, London, 1971, p201.
47 Quoted in Nicolson, 1974, p28.
48 Quoted in Banton, 1955
49 J. Banister, *England Under the Jews*, London, 1901, quoted in Holmes, 1988, p297.
50 See Virginia Berridge, 'East End opium dens and narcotic use in Britain', *The London Journal*, 4 (1), 1978; and Shang, this volume.
51 See Panayi, this volume.
52 Fryer, 1984, pp298–316.

53 Holmes, 1988, p300.

54 Quoted in Irene Scouloudi (ed.) *Returns of
    Strangers in the Metropolis 1593, 1627, 1635,
    1639. A Study of an Active Minority.* Huguenot
    Society of London, Quarto Series, vol. LVI,
    London, 1985, p1.

55 Paul Gordon and Francesca Klug, *British
    Immigration Control: A Brief Guide*, The
    Runnymede Trust, London, 1985.

56 Kiernan, 1978, pp52–3.

57 Holmes, 1988, p260.

58 The Act was found to be racially discrim-
    inatory by the European Commission on
    Human Rights. See Gordon & Klug, op cit,
    1985, p7.

59 Ibid, p.9.

60 The Mansfield Judgment, that a master could
    not by force kidnap an escaped slave and
    take him out of England, was heralded as a
    major step in the fight against slavery. It was
    many years, however, before slavery was
    abolished.

61 Fryer, 1984, pp99–112, 203–27; Fraser, this
    volume.

62 Roth, 1941, (rev. ed. 1978), pp241–66.

63 Holmes, 1988, pp241–2.

The Invisible Settlers

From Prehistoric Times to the Huguenots • Nick Merriman

Some groups, such as the Black, Jewish and Irish communities, have been established in London for many centuries and still retain a distinctive cultural identity today. Others have gradually assimilated themselves into the general population and, though they may express their common ancestry through membership of particular churches or societies, they are less readily identifiable as specific communities. This chapter examines the long history and contribution of some of these 'invisible' assimilated groups.

Before London

The London area had been inhabited, intermittently, for around half a million years before the Romans founded the city. Slowly spreading from their original homeland in Africa, early humans reached southern Britain during the Ice Age. They were able to enter the region on foot because much of northern Britain was under ice sheets, and the consequent lower sea level meant that the area now covered by the English Channel was exposed as dry land. For much of this half-million-year period, Britain was a relatively inhospitable peninsula of northern Europe and people could move freely into the area, probably seasonally, following the animals which provided their main source of food. Their presence in the London area is indicated by the many hundreds of flint hand axes (which they would have used for cutting plants and butchering animals), found in Thames-side gravel deposits. However, the severity of the climate during this time was such that for long periods the vegetation on which animals grazed could not flourish, and so the area was uninhabited. The last major period occurred between 25,000 and 15,000 years ago, during which time there is no firm evidence for human occupation in Britain.

The climate began to warm again about 15,000 years ago. With the rise in temperature, the vegetation cover increased, attracting game animals to migrate northwards into southern Britain to take advantage of this new food source. Following them came their human hunters, who walked across from Europe into an empty land. From this time, Britain has been continuously inhabited. It is possible to argue that, from these early immigrants to the refugees of today, everyone living in London is descended, however distantly, from people who have come from abroad.

Excavations by the Museum of London in Uxbridge have recently provided an insight into the life of these early settlers in the London area. The evidence

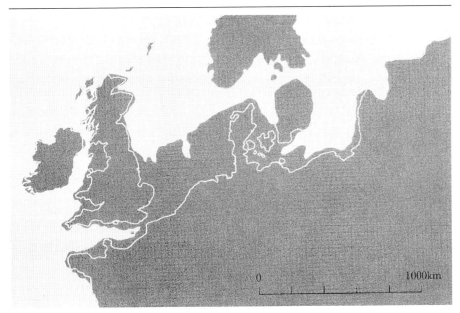

Map of Britain *c.* 8000 BC. Here, the land bridge to the Continent is still exposed, allowing colonists to walk into the Thames Valley to hunt herds of game

uncovered there revealed that 10,000 years ago hunters had lain in wait for herds of reindeer and wild horses as they migrated along the valley of the River Colne. Using flint-tipped weapons, they hunted them down and then butchered their carcasses on the riverside with flint knives manufactured on the spot.

During this time the sea level had been slowly rising as the ice sheets gradually melted far to the north. By 6000 BC the level had risen high enough to flood the Straits of Dover and form the English Channel. The land route which had connected Britain with the rest of Europe was finally severed, and from then on settlement could only be by boat.

In the absence of written records, we can only guess at the extent to which the London area was settled by people from overseas. That there was contact is shown by the presence of materials imported from Europe, such as rare stones for axes, and fine metalwork. It is likely that the adoption of farming around 4000 BC was accompanied by at least some settlement of peoples from overseas; no doubt other migrations occurred which have left no trace in the archaeological record. By the late Iron Age, there seems to have been close contact between the inhabitants of southern Britain and those across the Channel. If we are to believe the writings of Julius Caesar, there is some evidence for the large-scale movement of Celtic-speaking peoples into the region in the 150 years before the Roman invasion.

Roman London: a cosmopolitan city (AD 50—410)

Within ten years of the invasion of AD 43, London was founded as a new settlement by the Roman conquerors. London in AD 60 was described by the historian Tacitus, writing fifty years later, as 'filled with traders and a celebrated centre of commerce'. From the start, the town would have been thronged with a variety of peoples from all over the Empire. These would have included soldiers, administrators, traders and slaves, as well as people drawn to the town from the surrounding area. For the first time we can gain an insight into the nature of the population because the Romans have bequeathed us written records in the form of inscriptions, graffiti and writing tablets. There are now well over a hundred names recorded from Roman London. Some are probably the Romanised names of the local Celtic population who found employment in the new town, while many others belong to people from much further afield.

Part of a Roman soldier's tomb from London. He would have come from elsewhere in the Roman Empire to serve in the city

There is evidence of a significant military presence in London during much of the Roman period. For the first 150 years military personnel would have been recruited from outside Britain, as it was Roman policy not to station soldiers in their country of origin.[1] One of these was the unnamed soldier whose funerary monument was discovered in Camomile Street in the City in 1876; of mid-first-century date, this is our earliest known depiction of an inhabitant of London. Others, whose tombs were found in London, include Celsus, of the 2nd Legion Augusta, and Flavius Agricola, of the 6th Legion Victrix. Ulpius Silvanus, also of the 2nd Legion Augusta, is known from a plaque he commissioned showing the god Mithras slaying a bull. It also records that he was connected with Orange in France, either by being enlisted into the army there, or by being initiated into the higher echelons of the Mithraic religion.

Sometimes soldiers scratched their names on pieces of their equipment. A fine legionary helmet from London evidently had several owners, according to the inscriptions scratched into its rim: Lucius Dulcius, Lucius Postumus, Rufus and Aulus Saufeius all claimed ownership at various stages.[2] A spearhead from Bucklersbury House in the City has the words 'C.VER.VICT' punched into its blade, recording that it was the property of a soldier under the command of the centurion Verus Victor.[3] The presence of foreign auxiliaries has been shown in a letter from Chrauttius at Vindolanda (Northumberland) to Veldedeius in London. From their names, both were possibly from Batavia or Tungria, and of Germanic origin.[4]

Soldiers would have been recruited from all over the Roman Empire, including places quite distant from Britain. It is possible that soldiers from North Africa were stationed in, or passed through, London. A 'division of Moors' was stationed on Hadrian's Wall in the third century, and other Africans are recorded as having been present in Roman Britain, such as the Libyan-born Emperor Septimus Severus, who died at York in 211.[5]

As well as soldiers, the presence of Roman officials from overseas is also attested in London's archaeological record. Pre-eminent among these is Gaius Julius Classicianus, sent as procurator by the Emperor Nero to resolve problems in Britain arising from Boudicca's rebellion in AD 60. He originated from the Trier region in Germany, as did his wife, Julia Pacata, who set up his tombstone near Tower Hill. Another official, Marcus Martiannius Pulcher, the governor of Upper Britain in the third century AD, is known from an altar he set up in commemoration of the rebuilding of the temple of Isis in London.

Alongside the soldiers and officials of the Roman administration were larger numbers of civilians. Judging by the evidence that has survived, a significant number of these were Greek. The tombstone of Aulus Alfidius Olussa, found on Tower Hill, records that he was born in Athens and died at the age of seventy, an unusually long lifespan for the time. Although her birthplace is not recorded, the name of Aurelia Eucarpia, who set up a tombstone to her son in the cemetery area of what is now Moorgate Street, suggests that she too was Greek. A very recent find from Vintry, near London Bridge, is a silver plaque with a supplication written in Greek script by a certain Demetrius, asking for protection from plague, which would have been deposited with the river gods of the Thames. In addition, further examples of Greek writing, such as a child's shoe inscribed with the name 'HECTOR', and the word 'ORATOR' scratched on to some wall plaster from Pudding Lane, suggest that Greek, as well as Latin, was spoken and written in Roman London.

Not surprisingly, there are also signs of Italians living in London during the Roman period. One such person was Lucius Pompeius Licetus from Arretium (modern Arezzo), whose tombstone was excavated in 1988 on a cemetery site just outside the city walls on Hooper Street (see page 4).

Many more craftworkers, shopkeepers and labourers would have come to London from abroad for work. Their names are not recorded, and we can infer their presence only from the remains of their work which have survived. There is good evidence, for example, that a gemstone manufacturer was established in the area of modern Eastcheap around AD 55,[6] and a goldsmith a little later near present-day Cannon Street.[7] At this early date, both would almost certainly have come from abroad to set up their trade. The larger buildings, such as the 'Governor's Palace' and the Basilica and Forum, would have been embellished with paintings, mosaics and sculpture by workers from Italy and elsewhere in the Empire.

Slavery was integral to the functioning of the Roman Empire, and Britain exported large numbers of slaves to other provinces. Slaves could be anything from prisoners of war to household slaves who could ultimately buy their freedom. They would also have been brought to London from abroad to serve in various capacities, some holding positions of power far exceeding many 'free' officials. One such was Anencletus, described as a 'slave of the province' on the tombstone he set up to his wife Claudia Martina, a Roman citizen. He would have been in London to serve the provincial council that was responsible for the maintenance of the state cult of Emperor worship.

These are just a few of the surviving names of the Londoners of so many centuries ago, but they are enough to indicate the cosmopolitan nature of London's earliest population during the 360 years of Roman occupation. The clarity of focus provided by the inscriptions is unfortunately lost after the withdrawal of the Roman administration in AD 410, after which written records become virtually non-existent for over two centuries.

Saxons, Vikings and Normans (410—1066)

Tradition states that both in the century before and after the withdrawal of the Roman army the rulers of Britain employed mercenary soldiers from the Germanic lands to protect the country from raiders from the same areas, perhaps giving them and their families land in return for their services.[8] However, they seem to have rebelled and taken control, opening up the south and east of the country to their kinsmen from Angeln (an area around the mouth of the River Elbe), Saxony, Jutland and Frisia (an area including parts of modern Germany and Holland). These were the Angles, Saxons, Jutes and Frisians, whose invasions had such a great impact on the development of England (itself named after the first of these groups).

The Anglo-Saxons who sailed up the Thames were essentially farming people who wished to settle on land that they could cultivate. Initially, they avoided the walled city of London, which seems to have been abandoned as the Roman trading networks collapsed. Instead they farmed the countryside away from London at such places as Mucking, Hammersmith and Mitcham, where early cemeteries and settlements have been found.

The fate of the existing population of Romanised Britons is not certain. As the Anglo-Saxons increased their control of the area, some may have been forced west, ultimately to join the Celtic populations of Wales and the West Country. The majority probably remained, farming the land, and intermarried with the Anglo-Saxon population. Through time the influence of these Anglo-Saxon settlers has been such that their language forms the basis of English; the majority of local place-names in the London area are of Anglo-Saxon origin.

In 604, St Augustine sent the Italian bishop Mellitus to preach Christianity among the East Saxons. He was the first of a long line of overseas clergy to establish themselves in London, and upon converting the East Saxons he supervised the building of the first church of St Paul in the city.

By the early 600s, a new settlement, revealed in recent excavations, was springing up along Strand, outside the old Roman walled city. The historian Bede, writing in the 730s, describes London as 'a trading centre for many nations who visit it by land and sea'. A story he tells reveals that Frisian slave-traders had been present there in the late seventh century. Imported quernstones and pottery from the Rhineland, northern France and south-eastern Belgium, found in excavations, suggest that traders from these areas may have established some sort of presence in London in the eighth and ninth centuries.[9]

A much more emphatic presence was established from the ninth century onwards by Viking raiders from Scandinavia. Raids on London were recorded in 842 and 851, and a 'great army' of Danes overwintered in London in 871–2. Hoards of coins buried around this period may have been hidden in response to the danger posed by these attacks. By the 880s, Danes were settling in eastern England and an agreement was made between the English King Alfred and the Danish leader Guthrum by which the country was partitioned; an area to the north and east, its boundary running up the Thames and turning north along the Lea just east of

London, was recognised as Danish.

Though this territory, known as the 'Danelaw', was gradually recognised by the English kings, and its Scandinavian settlers incorporated into England, new Scandinavian attacks occurred in the late tenth century. In 994 Swein Forkbeard, son of the king of Denmark, and the Norwegian Olaf Tryggvason besieged London, an event recorded in the Anglo-Saxon Chronicle:

> 994. Here in this year came Olaf and Swein to London, on the nativity of St Mary, with ninety-four ships: and they were fighting constantly against the town and tried also to set fire to it. But there they sustained more harm and evil than ever they imagined any townsmen could do unto them.

Gradually the Danish campaign was stepped up and English resistance overcome. In 1016, after fierce fighting and after the death of King Ethelred, Londoners bought peace with the Danes, who set up their winter quarters in the city. On 30 November, Ethelred's son, Edmund, died, and the Danish leader Cnut was chosen as King of England. Thus began twenty-five years of Danish rule and strong Scandinavian influence on London life. Danish garrisons may have been set up at strategic points around Cnut's London, their presence later reflected by the church of St Clement Danes and a street in Strand known by 1246 as 'Densyemannestrete'.[10] The founder of the church of St Nicholas Acon in Lombard Street had the Scandinavian name Haakon, and a carved stone slab found in St Paul's churchyard has a runic inscription which translates as 'Ginna and Toki had this stone laid'. In west London, the name of the former village of Gunnersbury is derived from a Scandinavian woman called Gunnhuld.[11]

11th-century stone slab from St Paul's churchyard. The inscription, in Norse runes, reads 'Ginna and Toki had this stone laid'. It probably comes from the tomb of a member of the court of the Danish king, Cnut

Not surprisingly, Danish merchants are in evidence in London during this period. A document known as Ethelred's fourth law code, but which may date to the reign of Cnut, shows that they were accorded special privileges: as late as the twelfth century they were allowed to stay in the city for a year, while other foreign merchants were allowed to stay only forty days. The document also shows that merchants from Rouen, Flanders, Ponthieu, Normandy, the Isle of France, Huy, Liège and Nivelles all plied their trade in London.[12]

This period of strong Scandinavian influence ended in 1042 when Cnut's son Harthacnut died 'as he stood at his drink' at a feast in Lambeth. Twenty-four years later, after the death of Edward the Confessor, the age of invasions came to an end when William, Duke of Normandy, himself a descendant of Viking 'Norsemen', was crowned king at Westminster Abbey on Christmas Day, 1066 (see colour plate 8).

Merchants, moneylenders and craftworkers (1066—1550)

William's military success brought with it the control by the Norman aristocracy of political power and social administration. While we owe the terms 'alderman' and 'hustings' to the Scandinavians, the structure of London's municipal government, with its 'mayor', developed under Norman authority. Though William's initial charter guaranteeing the rights of the citizens of London was written in Old English, French became the language of the court and local administration, while Latin was the language of the Church and the law. Norman domination of the English population received physical expression in the building of castles: the White Tower in the east and Montfichet's Tower and Baynards Castle in the west.

Silver penny of William I, minted 1074–77

Contacts with northern France remained strong, and many settlers came to London from the Norman towns of Rouen and Caen. Among these was the merchant Gilbert Becket, whose son Thomas was born in Cheapside and went on to become Chancellor of England and Archbishop of Canterbury. His murder in Canterbury Cathedral in 1170 led to his adoption as patron saint of London, and thousands of Londoners made the pilgrimage to his shrine.

A number of monastic houses were founded during the medieval period which were linked to overseas orders. The Norman aristocracy, in particular, assisted with grants of land. In 1089, for example, four Cluniac monks from the priory of St Mary, Charité-sur-Loire, arrived to take possession of the abbey of St Saviour's, Bermondsey (founded seven years earlier by Alwin Child, a citizen of London). William Rufus granted them the manor of Bermondsey.[13] The Priory of Southwark was founded in 1106 by two Norman knights, William Pont de l'Arche, and William Dauncy. In 1221, three of the first Dominicans to enter England travelled to London to found the Black Friars priory, and in 1224 four Franciscans also came to set up a house which became the Grey Friars. The first members of the convent of the Minoresses-without-Aldgate, founded in 1293 by the Earl of Lancaster, were brought to England by the earl's wife, Blanche, Queen of Navarre.[14] St Bartholomew's Hospital and Priory was founded in 1123 by Rahere, who may have been of German origin.[15] The Knights Templar were established in London shortly after 1128 when Hugh de Payens, master of the order, visited England. The London Temple Church, consecrated in 1185, still survives. The Templars were used as financiers by the Crown and, with their widespread overseas contacts, played an important role in diplomacy. The Knights of the Hospital of St John of Jerusalem also established themselves in London in the early twelfth century at Clerkenwell.

The Jewish presence

A number of the settlers from northern France during the Norman period were Jews. They were the most distinct of the overseas, or 'alien', communities of medieval London, separated from the rest of the population by religion and restrictive laws, which forbade the Jews from owning land, carrying arms, or employing or having authority over Christians. Christians, on the other hand, were forbidden from undertaking moneylending which, together with medicine, became one of the few occupations open to Jews. Jews were encouraged to bring their capital from France and settle in England by William the Conqueror so that the king could benefit by taxing their moneylending operations. A document from 1128 mentions 'the Street of the Jews' in London, and about this time a flourishing community, led by the considerable scholar Rabbi Joseph, was established in the area between Gresham Street and Cheapside, which became known as the Jewry.[16] Excavations in 1985 revealed what might possibly be the remains of a *mikveh* or ritual bath, dating to the twelfth century.[17] The importance of the London settlement can be gauged from the fact that until 1177 the only cemetery in England where Jews were allowed to bury their dead was just outside Cripplegate, on a site now partially covered by the Museum of London.[18]

The position of the Jews was always a precarious one. The Crown relied on them because, through their moneylending consortia, they could finance military campaigns and advance large loans, as well as providing useful tax revenue. For this reason they enjoyed the special protection of the Crown, and for at least the first century of their settlement they were able to prosper. Aaron of Lincoln, for example, who also owned a house in Lothbury, was reputed to be the richest man in England in the twelfth century and financially assisted in the building of Lincoln Cathedral, Peterborough Cathedral, St Albans Abbey and nine Cistercian monasteries.[19]

At the same time, resentment and animosity towards the Jews was widespread among the general populace, partly through jealousy of this royal protection and partly because of the high rates of interest charged on moneylending (exceptionally, 60 per cent or higher; more usually between 22 and 43 per cent).[20] A religious dimension was added to this resentment with the preaching of a Crusade against the Infidel, and the blaming of the Jews for the Crucifixion. The combined factors of envy, financial anxiety and religious intolerance, which have commonly led in the history of London to the search for a scapegoat, were periodically turned on the Jews in outbreaks of violence and intimidation. In London the worst of these resulted from an incident in 1189 where Jews, normally excluded from admission, attempted to gain entry to the Coronation of Richard I to present gifts to the new monarch. The ensuing uproar sparked off a riot which resulted in the death of thirty Jews and the burning of Jewish houses in London.

King Richard and his successor John (1199–1216) subsequently attempted to give the Jews further measures of protection in order to safeguard their contributions to the Exchequer. In time, however, John's increasing need for finance led to ever greater pressures on the Jews, both through higher taxes and the official cancellation of large debts owed by the Crown to them. To supervise the taxation of Jews, a department of the Great Exchequer named the Exchequer of the Jews was set up. In 1210 a huge tax levied on Jews brought most to financial ruin, and many left the

Medieval Jew, shown wearing the 'Jewish badge' imposed in 1218 to distinguish Jews from Christians. There was a flourishing Jewish community in medieval London until their expulsion in 1290

country. From 1218 Jews were required to wear distinguishing badges, as they were over 700 years later in Nazi Germany.

Despite these restrictions, the Jewish community in London remained a significant presence. Documentary research on properties in Milk Street has shown that in the thirteenth century a number of Jews, such as Leo le Bland and Bonamicus, were property-holders in this area.[21] Despite the privations noted above, the scholarly life was at a peak during this period. Master Moses of London wrote a famous work on Hebrew pronunciation and grammar, and his son Elijah Menahem was a financier, physician and author of a celebrated religious commentary.

Under Henry III the Jews were financially squeezed even more tightly through forced contributions to projects such as the rebuilding of Westminster Abbey in 1245. By 1272, when Edward I succeeded to the throne, the Jews were almost penniless. Now that they were less useful to the Crown, royal protection was gradually withdrawn until the order came to expel all Jews from the country in 1290. The final chapter in the shameful treatment of the Jews occurred on 10 October 1290. A party of London Jews, with all of their property and Scrolls of the Law, set out to sail abroad. At Queenborough, at the mouth of the Thames, the ship grounded on a sandbank and waited for the tide to turn; meanwhile the passengers were invited to stretch their legs on the bank. When the tide turned, the master of the ship abandoned them to death by drowning and divided their property among the sailors.[22]

Alien merchants

Merchants from Europe had been a feature of London life from before the Norman Conquest. Some of the city's prominent families of the twelfth and thirteenth centuries, such as the Bucointes and the Bukerels, were probably descended from Italian settlers of the late eleventh century. The thirteenth-century alderman Arnald Fitz Thedmar, who wrote an important early chronicle of London, *Liber de Antiquis Legibus*, was of German descent.

In the late thirteenth and early fourteenth centuries, overseas merchants dominated London trade, attracted by English exports such as wool and grain (in 1273, six out of seven wool-exporters in London were foreigners.)[23] In return, Venetians and Genoese imported silks, velvets and spices. Spanish merchants, such as the Peres family of Burgos and Bilbao, brought iron and Cordovan leather (hence 'cordwainers', or shoemakers).[24]

Flemish and Dutch merchants traded their linen cloth, and those from northern France brought woad for dyeing. Gascons dominated the wine trade, particularly after Gascony was united with England in 1152, until the late 1320s when they were ousted by English merchants. The principal moneylenders, apart from the Jews, were from Italy and Cahors in France. After the expulsion of the Jews, the Lombards in particular came to play a central role in financing the operations of the Crown; their presence in the City is commemorated today by Lombard Street. In the reign of Edward III (1327–77) this role passed to the powerful Florentine companies of the Bardi, the Frescobaldi, the Riccardi and the Peruzzi.[25]

Eardley Junior School, Streatham: a typical mix of young Londoners

plate 1

Brick Lane Market on a Sunday morning

Fournier Street was named after George Fournier, a local benefactor of Huguenot extraction. The area now has a large Bengali community

London has long been a centre for the ethnic and international press

This mosque in Fournier Street started life as a Huguenot church and has also been a synagogue

Horse Guards and Banqueting House from St. James's Park, Giovanni Antonio Canale (Canaletto), 1749. Canaletto spent most of the period from 1746-55 in London, one of a long line of overseas-born artists who have influenced the development of English painting

Moroccan Information and Advice Centre, North Kensington

Opposite: Bengali shopkeeper, Brick Lane, 1978

plate 5

Chinese supermarket, Chinatown, Soho

Bloom's kosher restaurant, Whitechapel

Greek-Cypriot shop,
Haringey

plate 6

Portrait of Georg Gisze by Hans Holbein, 1532. Gisze was a German merchant at the London Steelyard

plate 7

Delftware plate with bust of William III, c. 1700

Glass beaker etched with a north Italian dialect inscription. The beaker probably belonged to an Italian merchant in London, c. 1500

William, Duke of Normandy, plans his campaign after landing in England

Stoneware bottle (1660-5) with medallion of Pieter van den Ancker, a Dutch merchant in London

plate 8

German merchants represented another trade axis. By 1130 the 'men of Cologne' had gained the right to reside in London, and later acquired a house or guildhall upstream from London Bridge. In 1157 they were granted royal protection.[26] After a long rivalry, in 1281 the various groups of German merchants, principally from Cologne, Hamburg and Lübeck, formed a single federation, the German 'Hanse', under the sign of the double-headed eagle. The group of buildings they occupied near London Bridge became known as the Steelyard. What drew the Hanseatic merchants to England was wool and woollen cloth, which in the fifteenth century together formed nearly 90 per cent of their exports from England. In return the Germans imported wine, wax, grain, copper, iron, timber and its by-products ashes, pitch and resin, together with the products of the Rhineland metal and ceramics industries.[27]

They took over responsibility for the maintenance of Bishopsgate, one of the entrances to the city, in the late thirteenth century, and enjoyed a number of privileges over other merchants. As a result, they dominated London more than any other overseas merchants in the fourteenth century. Something of their wealth and power can be gauged from the series of portraits of German merchants in London painted by Hans Holbein in 1532, even though the Hanse in England was in relative decline by then. One of the portraits shows the merchant Georg Gisze of Danzig sitting at his desk in the Steelyard, with his cashbox, account books and pen (see colour plate 7).

Throughout the fifteenth and sixteenth centuries, however, relations between English merchants and the Hanseatics were strained, as the English Merchant Adventurers attempted to gain the same privileges in the German city-states as were enjoyed by the Germans in London. In 1589, after the defeat of the Spanish Armada, the Hanse was accused of having supported the Spaniards and a number of their vessels were seized. From then onwards the Steelyard was almost deserted by the Germans, and it was closed by Elizabeth I in 1598. Although returned to the Germans in 1606, its greatest days were long past.

The importance of overseas merchants in the English medieval economy was such that when Edward II (1307–27) summoned the seven leading merchants of the land in 1314, four were foreigners: Antonio di Passano, fellow-Italian John Vanne, William Trente from the Agenais (France) and William Servat from Cahors.[28] The presence of these merchants and financiers was not wholly popular with other Londoners, who felt they had too much of an influence on the Crown, and as a result enjoyed business privileges denied to others. In 1255 the chronicler Matthew Paris complained that London was 'overflowing' with Poitevins, Provençals, Italians

Hanseatic League coat of arms. In 1281 German merchants formed a federation called the Hanse. Their premises in London were at the Steelyard near London Bridge

Weaver at work, 15th century. To develop the English textile industry, Edward III encouraged Flemish weavers to emigrate to England

and Spaniards. In 1457, a group of young men, incensed that a friend's wife had committed adultery with a Lombard named Galiot Scot, wanted to kill Scot and other Italians as 'fals extorcioners, common lechours and avoutres [adulterers]'.[29] They damaged several Italian houses, but fortunately there was no loss of life. Much more serious was an episode in 1517 which became known as 'Evil May Day'. A group of overseas financiers had gone bankrupt and fled the country, and just afterwards a leading Lombard merchant, Francesco di Bardi, humiliated an English merchant by seducing his wife. These two incidents triggered existing antipathy towards overseas merchants and craftworkers, and in the evening of May Day a large mob took to the streets, with the aim of attacking any foreigners they found and breaking into and ransacking the houses and workshops of foreigners in Leadenhall and Fenchurch Street. The ensuing riot culminated in the Lieutenant of the Tower showing his displeasure by firing ordnance into the City. By the small hours of the morning, the destruction had petered out. The City authorities, well aware of the economic benefits brought by the skills and capital of these foreigners, and anxious to stamp out any civil disobedience, punished the ringleaders severely. Three hundred were arrested and fifteen were hanged, drawn and quartered.[30]

Craftworkers from overseas

Unlike the merchants, who tended eventually to return to their home countries, workers who came to London from overseas to practise their craft often settled permanently. The majority of them came from the relatively overcrowded Low Countries. In the early fourteenth century, England produced a great deal of wool, but still imported finished cloth. Weaving skills were much in demand by those wishing to develop the English cloth industry, and a number of encouragements were offered to overseas weavers. As has often happened throughout the history of London, when there was a shortage of skills or labour people were invited from overseas to fill the gap. In 1337, for example, Edward III proclaimed:

> All the cloth workers of strange lands, of whatsoever country they be, which will come to England … shall come safely and securely, and shall be in the King's protection and safe conduct, to dwell in the same lands choosing where they will.

It is difficult to get a clear picture of the extent of overseas populations in London until 1440, when Richard II introduced a tax on all foreigners in the country. From this we can gain a snapshot of names and occupations of 'aliens' in London. In 1440, there were about 1500 aliens in the City and 350 in Southwark; these figures include Irish, Welsh, Scots and Channel Islanders, but exclude merchants with special privileges, such as the Germans.[31] The vast majority were 'Doche' (hence 'Dutch'), Latinised as 'Theutonici', a term which included Flemish, Dutch, Germans and Brabanters. The next largest groups were Italian and French, followed by a few Scots, three or four Greeks, some Icelandic servants, a few

Portuguese sailors and six Jews in London despite official expulsion. The majority were relatively wealthy and involved in business and trade, although one beggar, Henry Bem, is recorded.

Several of the Mediterranean residents, such as the Greek, Thomas Frank, continued a long tradition of medical practice. The Doche made significant contributions to goldsmithing, the leather trades, tailoring, haberdashery and in domestic service. In particular, they brought their expertise to pioneer new techniques in clockmaking, printing, spectacle-making and brewing. In 1484, all the alien printers and their servants are recorded as 'Theutonici'. John Saunders employed four Theutonici to run a brewery for him in Portsoken. There is interesting evidence, too, for the involvement of people from the Low Countries in brickmaking and bricklaying. At the London Charterhouse around 1415, the bricklayers were Arnauld Porter and Henry Bryker, both 'of Holland'. Henry Sondergyltes, a 'brykeman' at Deptford supplying 'bryktill' for use at London Bridge from 1418, was also probably from the Low Countries.[32] The high reputation of the Doche in this industry is suggested in a letter written in 1469 by a villager in Havering atte Bower to a friend near London asking him to find 'a mason that is a ducheman or a flemyng that canne make a dowbell chemeney of Brykks for they can best fare'.[33]

Although the majority of these medieval immigrants were men, a few independent women do appear in the records earning their own living at laundry, spinning and domestic service, and one schoolmistress is known. A good proportion of the men brought wives from their own countries with them and settled permanently, as did those who married local women.

While it is impossible to obtain an accurate picture of the number of overseas residents in London at this time, it has been estimated that in 1501 there were at least 3000 'aliens' in London in a population of about 50,000.[34]

During the reign of Henry VIII new industries grew up, and the need for new skills resulted in a considerable influx of people, especially from northern Europe, into the capital. Henry's reign was characterised by conscious attempts to develop a courtly culture appropriate to a major European power, through the employment of European artists and craftworkers. A new office of 'provider of the king's instruments of war' was created, and held continuously by foreigners for four reigns.[35] Milanese workers were brought over to work as court armourers in 1511, and in 1515 the Royal Armoury workshop proper was established, employing large numbers of Dutch and German workers. French artisans are recorded as making morris spikes, and an Italian cannon-founder, Arcana, had premises in London. Henry also employed foreign craftworkers to embellish his palaces, the most splendid of which was Nonsuch in Surrey. Among many others, an Italian, Nicholas Bellin of Modena, who had worked on the palace at Fontainebleau in France, was employed between 1542 and 1544. In 1542 he was paid 1s 4d per square foot to gild decorative slate work and a Dutchman, William Cure, was employed in carving stone.

At the court itself, painters such as Hans Holbein produced royal portraits and decorative paintings, and Lucas Hornebolte introduced the art of miniature

painting.[36] Henry VII and Henry VIII both employed a Black trumpeter, probably
from North Africa. He can be seen on the Westminster Tournament Roll of 1511,
the first known depiction of a Black person in London (see colour plate 10). The
King's Astronomer, Nicolaus Kratzer, introduced some of the important advances
made by German science and technical arts to the court of Henry VIII.[37] The reign
of Henry VIII is perhaps the most remarkable example of the long line of patronage
of overseas talent by the royal court. This tradition was continued by Elizabeth I,
who employed the female Flemish artist Levina Teerlinc as a painter of miniatures.
James I introduced a Scots presence at the court, while the close relations between
England and Holland in later centuries resulted in a wide circle of Dutch artists at
court, whose achievements have already been outlined in the previous chapter.

The Dutch (1550—1700)

Before about 1550 almost all overseas settlers in London had come for economic
reasons, with the expectation that their labour and skill could provide them with a
better living than they could earn in their homeland. The growth of Protestantism
in Europe, and the fierce attempts to suppress it in the Low Countries and France,
added a new factor to immigration into London: religious persecution. Henry VIII's
break with the Church in Rome from 1532 made England a haven for Protestants
fleeing harassment in their own countries.

In 1550 Henry's son, Edward VI, granted the use of the church of the former
monastery at Austin Friars to refugees from the Low Countries and elsewhere (see
colour plate 16). This freedom was disrupted during the reign of Mary, who sought
to restore the Catholic Church, and was tolerated rather than welcomed under
Elizabeth I. Nevertheless, in Elizabeth's reign there was a peak of Dutch immigration
to London as a result of the persecution conducted by the Duke of Alva in 1567 in
the Spanish Netherlands. Religious persecution was a strong factor in Dutch settlement in London, but it may not have been the only one. For many, moving to
London offered a chance to capitalise on skills that were much in demand or to
take advantage of new economic opportunities. An inquiry in 1573, for example,
showed that nearly half of the foreign-born population had migrated to London in
order to obtain work, rather than purely for religious reasons.[38]

The 'Dutch' incomers comprised two distinct groups: Walloons from Artois,
Hainault, Naumur and Luxemburg, who spoke a French dialect; and Flemings,
mainly from Flanders and Brabant, who spoke a Dutch dialect. By the early 1570s,
it has been estimated, overseas communities formed between 5 and 10 per cent of
London's population of around 100,000.[39]

As with so many overseas settlers, the Dutch were not initially welcomed. It was
felt that their presence would lead to unemployment and accommodation problems, and that they would drive prices up. However, the arrival of the Dutch in
larger numbers coincided with a time of general economic depression and a
dramatic rise in London's population, from around 50,000 in 1500 to 400,000
by 1650, and as much as 500,000 by 1700.[40] As has so often happened, the new

settlers were singled out as scapegoats by a disgruntled populace unable to differentiate between symptoms and cause. By the end of the sixteenth century the numbers of refugees dwindled as persecution abroad abated, and an attitude of tolerance prevailed.

The effect of these foreign workers on the development of London's industries was considerable.[41] Their influence was particularly great in the textile industry. Flemish silk-weavers practised in Cripplegate, and later Spitalfields developed as a centre for the craft. In East Anglia, in particular, the Dutch further developed 'New Draperies', light soft cloths which soon became more fashionable than the heavy English woollen ones. London played an important part in the dyeing and finishing of the cloths, and a dye works in Bow flourished from the 1630s under the Dutchman Kepler.[42] The Dutch were particularly famous for their tapestries, especially those from the Mortlake factory established around 1619 with the encouragement of James I.

New pottery styles and manufacturing techniques were also introduced to London, notably the tin-glazed ware popularly known as 'Delft'. The first Delftware factory in England was established in Norwich in 1567 by Jasper Andries and Jacob Janson, who moved to London in 1570 and stimulated a flourishing industry in Southwark and Lambeth.

Dutch and Venetians worked side by side in glass manufacturing in London. Jean Carré, an entrepreneur from Antwerp, set up a glass factory in the 1560s at Crutched Friars, staffed largely by overseas workers. After Carré's death, the manager of the glasshouse, Giacomo Verzelini, an Italian, who had practised in Antwerp, took over full control. In 1617 Sir Robert Mansell established a glass factory in Broad Street, probably in the old monastic church of the Austin Friars, and employed a number of Venetian craftsmen.

Expertise in drainage and water management was also put into good effect by the Dutch. The great engineer Cornelius Vermuyden, drainer of the Fens, carried out his first English project near London when he repaired a breach in the Thames embankment at Dagenham. The power of the Thames currents was used by Peter Mauritz in 1582 to turn waterwheels through the first arch at the City end of London Bridge. This in turn was used to pump up water to be distributed by pipes to local residents, a system that remained in use for about 250 years.

The Dutch also further developed the larger-scale end of the brewing industry, which they had dominated from the fifteenth century. Such was their influence that the previously used English word 'brewhouse' was replaced by the current Dutch term 'brewery'.

To their previous development of the art of printing, the Dutch in London in the late sixteenth and early seventeenth centuries added the skills of line engraving, mapmaking and the manufacture of scientific instruments. Almost all of the early prospects of London were produced by Dutchmen such as Hondius, Visscher, Kip and Merian.

A second phase in Dutch migration to London occurred during the later seventeenth century. The numbers may have been smaller, but their effect on the cultural and economic life of the city was enormous. Despite periods when the two countries were at war, the cultural influence of Holland over England had been growing increasingly close since the Civil War, when Charles II spent part of his exile in Holland and his court absorbed a great deal of Dutch culture. This influence was reintroduced into England with the Restoration of the Monarchy in 1660. Charles's niece Mary married William III of Orange so that after the 'Glorious Revolution' of 1688 there was a Dutch King on the English throne (see colour plate 8). In this climate of ever closer relations between the two countries, many Dutch merchants and financiers were attracted to London, and played a central part in England's financial revolution, methods dismissed by critics as 'Dutch finance'. Under William and Mary, much Dutch investment capital moved to London and a group of financiers including Sir Matthew Decker and the brothers Gerard and Joshua van Neck developed to handle transactions.

The Huguenots (1550—1750)

As we have seen, French-speaking Protestants had migrated to London from the mid-sixteenth century, the great majority being Walloons from the Netherlands. A separate place of worship for the French-speaking congregation was established in 1550 at the church of St Anthony in Threadneedle Street, and became a focus for the community. Around this time in France, the Protestants had become known as 'Huguenots'.[43] Huguenot immigration slowed down considerably after Henry of Navarre ascended the French throne. He had been brought up a Calvinist and, although converted to Catholicism, remained favourably disposed to Protestants. The Edict of Nantes, passed in 1598, offered French Protestants toleration, limited freedom of worship, and physical protection.

Never entirely safe from persecution in Catholic France, the Huguenots came under increasing attack under Louis XIV. Gradually the privileges granted by the Edict of Nantes were eroded as churches were burned and restrictions placed on Protestant worship. Expecting worse to come, from 1680 many Protestants began to flee abroad. In the anti-Catholic atmosphere prevailing in England, Charles II felt it right to offer them asylum in 1681. Many thousands took the chance to flee to England, and were joined by even greater numbers of their co-religionists after 1685 when the Edict of Nantes was formally revoked, and all Protestant churches were ordered to be destroyed. The word 'refugee', from the French *réfugié*, entered the English language at this time.

In the wake of this persecution, about 200,000 Protestants left France, of whom between 40,000 and 50,000 settled in England.[44] Being predominantly urban people, the refugees were attracted primarily to the towns. Half of them are estimated to have moved to the region now known as Greater London, and by 1700 Huguenots formed an estimated 5 per cent of London's population.[45] The Huguenots were received with relative sympathy by the majority of Londoners. A climate of receptiveness had been created by descriptions of their sufferings published in pamphlets, and through anti-Catholic sentiment spread by the clergy. Many Huguenots arrived in London destitute, and their plight provoked further sympathy from the general population. Five separate national appeals for the relief of the distressed French Protestants were launched, and such was their success (£50,000 was raised in the 1686 appeal) that the French Committee, a group of Huguenot noblemen, was set up to administer the funds. In time the Huguenots set up their own charities, their own schools, the first Friendly Societies in England and a French Hospital, which moved to Rochester in Kent in 1960.

However, the welcome accorded to the Huguenots was not universal. For those who practised the same crafts, the newcomers represented an economic threat, and others feared they would add greatly to London's overcrowding. In 1675, journeymen and apprentice weavers in London attacked French weavers and their property.[46] In 1685 it was again felt that 'weavers all may curse their fates/because the French work under-rates'.

Like many earlier immigrants, the refugees settled outside the City. One community grew up in the West End around the existing French community in Soho, focused on the Savoy church and its annex 'des Grecs', and another in the eastern suburbs around Spitalfields. By 1700 there were estimated to be around 8000 Huguenots in Westminster, served by fourteen churches, and 23,000 in Spitalfields, served by nine churches. Spitalfields was perhaps the more homogeneous community, with a large proportion of people involved in weaving (see colour plate 9). In Spitalfields, some 12,000 looms were in operation in the late eighteenth century, at the height of the silk industry's prosperity. The majority of the weavers were poor, hard-working craftsmen and -women employed by fellow Huguenot master-weavers. In whatever spare time they had, they cultivated gardens, being especially fond of tulips and dahlias.[47] Some were great pigeon-fanciers and breeders of songbirds. The presence of the Huguenots was so pronounced that some Londoners complained that they could walk through Spitalfields and hear only French being spoken.

Similarly, during the eighteenth century, Soho was described as 'abounding with French so that it is an easy matter for a stranger to imagine himself in France'. Those who set themselves up in this area were middle-class craftsmen, attracted and supported by their proximity to the court and parliament in Westminster. Here they engaged in, and made significant contributions to, a great variety of crafts. Huguenot skill in watch- and clockmaking was renowned, as was their gunsmithing, bookbinding and enamelling (see colour plate 9). The history of high quality gold- and silversmithing in the eighteenth century is essentially one of the Huguenot smiths, such as Paul de Lamerie, Pierre Harache, Pierre Platel and the Courtaulds, Augustin, Samuel and Louisa, whose descendant Samuel founded the textile firm. To support the insatiable demands of changing fashion, Huguenots brought their expertise in hairdressing, wigmaking, fanmaking, and boot- and shoemaking. By 1700 it was reported: 'The English have now so great an esteem for the workmanship of the French refugees that hardly any thing vends without a gallic name.' In Wandsworth, together with the skills of hatmakers from Caudebec in Normandy, Huguenots used their knowledge of dyeing to develop the felt hat-making industry.[48] They discovered a technique which prevented dyes from running even in the rain. Ironically, it was even claimed that the Catholic cardinals in Rome ordered their red hats to be made by the Protestant refugees at Wandsworth.[49]

In addition to their contribution to craft and industry, the Huguenots in London had a major impact on the development of science and technology. Hundreds of Huguenot academics who had fled the persecution congregated in London, and many became fellows of the Royal Society. Denis Papin invented the first pressure cooker (demonstrated in 1682) and attempted to harness the use of steam power. John Dollond, a silk-weaver in Spitalfields, showed the versatility of many of the refugees when he developed an interest in optics in his spare time. He set his son Peter up in business in 1750, and then joined him two years later. John Dollond reinvented the achromatic lens and became a Fellow of the Royal Society; the

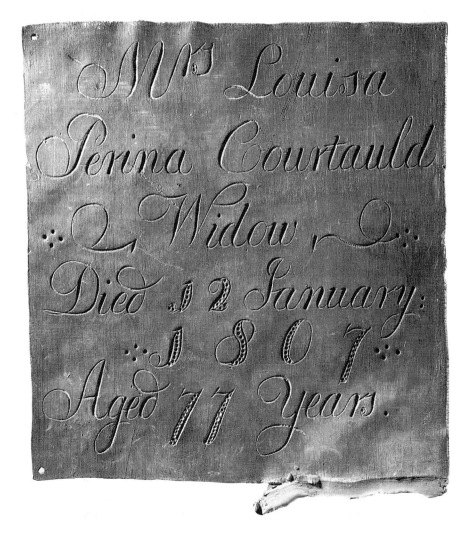

Coffin plate of Louisa Perina Courtauld. When her husband Samuel died, Louisa took over his gold-smith's business. Their descendants founded the Courtauld textile empire

firm he set up still exists as Dollond and Aitchison. A later Secretary of the Royal Society (from 1827 to 1849) was Peter Mark Roget, whose *Thesaurus* is widely used today.

Over three generations the Huguenots were gradually assimilated into English society. A distinct French Protestant community existed into the 1730s,[50] after which it slowly fragmented as the Huguenots moved into the mainstream of the middle classes and gave up everyday use of French. By 1800 only eight French Protestant churches remained in London, by 1900 only three, and today the only survivor is the French Church in Soho Square. Nowadays, the Huguenots of London are in many ways indistinguishable from other Londoners, although their French ancestry runs deep. For some, it can still be seen as a recognisable French name, such as the well-known ones of Bosanquet, Cazenove, Minet and Olivier. For many others, assimilation has brought Anglicisation of names – Blanc to White, de la Croix to Cross, for example – and only research of family trees can reveal the connection. Such was the impact of between 40,000 and 50,000 Huguenots on a population of around 5.5 million in late-seventeenth-century England, that through intermarriage, it has been claimed that up to 75 per cent of the current population can claim some Huguenot ancestry.

Endnotes

For full details of publications, see Bibliography.

1 J. C. Mann, *Legionary Recruitment and Veteran Settlement During the Principate*, Institute of Archaeology Occasional Publication No.7, London, 1983.
2 Collingwood & Wright, 1991, pp44–5.
3 Ibid, p51.
4 A. K. Bowman, J. D. Thomas and J. N. Adams, 'Two Letters from Vindolanda', *Britannia XXI*, 1990, pp33–52.
5 Fryer, 1984, p1.
6 Henig, 1984, p14.
7 Marsden, 1975, pp100–1.
8 Vince, 1990, p6.
9 Ibid, pp97, 101.
10 P. Nightingale, 'The Origin of the Court of Husting and Danish Influence on London's Development into a Capital City', *English Historical Review* 404, 1987, pp559–78.
11 J. E. B. Gover, A. Mawer and F. M. Stenton, *The Place Names of Middlesex*, Cambridge University Press, Cambridge, 1942, ppxvi, 91.
12 Loyn, 1962, pp93–4.
13 *The Victoria County History of Surrey*, vol. 2, Constable & Co. Ltd, London, 1905, p64.
14 *The Victoria County History of London*, vol. 1, Constable & Co. Ltd, London, 1909, pp502–84.
15 Brooke & Keir, 1975, p326.
16 Roth, 1941 (rev. ed. 1978) pp7–8.
17 Gabriel Pepper, 'An Archaeology of the Jewry in Medieval London', the *London Archaeologist*, vol. 7, 1992, pp3–6.
18 Honeybourne, 1961.
19 Fletcher Jones, 1990, p14.
20 Roth, 1941 (rev. ed. 1978) p106.
21 Information kindly provided by Colin Taylor in advance of the publication of J. Schofield, P. Allen and C. Taylor, *Medieval Building and Property Development in the Area of Cheapside*, forthcoming.
22 Information from Roth, 1941 (rev. ed. 1978) pp86–7.
23 Williams, 1963, p111.
24 Ibid, p182.
25 Ibid, p11.
26 Dollinger, 1970.
27 Ibid, p245.
28 Williams, 1963, p146.
29 Thrupp, 1969, p268.
30 Holmes, 1965.
31 See Thrupp, 1969.
32 Smith, 1985, p9.
33 Thrupp, 1969, p270.
34 Figures derived from Thrupp, 1969, p270.
35 Cunningham, 1897, p142; Watts, 1991, pp42–4.
36 Strong, 1984, pp12–44.
37 Hackmann, 1991.
38 Scouloudi, 1987, p44.
39 See Gwynn, 1985, p37 and Pettegree, 1987, p391.
40 Coleman, D.C., 1977, p20.
41 See Ormrod, 1973 and Cunningham, 1897.
42 Cunningham, 1897, p212.
43 The origin of the term is obscure. For a discussion of possible derivations, see Gwynn, 1985, p2.
44 Murdoch, 1985, p111.
45 Gwynn, 1985, p36.
46 Ibid, pp116–17.
47 The Huguenots introduced a number of new plants to Britain and popularised gardening. See Gwynn, 1985, p71 and Duthie, 1987.
48 Shaw, Gwynn & Thomas, 1985, p11.
49 Gwynn, 1985, p68.
50 Murdoch, 1985, p111.

PART II

London's Overseas Communities:
A series of personal views

Africans and Caribbeans in London • Peter Fraser

Although there is evidence for the presence of Black soldiers among the Roman legions stationed in Britain, and a 'black trumpet' at the court of Henry VII (see colour plate 10) and Henry VIII,[1] studies of African and Caribbean people in Britain usually start with the development of the English slave trade and plantation slavery in the English Caribbean. The long *continuous* history of Black people in London dates from 1555, when John Lok returned from Guinea with 'Certaine black slaves'.[2]

Yet can there be any justification for dealing with both Africans and Caribbeans together in one chapter of this book? In discussing the history of African and Caribbean people in London, we are not dealing with a single community, or even with two communities. Africans and Caribbeans both come from a multitude of religious, cultural and linguistic heritages. Indeed the Caribbean, as a spectrum of identities, can be said to fade into Africa, Asia and Europe with an older base in native American cultures and a new, debatable, middle constituting what is uniquely Caribbean. Yet two features bind people from the two regions together: the existence of slavery and the persistence of racism. The majority of Commonwealth Caribbean people have African ancestry because of the slave trade to the Caribbean. Caribbean people of African descent suffer the effects of racism just as much as those who are visibly, and actually, from Africa.

During the seventeenth and eighteenth centuries, the forces that propelled African and Caribbean people to settle in London were very similar. Until about 1800 slavery was the main force, whether they came directly or via the Caribbean. After the effective ending of slavery in Britain at the end of the eighteenth century, broad similarities between the two communities do exist but the chronology and scale of immigration differ greatly. Nineteenth-century African and Caribbean arrivals in London were mainly students or sailors who decided to settle, but among the Africans there was also a significant number of businesspeople. In the twentieth century, the pattern remained the same until 1945, with the addition of servicemen and -women in the two world wars and a variety of workers, who were recruited mainly from the Caribbean. After the Second World War, emigration to the USA became more difficult for Caribbean people, but unemployment continued to stimulate them to leave. Active recruitment of Caribbean people by the National Health Service and London Transport meant that for the first time Britain, and

Collared slave in the service
of James Drummond, 3rd
Duke of Perth

especially London, became the destination for large numbers of people. Emigration
from Africa in the same period was not driven purely by economic motives; the
political uncertainties and difficulties of post-independence Africa weighed more
heavily. The Caribbean was not entirely immune to this and emigration from
Guyana, especially from the 1960s, was mainly political. In the long run, political and
economic motives were indissolubly linked as instability in either the economy or
the political system affected government and people's livelihoods.

The history of African and Caribbean people in London can be divided into four
main periods. During the era of slavery from the seventeenth to the early nineteenth century, the Africans and Caribbeans who migrated to London and settled
there did not do so voluntarily. The lives of many of them in domestic service may
have been lived out in relatively good conditions, compared with those of the poor
of London and the slaves on the Caribbean sugar plantations, but they remained
slaves. If they ran away, dangerous and often short lives awaited them. In the seventeenth and eighteenth centuries, Black people in London were drawn from several
different groups: domestic slaves of varying degrees of privilege; slaves brought
directly from Africa or the Caribbean, and usually destined to return there; princes,
students and scholars (usually visitors); sailors; and a growing number of free

people living precarious existences. Towards the end of the eighteenth century, the status of the domestic slaves changed into that of servants; many ran away or bought or were granted their freedom, and by the end of the century they lived as free people.

A few, well known at the time, have been rediscovered in recent years. Francis Barber was Samuel Johnson's servant and features in a portrait by Gainsborough. Johnson left him £70 in his will, and Barber ended his days as a schoolmaster.[3] Ignatius Sancho was born a slave in 1729 and brought to England when he was two. While butler for the Duke of Montagu he wrote poetry, two plays, and a number of musical pieces. A friend of Garrick, Samuel Johnson and Laurence Sterne, he opened a fashionable grocery in Westminster. After his death in 1780 his *Letters*, published in two volumes, were so popular that they were reprinted five times. George Bridgtower was another musician of African parentage, who came to London as a child prodigy and was first violinist in the Prince of Wales's orchestra. Beethoven admired his talent greatly and originally dedicated the Kreutzer sonata to him, changing the dedication only after quarrelling with Bridgtower.[4]

One of the earliest Black political leaders was Olaudah Equiano (see colour plate 10). Born in Nigeria around 1745, he was kidnapped at the age of eleven for the slave trade, and brought to England a year later. After thirteen years of servitude he managed to buy his freedom, and worked in a great range of occupations, including hairdresser, servant, coalminer and ship's steward. He even visited the Arctic as a crew-member of a ship attempting to find a passage to India. In London, he became involved in the struggle against slavery and proved to be an effective speaker and lobbyist. In 1789 he published *The Interesting Narrative of the Life of Olaudah Equiano, or Gustavus Vassa, the African*, which detailed his life story and put forward the case for the abolition of slavery. It went through a total of fourteen editions and was the first example of the case for abolition being put to a popular audience by a Black person. A tireless advocate of the cause, he died in London in 1797, when slavery had almost ended in Britain.[5]

Jamaican-born Robert Wedderburn was another Black person famous for his belief in social justice. A member of a radical group called the Society of Spencean Philanthropists, he was imprisoned for two years after distributing revolutionary propaganda. Although a champion of the general liberation of the working classes, he spoke out strongly against slavery, publishing an autobiographical pamphlet, *The Horrors of Slavery*, in 1824.[6] Of milder disposition was the Bermudan-born Mary Prince, whose autobiography, published in 1831, was part of the final assault upon slavery in the colonies.[7]

London parish records in the 1780s and 1790s show the baptism of babies like Catherine Abraham and Christiana Stewart, of young adults like George Hamilton and Charles Bollin, both African-born, and Thomas Brown from Antigua, Richard Ashington from St Kitts, and Alice Jane from Dominica, as well as of mature adults

Portrait of Ignatius Sancho (1729–80) engraved by Francesco Bartolozzi, after Thomas Gainsborough

West African seamen pictured aboard SS *Barrabool* in London docks, *c.* 1935

like Bermudan Samuel Sanders, Jamaican John Francis, and Joseph Blakeman from St Kitts.[8] Several of these adults were sailors. Those working in the navy were not always eligible for pensions, and some were unable to find work after being discharged. A number, such as the one-legged fiddler Billy Waters and the street singer Joseph Johnson, became famous beggars. Waters was elected 'King of the Beggars' shortly before his death in 1823, and is depicted in many illustrations. Others like Joe Leashley, Massa Kendrick and James Wharton took up prize-fighting, the start of a long tradition of Black boxers.

The second period starts in the early nineteenth century and ends towards its close. Without the stimulus to mutual support and the publicity that the fight against slavery provided, a more complex picture emerges. A few figures stand out, but on the whole little is still known about Black people during this period. William Cuffay was born in Chatham in 1788, and became a journeyman tailor. From 1839 onwards he was involved in the Chartist movement. In 1848 he chaired the committee organising the great procession to present the People's Charter to parliament. After its rejection his continued prominence led to his trial and conviction for conspiracy to commit arson and he was transported to Australia.[9] More conventional politics were practised by Mary Seacole, who moved to London at the time of the Crimean War to offer her services to the British army. Rebuffed officially, she journeyed independently to the Crimea. Once there, she set up a store and a small 'hospital' for the troops, and worked tending the wounded. Her work was made famous in Britain by W. H. Russell, the first war correspondent. After the war she was rendered bankrupt by her unsaleable stock and had to be rescued by grateful officers, who organised a four-day musical festival to raise funds for her.[10] Ian Duffield's work on Black people transported to the Australian colonies shows the continued existence of Black people among the London poor to the mid-1850s, although they also seem to have worked in skilled occupations.[11] Sailors continued to arrive, like the Kru seamen from West Africa who stayed at Green's Home in East London from the 1850s to the 1870s, part of a transient population of sailors.[12]

The end of the nineteenth century to the late 1940s constitutes the third period, when locally born Black people begin to make a mark within the mainstream of London life. At the end of the nineteenth century some prominent people of African descent appear. Samuel Coleridge-Taylor, the son of a Sierra Leonian doctor and an Englishwoman, became a highly respected composer who died prematurely aged thirty-seven in 1912. His most famous work, *Hiawatha's Wedding Feast*, was one of the most popular English choral-orchestral works in the first decade of this century.[13]

Almost exactly overlapping with Coleridge-Taylor's lifetime, a small but interesting group of people from the Gold Coast (now Ghana) lived in Britain, mostly in London. They can be divided into three groups: students, businessmen and a mixed group of sportsmen, theatrical impresarios and ministers of religion. The well-known Hayford family first came to London for professional education and to

Samuel Coleridge-Taylor
pictured at his piano with
the score for *Hiawatha's
Wedding Feast*

obtain gold concessions,[14] and London was also important in the career of John
Mensah Sarbah, author of *Fanti Customary Law* (1897) and *Fanti National Constitution*
(1906).[15]

During this period, people from the Caribbean also began to occupy professional
positions, such as doctors. Ernest Goffe from Jamaica was the pioneer, serving in
London hospitals for many years. Dr J. J. Green of Hackney was also well known,
but the most famous was Dr Harold Moody, the founder of the League of
Coloured Peoples (LCP), from the 1930s to the late 1940s the most influential
organisation struggling for the rights of Caribbean people both in Britain and in the
Caribbean itself.

The LCP and Dr Moody preferred to function as a pressure group that worked
discreetly if possible; others took a more openly political stance.[16] John Richard
Archer, born in Liverpool in 1863 to a Barbadian father and an Irish mother, moved
to Battersea in the 1890s and became mayor of the borough in 1913. He pioneered

African and Caribbean involvement in local politics, though it was not until 1987 that Black people were elected to parliament.[17]

Various memoirs and oral histories recall the small size of the Black communities in London in the first half of the twentieth century. Esther Bruce, born in 1913 to a Guyanese father and an English mother in Fulham, recalls that, growing up, she knew few Black people: one, Augustus Greenidge, had been a witness at her parents' wedding in March 1912; another, an Egyptian, Mr Fammi, worked as a film extra; and a third, her stepmother, Jennie Edwards, also Guyanese, worked as a children's nurse in South Kensington. Two others were better known: she also met the racing tipster Prince Monolulu (despite his name another Guyanese) and occasionally visited the home of Marcus Garvey, the Jamaican Pan-Africanist who ended his days in London. Her own father was a labourer at the time of his marriage and later worked as a coach painter, and sometimes as a film extra. Esther Bruce herself was employed mainly as a dressmaker, and during the Second World War started work as a cleaner and later became a laundry worker.[18]

London remained important for the more privileged and transient student populations. In the twentieth century the small African student body in Britain numbered about thirty in 1913, about seventy in 1940 and about two thousand from west Africa alone in the 1950s, when about half lived in London. The West African Student Union was founded in 1925 and was important in the nationalist struggles of the 1940s and 1950s.[19] The Italian invasion of Ethiopia in 1935 brought together in London two famous Trinidadian schoolfriends, George Padmore and C.L.R. James, in the International African Service Bureau. After James's departure for the USA, Padmore remained involved in the struggle for African and Caribbean independence and organised the 1945 Pan-African Congress. Another friend of James, the cricketer Learie Constantine, found a career in race-relations after his cricketing days ended. The most famous of the students was Kwame Nkrumah (in London between 1945 and 1947), who helped to form the West African National Secretariat.[20]

The fourth period starts with the arrival of nearly 500 immigrants on the *Empire Windrush* in 1948. From then until the 1962 Commonwealth Immigrants Act reduced numbers, thousands of Black people arrived to settle in London. The majority were Caribbeans coming mainly for work; most Africans came to study. In both cases the populations were relatively youthful, a characteristic that has remained constant. In the late 1980s over half the 150,000 Africans and 456,000 Caribbeans in Britain were under thirty years of age.[21] If the main reasons for Caribbean emigration were economic, individuals had personal reasons. Randolph Moses was in his mid-thirties when he arrived in 1962:

> It was a craze; everybody was getting out. When they were coming to Britain, they were sending back some nice tall stories. So you just said, I'll have to go. The boys, my friends, were coming over, so I decided to take a shot.

Caribbean-born bus conductor and driver, Crystal Palace, 1962. In the 1950s London Transport organised recruitment drives in the Caribbean

Cecilia Wade, from Montserrat, was roughly the same age as Randolph Moses when she arrived in 1956, and she gave much the same reason:

> I left my home because there was the England rush going on. People were coming to England, sending back for their families, and I thought of some of the people who sent money to take their family over to England. If they, just ordinary labourers, could do so well in England, then I can go there and do just as well or even better.

Gwen Thomas from Grenada left a good job there 'out of curiosity'; Connie Mark from Jamaica joined her professional cricketer husband; Christiana Wilson from Nigeria arrived to study midwifery, intending to return, but never did. All these people and many others began to create Caribbean, and to a smaller extent, African communities in London, often without intending to stay.[22]

Christiana Wilson's experience suggests one large difference between African and Caribbean migration: the primary motive for most African migration was educational. On the whole, independence created a demand for new skills and higher levels of education that could not be met locally. From the late 1960s, however, a combination of civil and political unrest and blighted economic hopes has also led to a large number of refugees.[23]

The development of the Notting Hill West Indian community (see colour plate 10) and the riots of 1958 marked a crucial stage in the development of the post-Second World War Caribbean communities in Britain.[24] These were the last large-scale riots by White people directed at Black people, and the area once seen as hostile territory for Black people is now one of significant Black settlement. Also in 1958, the *West Indian Gazette* was founded, further evidence of the growth of the Caribbean community since the late 1940s. It was edited by the Trinidadian-born but US-bred radical Claudia Jones, who in 1964, the year of her death, wrote denouncing new legislation intended to restrict non-White immigration and described the Caribbean community:

> Throughout Britain, the West Indian contribution to its economy is undoubted. As building workers, carpenters, as nurses, doctors and on hospital staffs, in factories, on the transportation system and railway depots and stations, West Indians are easily evidenced. Lest the younger generation be omitted (without commenting here on the social mores 'guiding' the cultural orientation of today's youth) one of the most popular current pop singers is a sixteen-year-old girl from rural Jamaica.[25]

By the 1980s, the cultural strand that Claudia Jones had mentioned had become more prominent. The Notting Hill area of London became famous for its West Indian carnival which, after being marred by rioting in earlier years, now re-creates in London some of the atmosphere and excitement of the Trinidad carnival, the biggest in the Caribbean. The re-creation goes further than this: the music of Jamaica plays a greater role in London than in Trinidad, and many of the bands are faithfully based on African culture.[26] In many ways, young Blacks set the style for fashions in clothing, music and dance in the wider youth culture.

By the 1980s too, the African and Caribbean communities in London boasted a number of prominent personalities. The Members of Parliament, Diane Abbott, Bernie Grant and Paul Boateng, were the best known of the politicians, the majority of whom were involved in local government, like the late Janet Adegoke, the first African woman to become mayor of a London borough. In the national media, Trevor McDonald and Moira Stuart worked as television newscasters; other well-known figures include sportsmen like the athlete Linford Christie and numerous footballers and cricketers; Dame Jocelyn Barrow, a former teacher and lecturer, once BBC governor and now on the Broadcasting Standards Council; Darcus Howe in television production and presentation and the film-maker Horace Ove; the trade unionist Bill Morris, head of the TGWU; publishers like Margaret Busby, John La Rose, Jessica and Eric Huntley, Buzz Johnson, and Arif Ali; Directors of Education like Bebb Burchell and Gus John. In the arts writers, painters, sculptors, actors and actresses of Caribbean and African descent played a lively part in the cultural life of Britain, Africa and the Caribbean: Ben Okri, novelist, poet and Booker Prize-winner, might stand as one example of this large and diverse group.

But supporting these prominent individuals were large numbers of organisations either regionally or nationally based, some concerned with welfare, others with education. The West Indian Standing Conference was one of the oldest of these but has never become the umbrella organisation for the Caribbean groups that it had hoped to be. One of the most vital areas of concern has been education. Research suggested that while the children of Africans in London schools did better than average, those of Caribbeans did worse in London schools. Even so, Remi Kapo, an African educated in British schools, has denounced the tendency of teachers to perpetuate myths of the special aptitude at music and sports of Black people in general.[27] Despite some improvements in education, the high levels of unemployment of the 1980s and the 1990s do not afford much optimism for those of Caribbean and African parentage.

A service at Ritson Road Church, Hackney, 1968

In another area of their lives African and Caribbean people have been ready to develop their own institutions by establishing African or Caribbean churches. Caribbean people have on the whole remained faithful to forms of worship originating in the USA when they have withdrawn from mainstream British ones. Africans, on the other hand, have developed their own particular forms of Christianity in Africa and transported them to Britain. The Aladura Church, which developed in Nigeria, for example, has begun to spread among African and Caribbean Christians in Britain.[28] Indeed, the development of churches which cater mainly for people of African or Caribbean descent has been one of the most obvious but least studied features of the post-Second World War patterns of settlement and social life in London.

In the early 1990s, the shape of the African and Caribbean communities in London differs greatly from that of earlier years. The 1991 census showed 534,300 Black people living in Greater London, of whom an increasingly large proportion are London- or British-born. Though still concentrated in several distinct areas, Brixton, Shepherds Bush, and in the north and east of London, African and Caribbean people can be found throughout the capital. Increasingly, too, occupations demanding higher levels of skill and education are no longer closed to them or open only to a few specially privileged people, and the association with slave origins has become historical rather than contemporary. Discrimination still remains, and a depressed and declining British economy cannot provide the certainty of employment to compensate. The resilience of the communities and the institutions created over the years will at least provide a base for progress and some protection against continuing economic crisis.[29]

Endnotes

For full details of publications, see Bibliography.

1 Fryer, 1984, pp4–5.
2 Walvin 1973, p1; Shyllon 1977, p4; Fryer, 1984, pp1–7.
3 Fryer, 1984, pp424–26.
4 Ibid, pp428–30.
5 Ibid, pp102–12.
6 Iain McCalman, *The Horrors of Slavery and Other Writings by Robert Wedderburn*, Edinburgh University Press, 1991.
7 Mary Prince, *The History of Mary Prince, West Indian Slave, Related by Herself*, 1831, reprinted Pandora, London, Moira Ferguson (ed.), 1987.
8 Peter Fraser and Rozina Visram, *The Black Contribution to British History*. Report Commissioned by CUES Community Division and the Geffrye Museum, CUES/ILEA, London, 1988; Fryer, 1984, pp231–2, 445–54.
9 Fryer, 1984, pp237–46.
10 Mary Seacole, *The Wonderful Adventures of Mrs Seacole in Many Lands*, 1857, reprinted Falling Wall Press, Bristol, Ziggi Alexander and Audrey Dewjee (eds), 1984.
11 See Ian Duffield's paper to the Conference on the History of Black People in London, 1984; and his 'Skilled Workers or Marginalised Poor? Some Evidence on the Afro Population of the United Kingdom, 1812–1852', delivered at the Conference on the African Presence in Britain, 1991.
12 Walvin, 1973, p198.
13 Marjorie Evans, 'I Remember Coleridge: Recollections of Samuel Coleridge-Taylor (1875–1912)', in Lotz & Pegg, 1986.
14 See Ray Jenkins's paper, 'A Talented Minority: Enterprising Gold Coasters in Britain: 1880–1920', delivered at the Conference on the African Presence in Britain, 1991; see also his paper 'Gold Coasters Overseas, 1880–1919: With Special Reference to Their Activities in Britain', *Immigrants and Minorities*, 4(3), 1985.
15 Ray Jenkins, 'In Pursuit of the African Past: John Mensah Sarbah (1864–1903) Historian of Ghana', in Lotz & Pegg, 1986.
16 File & Power, 1981; Jeffrey Green, 'Dr J. J. Green of Hackney (1882–1953)', in Lotz & Pegg, 1986; Fryer, pp326–34.
17 Fryer, 1984, pp290–4.
18 Stephen Bourne and Esther Bruce, *The Sun Shone on Our Side of the Street: Aunt Esther's Story*, Ethnic Communities Oral History Project, London, 1991.
19 Hakim Adi, 'West African Students in Britain, 1900–1960: the Politics of Exile',

paper presented to the Conference on the African Presence in Britain, 1991.
20 Paul Buhle, *C. L. R. James: The Artist as Revolutionary*, Verso, London, 1988; Imanuel Geiss, *The Pan-African Movement*, Methuen, London, 1974, pp340–62, 385–408; Marika Sherwood, 'Kwame Nkrumah in London, 1945–1947', paper presented to the Conference on the African Presence in Britain, 1991.
21 *Social Trends* 22 HMSO, London, 1992, p28; *Social Trends* 23 HMSO, London, 1993, p16.
22 James Barry et al., 'Sorry, No Vacancies': Life Stories of Senior Citizens from the Caribbean, Notting Dale Urban Studies Centre and Ethnic Communities Oral History Project, London, 1992.
23 Esther N. Goody and Christine Muir Groothues, 'The West Africans: The Quest for Education' in James L. Watson (ed.), *Between Two Cultures: Migrants and Minorities in Britain*, Basil Blackwell, Oxford, 1977; Mary Dines, 'African Refugees in the United Kingdom', paper given to the Conference on the African Presence in Britain, 1991.
24 Edward Pilkington, *Beyond the Mother Country: West Indians and the Notting Hill White Riots*, I. B. Tauris, London, 1988.
25 Buzz Johnson, *'I think of My Mother': Notes on the Life and Times of Claudia Jones*, Karia Press, London, 1985, pp145–6. The singer in question was Millie, with her song 'My Boy Lollipop'.
26 Kwesi Owusu, 'Notting Hill Carnival: Image and Text Take a Walk with Masquerade' in Kwesi Owusu (ed.), *Storms of the Heart. An Anthology of Black Arts and Culture*, Camden Press, London, 1988.
27 *Education for All: the Report of the Committee of Inquiry into the Education of Children from Ethnic Minority Groups*, Cmnd 9453, HMSO, London, 1985; Dilip Hiro, *Black British White British. A History of Race Relations in Britain* (rev. ed.), Grafton Books, London, 1991, p324; Remi Kapo, *A Savage Culture: Racism – A Black British View*, Quartet, London, 1981, p79.
28 Most Revd Father Olu A. Abiola, 'The Work of the Aladura Church in Britain', paper delivered at the Conference on the African Presence in Britain 1991.
29 Further sources on the African and Caribbean presence in London include Dabydeen, 1987; Edwards & Walvin, 1983; Greater London Council, 1986; Lorimer, 1978; Scobie, 1972 and Shyllon, 1974.

Americans in London · Richard Tames

London's first American was Pocahontas, who received, quite literally, a right royal welcome but died from the effects of the climate within a year (see colour plate 15). Americans have never much liked London's weather nor, until the present century, the food. However, they have usually felt comfortable enough for the institutions they have created for themselves to be geared to sociability rather than survival. If their attitude to the native culture was usually ambivalent, this seldom sprang from insecurity. For Americans, the preservation of individual identity has not depended crucially on the preservation of a distinct social identity. Feeling relatively 'at home', they have been less strongly impelled than other ethnic groups to develop their own separate social infrastructure.

Informal networks of Americans in London go back to the Pilgrim Fathers. The Puritan ascendancy of the 1640s lured back both Edward Winslow, founder of Massachusetts, and Roger Williams, founder of Rhode Island. Clubs of Americans date back to the eighteenth century and *The American* newspaper is now a century old. Oddly enough, American schools and an American church date only from the latter half of the twentieth century. The extent to which Americans have in the past constituted a 'community' (and do in the present) is therefore problematic; the boundaries of that community have always been blurred by intermarriage with the local population, and by the constant to and fro of temporary residents motivated by business, study or tourism.

The first American tourist to have left a detailed account of his stay in London is Samuel Sewall, who in 1689 visited St Paul's (still under construction), the Guildhall, the Tower and Westminster Abbey, the courts at the Old Bailey, the hangings of Tyburn and a 'consort of musick' at Covent Garden. This itinerary, repeated by generations of Americans, featured the courts and parliament as essential for young men hoping to cut a figure in the law or politics. A century later, Benjamin Rush reassured his son, a medical student, 'That great city is an epitome of the whole world. Nine months spent in it will teach you more by your eyes and ears than a life spent in your native country.'

Eighteenth-century Americans who committed themselves to more than a lengthy visit could enter fully into the life of the capital. Virginia grandee William Byrd was received at court, attended meetings of the Royal Society, became a friend of the dramatist William Congreve and had his portrait painted by the royal

Benjamin Franklin, 1783
(after J. S. Duplessis). The
American statesman and
scientist spent over 16 years
in London

painter, Sir Godfrey Kneller. Between 1763 and 1783, five Americans sat in the
Commons, with Barlow Trecocthick of Massachusetts representing the City of
London from 1768 to 1774.[1]

An informal network of Harvard alumni was already in existence in London by
the early eighteenth century. Numerous larger networks focused on the City coffee
houses favoured by merchants specialising in the Atlantic trade, notably the New
England in Threadneedle Street (one of the oldest, dating from 1689), which took
the New York newspapers. Other social centres for Americans included Dilly
Brothers in Poultry, who specialised in publishing Americana, and the homes of
'agents' representing the various colonies, who helped their countrymen with
advice, contacts and credit. The most celebrated was Benjamin Franklin's house
in Craven Street, currently being restored as a future focus for Anglo-American
cultural relations.

A large proportion of eighteenth-century London's temporary residents came to
study. Westminster School had a strong connection with the American colonies,
and there are known to have been American boys at Charterhouse and Harrow, as
well as at humbler establishments in Putney, Islington, Mile End and Hackney.
Almost 200 Americans enrolled at the Inns of Court, particularly the Middle
Temple, including six signatories of the Declaration of Independence and George
Washington's aide de camp.[2] They were overwhelmingly from the South, forty-nine
from South Carolina and forty-six from Virginia. Many Americans favoured
Edinburgh for medical studies, but London offered the chance to study under the
eminent anatomist, John Hunter, as well as practical experience. John Collins

Warren, a future professor of Harvard Medical School, trained at Guy's as late as 1799 and the chemist Benjamin Silliman was studying in London in 1805.

Americans undoubtedly figured among the city's 10,000-strong Black population of the late eighteenth century. Newspaper advertisements for runaways testify that many were temporary residents hoping to become permanent ones. Other advertisements reveal that Black slaves were offered for sale in coffee houses. James Somerset, subject of a famous judgment by Lord Mansfield, who ruled that runaways could not be returned to slave countries by force, had himself come as the 'property' of a Boston customs official. A Black minister from Nova Scotia is also recorded.[3]

The outbreak of revolution in the American colonies led to a refugee exodus which decisively altered the character of the American community in London. The 'Loyalist' population is estimated to have numbered between seven and eight thousand, of whom some 5000 submitted claims for compensation to the government and over 700 received Treasury allowances or pensions.[4] As 'Loyalists' rather than 'Americans', they tended to cluster together according to their colonies of origin: Soho was favoured by families from the middle colonies, the Strand by Southerners and the Westminster/Haymarket area by New Englanders, with a sub-colony out at Brompton Row. In 1779 they formed a Loyalist Association under the Presidency of Sir William Pepperell of Portman Square. On the whole, the exiles hated London, finding it cold, damp, smoky, foggy, expensive, inhospitable and vice-ridden. In the words of one of the luckless uprooted, J. H. Cruger, 'this huge unwieldy town swarms with Americans grumbling and discontented'.

This is the more surprising as the City, bound to the colonies by profitable ties of trade, took a sympathetic view of their grievances. Lord Mayor John Wilkes was particularly outspoken, to the 'utter astonishment' of George III. One distinguished American resident who remained unmoved by the turmoil was Benjamin West, History Painter to the King, who continued to enjoy royal favour and eventually succeeded Sir Joshua Reynolds to become the second President of the Royal Academy. His studio in Newman Street became the forcing-house for a stream of American artistic talent, including portraitists John Singleton Copley and John Trumbull, and inventors Robert Fulton and Samuel Morse. At his death in 1820, West was honoured with a state funeral and burial in St Paul's Cathedral.[5]

After the American War of Independence, some of the exiles found situations in Britain, taking over a parish or going on the half-pay list of reserve officers; many re-emigrated to Canada or the West Indies. A special problem was posed by the former Black slaves who had chosen to fight for the British in return for their freedom. In 1786 there were over 1100 of them on the streets of London, mostly penniless. A Committee for the Relief of the Black Poor established a hospice for the worst-off in Warren Street, and distributed food, clothes and some £20,000 in cash among the rest, all but £890 of it coming from government funds. Unwilling to support this situation indefinitely, the authorities invoked the vagrancy laws to coerce 'volunteers' to resettle in Sierra Leone. About 400 eventually went, but after four years only sixty were still alive. One, at least, is known to have stuck it out in London with some success: prize-fighter and cricketer Bill Richmond (1763–1829) of New York ended up with his own pub and boxing academy.

The creation of an independent United States meant the establishment of permanent diplomatic representation in London. The first minister to the court of St James's was John Adams, who established the Embassy's long connection with Grosvenor Square by taking a house there in 1785. 'Prince Saunders', a Black New Englander, represented Haiti in 1816, and there was a separate Texas Legation in St James's Street from 1843 to 1845.

The most significant figure in the nineteenth-century business community was undoubtedly George Peabody (1795–1869). Arriving in London in the aftermath of a major banking crisis which had wrecked the creditworthiness of American states and finance houses alike, this dour workaholic restored Americans' reputation for probity, and in so doing made himself a fortune. His efforts to foster closer Anglo-American relations included personally sponsoring the American display at the Great Exhibition of 1851, and inaugurating a highly successful annual Fourth of July dinner. He also donated £500,000 to establish a charitable trust which pioneered the provision of 'cheap, cleanly, well-drained and healthful dwellings for the poor'. Even before his death he was honoured with a statue near the Royal Exchange, and when he did die he was accorded the unique honour of temporary burial in Westminster Abbey before being returned to his native Massachusetts aboard the Royal Navy's latest and largest warship.[6]

British interest in the American slavery issue attracted distinguished visitors and occasional refugees. Frederick Douglass, a former slave who went on to become an important political leader, made an extended stay between 1845 and 1847. In 1851

Peabody Buildings, Westminster. The Peabody Trust was founded in 1862 by the American banker George Peabody 'to ameliorate the condition and augment the comforts' of the London poor

there was a London meeting of fugitive American slaves which was attended by Tennyson. In 1853 Harriet Beecher Stowe, author of *Uncle Tom's Cabin* (1852), was fêted at Lancaster House in the presence of Lords Palmerston, Granville and Russell. Her book sold three times as many copies in Britain as in America and the capital was in the grip of 'Uncle Tom' fever, with slave dramas running at the Adelphi, Royal Victoria and Drury Lane and shopkeepers plastering 'Uncle Tom' on products as various as coffee, china, flageolets and unshrinkable woollen stockings. This may explain William Wells Brown's success the same year finding a publisher for *Clotel*, the first novel by a Black American. Other Black refugees of the period included William and Ellen Craft and William G. Allen, who became headmaster of a school in Islington.

The Fisk Jubilee Singers toured Britain in 1873 to raise funds for Fisk University, a university for Black students in Nashville, Tennessee, and introduced spirituals to the country. They are pictured here on a return tour in 1884

London remained the literary and theatrical capital of the English-speaking world throughout the century, and as such exerted an irresistible attraction to culture-conscious Americans. Washington Irving, the first American writer to gain a reputation outside his native country, did so while serving as a junior diplomat in London. Other major literary pilgrims included Fenimore Cooper, Nathaniel Hawthorne, Ralph Waldo Emerson, Herman Melville, Mark Twain, Stephen Crane, Robert Frost, Oliver Wendell Holmes and Jack London. Literary settlers included Frances Hodgson Burnett, Henry James, Bret Harte, Ezra Pound, T. S. Eliot and *New York Tribune* correspondent George Smalley. New York-born Ira Aldridge made his London stage debut in 1825 but fell victim to the brutal racism of the local press, although he later achieved a brilliant reputation as a tragedian throughout Europe. The dancer William Henry Lane came to London in 1848, 'dazzled' Dickens and stayed until his death in 1852. Queen Victoria appears to have been a consistent patron of Black American performers: in 1838 she presented the versatile Frank Johnson with a silver bugle, in 1853 she applauded the soprano Elizabeth Taylor Greenfield, and in 1873 and 1881 she commanded special performances from the Fisk Jubilee Singers and Haverley's Colored Minstrels respectively. (The Fisk troupe, singing to raise money for their college, introduced spirituals to Britain.) In 1903 the cast of the American musical *In Dahomey* popularised the 'cakewalk'. In the intervening years, the British stage benefited enormously from the managerial talents of long-term residents Knoblock, Boucicault and Ryder Fiske.

With the onset of agricultural depression in the 1870s, the British aristocracy looked westwards to remedy their misfortunes through matrimony. Between then and the outbreak of the First World War, nearly 100 American heiresses married into Britain's social elite; Jennie Jerome, mother of Winston Churchill, was one of the earliest. Around the turn of the century, Charles Street, Portman Square, Berkeley Square and Great Cumberland Place each numbered three transatlantic *grandes dames* among their residents; Chesterfield Gardens had four and ultra-exclusive Carlton House Terrace no fewer than eight. Most London Americans were, however, more concerned with making money than spending it. Prominent among the business community were the shady but energetic Charles Tyson Yerkes, promoter of the Northern, Bakerloo and Piccadilly lines, department store supremo Gordon Selfridge, financial mogul J. P. Morgan, inventor Hiram Maxim and would-be English milord Waldorf Astor.

The prominence of Americans in London at the beginning of the twentieth century was sufficient to support the publication of an annual Directory from 1901 to 1906. The Residential section of the first edition included some 400 names, including several people of Canadian origin; these represented only a small, prominent fraction of a community which a contemporary American journalist estimated to be 20,000 strong.[7] Heading the 'glitterati' were the distinguished painters Edwin Austin Abbey, John Singer Sargent and J. A. M. Whistler, the principal baritone of the Royal Opera, the Principal of the Normal College for the Blind, the wife of the Fleet Paymaster and two Fellows of the Royal Geographical Society. Many listed their addresses as c/o such clubs as the Savile, Savage and Athenaeum, or hotels, the Cecil and the brand-new Russell being particularly favoured. A separate section listed some eighty-six titled Americans, including ten with French titles, three with German ones and the Princesses Cantacuzene, Colonna (two), Poggio-Suasa, Poniatowska and Vicovaro. Serving the needs of these 'swells' was a sub-elite of specialised professionals, including firms of lawyers and accountants and no fewer than fifteen dentists.

The humbler, but still no doubt prosperous, members of the North American community were indirectly represented through the listing of the companies that employed them. Running to over fifty pages, the Business Directory section lists such household names as American Express, Armour, Heinz, Horlicks, Libby, Ponds, Quaker Oats and Shredded Wheat. The largest category of companies listed (more than fifty of them) were connected with engineering, machinery, steel and railways. The next largest categories were chemist's goods, office equipment (including seventeen typewriter importers), canned goods, shoes and boots, sewing-machines and cars and bicycles. To service this commerce, there were thirty-four specialised firms of British–American merchants and twenty-one American banks.

No doubt the social and commercial élites mixed at the various occasions organised by the American Society in London or the Society of American Women in London (for 'the thinking women of the US'). The Anglo-American League was established in 1898, and the Atlantic Union in 1900. There were also two lodges of Freemasons: the Columbia, whose members were both British and American, and the America, which was restricted to Americans only. In 1913 alumni of America's oldest university formally institutionalised themselves as the Harvard Club of London.

Cultural relations were also served by representatives of twenty-two magazines and thirty-six publishers, and by two weekly newspapers, *The Anglo-American* and *The London American*. In a slightly different way, they were doubtless also furthered by the capital's nine self-styled American bars, including that of the Queen's Hotel, Leicester Square, which boasted bartender Arthur E. Mullens of New York.

American entertainment in London was especially strong but had two separate lists — one consisting of forty-three musical and dramatic artistes, the other of 162 vaudeville performers. Many of the latter were doubtless seasonal visitors, giving as accommodation addresses the theatres and music halls which employed them, principally the Alhambra, Palace and Hippodrome. Although the majority were singers or comedians, the vaudeville listing contains a remarkably high proportion of speciality acts, including several sharpshooters and bicycle experts, as well as such curiosities as barrel-jumpers, 'musical blacksmiths' and Houdini, Handcuff King.

The outbreak of war in 1914 saw 150,000 American tourists stranded in Europe. Of these, 120,000 were safely repatriated through the good offices of a relief committee headquartered in the Savoy Hotel and headed by London-based consulting engineer Herbert Hoover.[8] By 1917 the flow was in the reverse direction as London welcomed American servicemen as allies. Special permission was granted for men on leave to sleep overnight in the Royal Courts of Justice and Eagle Hut, at the Aldwych, supplied suitable refreshments. (An inscription on the north wall of Bush House, itself an American development, marks its site.)

An American Chamber of Commerce was established in 1916 and in 1919 the American Club opened its doors at 95 Piccadilly. Other organisations catered more particularly for social, charitable and leisure interests. There was the American Golfing Society, the American Circle (a women's group), the Pilgrims of Great Britain, the English-Speaking Union, the Old Colony Club (for businessmen) and the Sulgrave Institution (preserving the ancestral home of George Washington), as well

The Rainbow Club,
Piccadilly, 1942

as European representative offices for the American League, the YMCA, the Red
Cross and Relief Administration. The office of the American University Union in
Europe was a portent of what was to come.

The Second World War witnessed the same pattern of civilian evacuation and
service influx. The Grosvenor Square area became known to Londoners as
'Eisenhowerplatz'. Former fashion artist Francis Marshall described leaving Piccadilly
Circus Underground station: 'Coming out in the black-out American voices were all
around.'[9] A stone's throw away was 'Rainbow Corner', a reception centre which
was a mecca for Yanks on leave. On the north side of Shaftesbury Avenue, in the
Bouillabaisse on New Compton Street and at Frisco's, American voices added to
the multi-lingual hubbub. The jazz scene was undoubtedly enriched by the American
presence. Less happy was the temporary importation of the 'colour bar' still oper-
ating in the US forces. In October 1942 the first five Black girls arrived with a specific mission to care for off-duty Black GIs. An Albert Hall concert of spirituals by
200 Black servicemen in October 1943 was widely covered in the press. Just as the
aftermath of the First World War saw the celebration of the 'special relationship'

through the raising of London statues to Washington and Lincoln, so the Second World War led to the raising of a statue to Roosevelt, a memorial to the American volunteer Eagles squadrons of the RAF, and the rededication of the rebuilt Jesus Chapel of St Paul's Cathedral as the American Memorial Chapel.

London's American community is now estimated to be 50,000 strong, though many of these are, as ever, temporary residents. (The American Church in Tottenham Court Road reckons on a one-third annual turnover in its 400-strong congregation.[10]) Many of the community's old-established institutions – the American Chamber of Commerce, the American Club, the American Women's Club – are still in business. Networking is as vigorous an impulse among London Americans as it was in Benjamin Franklin's day, with new initiatives including a singles organisation, a newsletter for bankers, an American Society of Composers, Authors and Publishers, and an Anglo-American Medical Society. The traditional commercial interests, in finance and manufacturing, have been diversified by the growth of companies representing the oil industry and media services. The educational and academic presence in the capital grows annually stronger, through the success of schools catering primarily for the American community and also through the dozens of centres administering 'study abroad' programmes for US universities. London at last seems to be taking notice of American sports. If Americans feel as comfortable in London as they have in the past, particularly now following the post-war Americanisation of London's high streets, they still represent a culture with distinct standards of its own in some vital aspects, hence the specialist American drycleaners, doughnut-makers – and dentists.

Endnotes

For full details of publications see Bibliography.

1 Bailyn and Morgan, 1991, p403.
2 E. A. Jones, 1924.
3 Fryer, 1984.
4 National Maritime Museum, 1976, p131.
5 Kenin, 1979, p1.
6 Ibid, p105.
7 MacColl and Wallace, 1989, pp360–4.
8 Elizabeth L. Banks, 'American in London', in George R. Sims (ed.), *Living London*, Cassell & Co, London, 1902, p126.
9 Francis Marshall, *London West*, The Studio, London, 1944, p95.
10 Interview with Rev. Vern Frazier.

Arabs in London · Camillia Fawzi El-Solh

In certain areas of London, one almost inevitably stumbles upon evidence of the presence of Arabs in the British capital: newsagents, bookshops, art galleries, grocery stores, restaurants, community centres, cultural clubs, schools, estate agents, consultancy firms, banks, mosques and churches. To the uninitiated, these venues are part and parcel of an immigrant culture perceived in largely undifferentiated terms as 'other', ie outside White British mainstream society. To the more knowledgeable, they are links with the Arab world, even when their names or other forms of identification only hint at such a relationship.

On one level, this visibility justifies the use of the term 'Arab' as a collective category, in which history, culture and consciousness of belonging function as common denominators. A collective consciousness surfaced during the Gulf War in 1991, when Arabs in Britain from all walks of life reactivated commonalities binding them, not least because of the way they were negatively stereotyped in the British tabloids. A similar 'Arab' identity has emerged over the question of the Palestinians' right to self-determination.

However, this collective identity goes hand in hand with important distinctions between and within Arab communities, based on such variables as country of origin in the Arab world,[1] religious, ethnic and political affiliations, socio-economic status, language and dialect, age group and gender, the numerical strength of the community and whether its members are scattered in various parts of London or concentrated in particular areas.[2] Moreover, while this visibility may tell us something about the contemporary Arab presence in London, it reveals little about the settlement history of various Arab communities or the multitude of reasons which brought their members to Britain in the first place.

Unearthing the history of Arab communities in Britain is difficult, partly because of the hitherto inadequate data, which for the most part lumps Arab communities together under the category 'Middle East'. Published material on early immigrant communities in Britain is relatively limited, affording few glimpses of the first Arab settlers.[3] In addition, the term 'Arab' has all too often tended to be used almost synonymously with the term 'Muslim', neglecting to distinguish between Arab and non-Arab Muslims, as well as overlooking non-Muslim Arabs. More often than not, the association of the term 'Arab' with oil wealth conjures up in the popular Western images of affluence spiced with the exotic, thereby overlooking those

Arabs in Britain who are trapped in menial employment or are subject to the restrictions of their asylum status.

The earliest wave of immigrants from what is today known as the Arab region are believed to have arrived in Britain during the second half of the nineteenth century, perhaps even earlier. As with other immigrant groups, they came from countries which had colonial or other political or economic links with Britain. Yemeni seafarers recruited by the British merchant navy began to settle in areas nearest their source of livelihood, namely London's docklands.[4] By the beginning of the twentieth century, they had established their own distinct community in London's East End, maintaining social links with relatives settled in other British ports such as Cardiff, Liverpool and South Shields. Lodging houses and seamen's cafés provided many Yemenis with a niche which served to reinforce their sense of identity. In the absence of Yemeni women, they were apparently inclined to marry indigenous British women, at least during the earlier settlement phases, but the minority who did inter-marry continued to find themselves as socially marginalised as those who did not. This was partly due to manifestations of racism against them

A rhubarb and spice seller, 1850s. From Mogadore in Morocco, this 73-year-old street seller interviewed by Henry Mayhew called himself an Arab. He was of the Jewish faith, and married a Christian

as newcomers, partly because of their socio-economic status as a largely unskilled migrant labour force, but also a consequence of their seafaring life. Their British wives, some of whom are said to have converted to Islam, were for the most part incorporated into the Yemeni community, often losing their links with their own families. This social marginalisation prevailed, in spite of the Yemenis' labour contribution during times when the British economy needed every available hand, particularly during the two World Wars.

By the end of the 1950s, the declining fortunes of the British merchant navy had begun to push many Yemenis into seeking employment elsewhere in London, or in industrial and manufacturing centres in other parts of Britain. This eventually led to the shrinking of the Yemeni community in London's East End, a trend poignantly reflected in the closure of the last Yemeni-owned café and in the dwindling number of *qat*-sellers.[5] Those who have remained are scattered throughout Greater London, and the Yemeni community in the East End appears to have been consigned to history.[6]

Moroccans are another Arab community with a more or less distinct history of settlement in London. As with many economic migrants who found their way to Britain during the 1950s and 1960s, they were recruited to fill job vacancies in the British labour market, in this case in the hotel and catering industries, and to some extent the National Health Service. Because of their limited market skills and lack of English, they almost inevitably did the lowest-paid jobs, providing little scope for career mobility. The increasingly restrictive immigration rules set in motion by the late 1960s and early 1970s encouraged many to bring their families over from Morocco, thus transforming what was originally a temporary migration in search of a livelihood into longer-term settlement. They lived mainly in north Kensington and, to a much lesser extent, in east London.

The Moroccan community's main problems today are related to its relatively low educational and skill levels, and its high level of unemployment. These have served further to relegate Moroccans to the margins of British mainstream society, a position from which they find it difficult to move. Added to these problems are the almost inevitable tensions between the first generation holding on to the cherished dream of returning to the homeland, a dream regularly replenished through visits to the home country, and the younger generation socialised in Britain. These tensions tend to find expression in the search for a meaningful Muslim identity within a Western culture that all too often views Islam as a cultural intrusion. They are also reflected in debates concerning culturally appropriate roles for women.

The Egyptians are a community of particular interest. In contrast to the Yemenis and Moroccans, who are almost exclusively Muslim, there are both Muslim and Christian (Coptic) Egyptians settled in London. Again in contrast to these other two communities, whose members are predominantly working-class within the British social context, the Egyptian community includes working, middle- and upper-middle-classes. Their settlement dates back to the 1940s and 1950s, when skilled and semi-skilled Egyptians came in search of employment in Britain, or remained after completing their studies. Eventually, less skilled Egyptians found their way to Britain, and today the Egyptian community is believed to be one of the largest Arab groups in London.[7] It includes such names as Magdi Yacoub, the internationally renowned heart specialist, and the Al-Fayed brothers (of Harrods fame). Egyptian influence is further evident in, for example, the leadership of the Council of Imams and Mosques and the Islamic Society for the Promotion of Religious Tolerance in London.

The Iraqi community deserves to be singled out because it contains a large number of political refugees. Iraqi settlement in Britain dates back to the 1930s when, because of their association with Britain's political influence in Iraq, Assyrians (a Christian sect) began to settle in Britain. Their pre-emigration history has served to encourage the disassociation of this relatively small community from non-Assyrian Iraqis in particular, and other Arab communities in general. By the 1940s and 1950s, skilled and professional Iraqis also began to settle in Britain, their numbers augmented by those fleeing the repercussions of the revolution which had toppled the monarchy in Iraq in 1958. Like, for example, the Egyptian community during this period, Iraqis generally did not cluster in particular areas of London. It was only with the influx of Kurdish and Shi'a Iraqis fleeing political persecution in Iraq during the 1970s and 1980s that a discernible Iraqi community, divided into sub-groups differentiated by political and religious ideology, began to emerge.

Other Arabs who began to settle in Britain during the 1940s and 1950s included Palestinians after the creation of Israel in 1948, and Sudanese. The latter were predominantly professionals who remained after completing their studies. As with the Iraqis and Egyptians during this period, they were numerically too insignificant to form distinct communities.

To some extent, the 1970s were a turning-point in the history of Arab settlement in London. The economic boom in the aftermath of the 1973 oil crisis, coupled with political instability in parts of the Arab world (in particular the repercussions of the Lebanese civil war), encouraged many Arab nationals to seek a new life and investment opportunities in the West. Arabs in London began to include Lebanese, Syrians, Palestinians and some Jordanians, mainly of middle- and upper-middle-class origin. They brought with them their capital and/or expertise, which led to the proliferation of many Arab businesses and the establishment of London as an important centre for the Arabic-language press. Arab writers and poets, some of them escaping censorship in their country of origin, helped to further the impression of London as an Arab 'cultural centre'. Nationals from Saudi Arabia and other Arab Gulf states added their share to the proliferation of Arab investment in Britain,[8] though their presence has tended to be temporary and seasonal. By the late 1970s and during the 1980s, the diversity which was becoming more characteristic of Arab communities in London was enhanced by the arrival of refugees from countries such as Somalia, Lebanon and the Sudan, and, as mentioned above, from Iraq. The varied class origins and educational or skill levels of these refugees, the increasingly restrictive immigration controls and the repercussions of

Arabic newspaper stand in London. The city has become a centre for the Arab press

the economic recession have all affected their socio-economic status in Britain.[9] Generally, unless they can prove a connection with relatives living in London, refugees are housed in the borough whose turn it is to provide them with social services and housing. This practice has inadvertently led to the increased dispersal of Arab newcomers over many parts of London and its suburbs.

The contemporary diversity of Arabs in London is reflected by the various community associations which have proliferated all over the capital. Some, for example the Arab Club of Britain, attempt to cater to a wide Arab audience, organising cultural events and activities, youth clubs and Arabic-language schools and publishing a regular newsletter. Although in reality the club mainly attracts middle-class Arabs from the eastern Arab world and most working-class Arabs remain outside its orbit, it does try to foster an Arab consciousness divorced from any particular ideology. Other organisations tend to focus on their own nationals. For example, the Moroccan Information and Advice Centre (see colour plate 5) directs its services and activities mainly towards working-class Moroccans living within the vicinity of its premises in north Kensington, although outsiders seeking advice are not turned away; the existence of the Hasaniyya Moroccan Women's Centre nearby indicates some factionalism within the Moroccan community, in this case reflected in ideological differences over gender issues. Other organisations, such as the Iraqi Community Association, reflect changing alliances in response to political developments in the country of origin: Iraqi Kurds and Iraqi Shi'a have formed their own associations, which address issues of special concern to their needs and priorities, for example, the Kurdistan Solidarity Committee and the Shi'a Ahl Ul-Bayt.

Parallel to these associations, whose membership is almost exclusively Arab, are those which actively seek to cultivate contacts with the host society. The Council for the Advancement of Arab-British Understanding (CAABU), the Anglo-Jordanian Society and the British Lebanese Association, for example, are all keen to promote relations between Britain and segments of the Arab world. Arab membership in these associations is largely confined to middle- and upper-middle-class Arabs, ie precisely those who, because of their economic background, generally have less of a problem maintaining links with the home country.

Arab women in London, 1992

The affiliations that may both bind and divide Arab communities become even more complex when religious persuasion is taken into consideration. Arab Christians such as the Egyptian Copts and the Iraqi Assyrians have their own churches, in Kensington and Ealing respectively, reflecting their longer settlement history as well as their community cohesion in London. In contrast, Catholic, Greek Orthodox and Protestant Arabs of mainly Jordanian, Lebanese, Palestinian and Syrian origin generally attend the churches of their respective co-confessionals in London, although they may hold separate services. The national origin of the leaders of some Muslim organisations in London is also indicative of Arab efforts and activities in this sphere. Arabs tend to predominate in the Central Mosque in Regent's Park, perhaps the most visible indication of the presence of Muslims in Britain, given its location in the heart of London (see colour plate 11). However, Arab-dominated religious venues do not exclude non-Arabs of the Muslim faith and Asian mosques are generally open to Arab worshippers living in their vicinity. In effect, church and mosque tend to function as the place where Arabs from different communities affirm their religious identity and, to some extent, the bonds they have in common, regardless of the many factors that may separate them.

Like so many other ethnic communities settled in London, Arabs from all walks of life wish to secure for themselves a position in British society that they feel comfortable with. Not surprisingly, given the diversity of Arab communities, the search can be a complex one. For some, in particular those whose social status tends to perpetuate their marginalisation within the British social hierarchy, it can be painful and disheartening. All too often, the world beyond the divide which separates them physically and culturally from British mainstream society is perceived as unwelcoming, if not hostile. For the middle- and upper-middle-class Arab, British mainstream society may seem less intimidating. The better-educated Arabs often find integration easier, and enjoy greater flexibility in deciding whether to remain in Britain, to return to their country of origin or to seek opportunities elsewhere. Their unskilled working-class compatriots have less prospect of earning a living back in their home country, or of emigrating elsewhere for employment. Thus, it is often the socio-economically marginalised Arabs who, for lack of viable alternatives, are most likely to end up settling more or less permanently in Britain, however pervasive the myth of return.

Endnotes

For full details of publications, see Bibliography.

1 For the purpose of this essay, Arabs are defined as nationals from countries which are members of the League of Arab States: Algeria, Bahrain, Djibouti, Egypt, Iraq, Jordan, Kuwait, Lebanon, Libya, Mauritania, Morocco, Oman, Palestine, Qatar, Saudi Arabia, Somalia, Sudan, Syria, Tunisia, United Arab Emirates and Yemen. This list includes some countries in which Arabic is not the main or official language.

2 For a wider discussion of the multitude of differences and commonalities between and within Arab communities in London, see Fawzi El-Solh, 1992.

3 See, for example, Little, 1948; Banton, 1955; Collins, 1957. The very titles of these volumes unconsciously reflect the view of what at the time were perceived to be non-indigenous communities in Britain, where race and skin colour, rather than ethnic differences per se, were the main markers of differentiation.

4 See Fawzi El-Solh, 1991. Another important immigrant group during this period were merchants from the Ottoman regions of present-day Lebanon and Syria, as well as from Morocco, who settled in such urban trading centres as Manchester. A descendant from this merchant community is the eminent late historian Albert Hourani, whose recently published book *A History of the Arab Peoples* (Faber, London, 1991) topped the bestseller list for many weeks.

5 *Qat* is a mildly narcotic plant which may be legally imported into Britain (mainly from Kenya). Djibouti, Somalia and Yemen appear to be the only Arab League countries in which *qat* is legally grown and/or chewed (Ethiopia and Kenya being the other East African countries where its consumption is widespread). It is legally prohibited in Saudi Arabia and other Arab Gulf countries where the bulk of Yemeni migrants used to settle. *Qat*-dealers in London's East End are now mainly Somalis, including a number of Somali women who derive an income from this informal sector activity.

6 For historical details of Yemeni settlement in Britain, see Halliday, 1992.

7 Egyptians in London maintain that their community numbers at least 60,000, while the estimate for all Arabs in the UK has been variously set at between 230,000 and 500,000. The 1991 Census, however, recorded 9301 Egyptian-born people living in London.

8 For example, the Kuwait Investment Office in London is believed to have invested billions of pounds sterling in Britain over the past two decades, and members of the ruling family in the United Arab Emirates have invested millions in the British race horse industry.

9 A pertinent example of the implications of loss of socio-economic status is that of Iraqis in London, described by Al-Rashid, 1992.

Australians and New Zealanders in London · Rick Bouwman

Many commuters in London will have seen, and possibly read, one of the free magazines produced for Australians and New Zealanders, available all over London: *TNT*, *Southern Cross* or *New Zealand News* (see colour plate 12). They contain news and information for expatriate Australasians,[1] specifically young Australasians in London on working-holiday visas, as well as advertisements for jobs in nursing, accountancy, catering, teaching and engineering, and for accommodation, travel and entertainment.

For many Londoners, the presence of these young expatriates in visible occupations (bar attendants, agency nurses, office 'temps' and supply teachers) reinforces the long-lived stereotype of Australasians as young, carefree, self-reliant and transient, here to have a good time, travel around Europe and socialise with fellow-compatriots. This stereotype has developed over a period of three decades or more, beginning in the 1950s when the first groups of Australasians settled in London, most notoriously in bedsits in Earl's Court.

British familiarity with the Australasian community has increased through images of Antipodean (mainly Australian) life in the British media: television programmes such as 'Neighbours', 'Clive James on Television' and 'The Dame Edna Experience', beer advertisements and the renown of the All Blacks and cricketers. It is certainly not based on numbers – the 42,000 Australians and New Zealanders in London in 1991 made up merely 0.6 per cent of the population.

Australia and New Zealand are both young countries, settled and culturally formed by their 'mother country', Britain. New Zealand took its first step towards independence in 1840 with the signing of the Treaty of Waitangi between British representatives of the Crown and the native Maori, with whom they had been at war. Australia was a collection of colonies, each ruled from Westminster via a governor until 1901, when the colonies federated. Subsequently, each country has passed through various stages more or less simultaneously, from colony to dominion to member of the Old Commonwealth. Today the link with Britain is tenuous, with republican sentiment strengthening, particularly in Australia. Periodic outbursts of anti-royal feeling also surface in New Zealand, most notably during Waitangi Day celebrations and royal visits.

Although cultural ties with Britain have loosened, the process of cultural independence is complicated, uncertain and far from complete, and certainly differs

between Australia and New Zealand. Profound social changes in both countries include migration, recession, the influence of nationalism and policies promoting multi-culturalism. These have changed them from the monocultural and, some felt, complacent societies they were, even two decades ago. In both countries, a significant proportion of the population now has no social or cultural links with the UK. Encouragement of identification with local regions (the Pacific for New Zealand, South East Asia or Japan for Australia) is having an effect; many people, including those with an Anglo-Celtic heritage, now look towards Europe or the United States rather than Britain. This trend has been accentuated by the widely held perception that when Britain joined the EEC in 1973 it was Britain who cut the apron strings and, in the words of a New Zealand historian, 'Mother deserted'.[2]

Young Australians touring in London, Market Road, Islington, 1992

Even so, in both nations significant segments of the population are broadly Anglo-Celtic in culture and sympathies, and feel drawn to Britain in some way. Language is an important link, as is 'high' and popular culture, including film and television. 'Refined' accents are still valued socially, with regional or demotic speech often used for comic effect. But this cultural link with Britain is most strongly felt by older generations. A young New Zealander is just as likely today to look to the west coast of the United States or to Sydney or Brisbane for culture, adventure and new experiences, and a growing number of Australians are exploring South East Asia rather than routinely setting off to London. For those who do come to London, Britain is certainly no longer 'home'.

The change in the relationship between Australians or New Zealanders and Britain can be traced to the time when young people spoke less of going 'home' and started planning to go 'overseas' or, more recently, 'OS'. The time has long since passed when it was a compliment to be described, as the nineteenth-century cricketer Fred Spofforth was, as being 'like all the better class of Australians, not distinguishable from an English gentleman'.[3]

The first Australians to visit London were the Aborigines Bennelong and Yemmerawanyea, who went to England with Governor Philip in 1792 and were feted as exotic Noble Savages. Yemmerawanyea died in 1794, and is buried at Eltham churchyard (see colour plate 12). Bennelong lost most of his curiosity value after a year or two and returned to Australia in 1795.[4] Governor Philip was an Englishman, as were his successors, at least until the turn of the century; Australia did not have a native-born governor-general until the 1960s. Until at least the 1870s, 'New Zealander' meant Maori; Whites were British settlers, aiming to create a genteel 'second Britain'. In the 1920s, when 50 per cent of New Zealand's population were not New Zealand-born, the relationship to Britain as 'home' was particularly strong. The 'establishment' and the 'respectable' loyally cultivated an emotional bond with the 'green and pleasant land' (although there were fierce patriots in both countries after 1900). The future Australian prime minister Robert Menzies (son of a Scottish father and a Cornish mother) wrote this in his diary on his first visit to England in 1935: 'At last we are in England. [The] journey to Mecca has ended ... for souls ... who go home to a land they have never seen.'[5]

Between the wars, there was a steady artistic and professional exodus from both Australia and New Zealand. It has been said that New Zealand's greatest export at this time was brains and talent, among them physicist Ernest Rutherford, writer Katherine Mansfield and artist Frances Hodgkins.

Sport and, especially, war contributed to the maturing of the relationship. The Anzac experience provided a powerful oppositional myth for both Australians and New Zealanders; Stuart MacIntyre writes of the Australian soldier, 'His confidence in the British Army suffered an initial shock at Gallipoli from which it never recovered.'[6] Even today, the Anzac celebrations draw large numbers of young Australasians to the Gallipoli peninsula, motivated by a mixture of national pride and contempt for the British.

After the Second World War cheap sea and, later, air travel and increased afflu-ence meant that what had been available only to the rich could now be enjoyed by the middle classes. Barry Humphries, the son of a suburban bank manager, longed to escape from the narrow confines of Melbourne life to the imagined riches of London, in his mind the centre of world culture. Many of the artistic and creative expatriates who came to London in the 1950s and 1960s – Peter Finch, Clive James, Germaine Greer, Richard Neville, John Pilger, John Williams, Charles Mackerras, Joan Sutherland, Peter Porter – felt themselves to be, to some degree, escapees from the periphery to the centre, like country people making the break to the city. Some felt they had little choice. Clive James describes the atmosphere in 1950s Sydney student circles, where going to London was as much a rite of passage as buying a duffel coat or learning how to fall in love or get drunk.[7] Australian news-paper journalists, as Stephen Alomes has shown, could reach a dead end at the top of their careers in the Australian press by their early twenties, and were then attracted to London at a time when Fleet Street truly was Mecca; some Australian papers refused to send correspondents to England, but employed them once they had arrived.[8] Musicians and academics were attracted by the still very high reputations of British institutions. As Commonwealth citizens travelling on British passports, they were free to support themselves once they arrived; all they needed was the cost of their passage. A small number came on academic scholarships, including Germaine Greer and the future MP Bryan Gould, and many stayed on. As early as the 1960s, a pattern had emerged within the expatriate community: a divi-sion between professionals, who came to London to 'make it' in their chosen field, and travellers, on whom the reputation of Australasians has largely rested. This pat-tern continues. However, from the mid-1960s neither group believed it was return-ing 'home' – London was, and is, a means to an end, to fun, freedom or fulfilment.

Historically, the great period of Australasian presence in London, for prof-essionals and travellers, was between about 1963 and 1973. This can be explained by four factors. First was the growing affluence in Australia and New Zealand, the associated expansion of higher education, the development of youth culture and the ideology of youthful independence. Second, in Australia at least, was the so-called 'cultural cringe' away from provincialism and isolation. Third, the growth of 'swinging London' was a magnet for adventurous youth, as well as for those who aspired to work in the media, fashion or music. Finally, there was the virtually com-plete lack of immigration restrictions; a New Zealand passport of this period was marked 'New Zealand citizen and British subject', and Australians enjoyed similar freedom. This situation ended in 1973 when the UK entered the European Common Market.

The centre of Australasian life in London was Earl's Court, 'a neighbourhood of strangers washed over by a steamy monsoon of laundromats', 'a poisoned water-hole of bedsitterland [whose] littered pavements teem with other people's grown-up children'.[9] Its bohemian atmosphere and faded gentility contrasted with the wealth and respectability of most of the rest of the borough of Kensington and

The *Earls Courtier*, 1962. 'The Newspaper for Overseas Visitors' captures something of the cosmopolitan atmosphere of Earls Court

Chelsea. It was an area of bedsits and cheap hotels, first popular with Italian hotel workers, as well as Caribbean immigrants who gave it its early nickname of 'Jamaica Inn'. The first 'colonials' to be associated with the neighbourhood were South Africans, and as late as the mid-1960s South Africans and Rhodesians rather than Australians and New Zealanders were the dominant 'White Commonwealth' group. The Overseas Visitors Club (OVC), founded in 1955, originally catered for South Africans, who also had their own Voortrekkers Club, but its appeal for young travellers widened. In the following decade the OVC welcomed more than 100,000 of them, meeting visitors from ships at Tilbury and Southampton and bringing them to Earl's Court, where it organised tours, accommodation and employ-ment. Those who intended to stay longer rented a bedsitter or a flat. At a time when it was unusual for young people to live on their own before marriage, a bedsit meant independence and excitement; the pattern of many people experiencing this in a relatively small area gave Earl's Court its bohemian and, in the 1960s, risqué atmosphere. It soon became a favourite haunt of journalists looking for stories with a sensational 'youth' angle. Colonials stood out, clean-cut, short-haired, wide-eyed, thirsty – a contrast to the beatniks and hippies who also populated the area.

In the late 1960s, the character of the area as a centre of the 'meet-and-greet' agencies and of accommodation and services was reinforced by the growth of air travel, following the development of Heathrow Airport. The Piccadilly line to Heathrow brought travellers right into Earl's Court Road. This led to more OVC-type travellers' support organisations, some of which, like Trailfinders and Top Deck, still trade from premises in the area.

Despite being known as 'Kangaroo Valley, SW5', Earl's Court was never an exclu-sively Australasian enclave, nor were all Australasian visitors and settlers, especially the professionals, drawn there. For instance, Clive James lived in Cambridge, on a houseboat in Richmond and in Tufnell Park, while Barry Humphries lived in Notting Hill Gate and Little Venice. According to some sources, after a time some Australasians, perhaps the better-off ones, did not want to live in Earl's Court.

However, it was close to the West End, with relatively cheap accommodation and, more important, late-night clubs and pubs, and hence became associated with the group identified as 'well-heeled, hard-drinking and short-staying young colonials'.[10]

While this group took tours around London to see sights glimpsed only on calendars or biscuit tins, homecoming sentiments like those expressed by Robert Menzies in 1935 were rarely felt. Expatriate Australian actor Bill Kerr made a more realistic appraisal of the Australasian attitude to the 'mother country': 'It's a lot of nonsense that England is the natural home for all Australians. Let's face it, London is a good place to get a job, save up some shekels, buy an old banger and do the Continent.'[11]

Earl's Court changed markedly in the 1970s and 1980s in response to local concern about the area and its perceived social problems (drug use, crowded housing, public drunkenness and the gay scene). From the early 1970s the number of bedsits and hotel beds was reduced. Between 1971 and 1981 the private rental sector halved, as did the number of young adults in the area, while the overall population fell by 30 per cent, a decline which has continued. Earl's Court still has the largest number of hotel bedrooms in the borough of Kensington and Chelsea (in the summer an estimated one-third of its residents are tourists), but it is no longer the magnet for expatriates and travellers it once was, mainly because it has become too expensive. Australasian pubs, clubs, travel services and agencies now serve young tourists of all nationalities and Australasian facilities are common elsewhere, especially in west London, in Acton and Ealing for instance. In terms of residents, the numbers of Irish, Filipino, Polish, Iranian and Egyptian households match or outnumber Australasian ones.

The number of Australasians resident in London has risen in the last decade, from just under 27,000 in 1981 to almost 42,000 in 1991, but they are much more evenly distributed than in the past. Large groups now set up shared houses in areas such as Golders Green, Acton or Willesden. The top boroughs for Australasian residence in 1991, making up about 30 per cent of the total, are all in inner London and virtually abut one another: Kensington and Chelsea, Hammersmith and Fulham, Westminster and Camden. Australasians are fairly evenly spread throughout the remaining boroughs of Greater London. The majority are under the age of twenty-seven, and stay in the UK for up to two years on a so-called working-holiday visa. These visas forbid full-time or permanent work and residence to all but the tiny minority of Australasians who have family links with the UK. They permit work for no more than half the year. This restriction is the most obvious difference between the status of Australasians today and those who came in the 1960s and settled permanently.

Ironically, this status of working holiday-makers probably does a great deal to preserve aspects of the 1960s Earl's Court culture. The 'escape' nature of the working holiday and the youth of the travellers supports a culture, much like that of past times, based on partying and travel, and supported by part-time work in the traditional travellers' occupations of nannying, nursing, teaching and temporary

THE COOLABAH
ENTERTAINMENT NIGHTLY!

3 NORTH END CRESCENT
WEST KENSINGTON, W.14

TELEPHONE: 01-603 3621

OLYMPIA
HAMMERSMITH ROAD
BUS ROUTES
9, 9A, 27, 28, 73
NORTH END ROAD
WEST CROMWELL ROAD
West Kensington
200 yards from West Kensington Tube Station

Get your ass into gear and
come along and see US !!!

☆ OPEN 7 NIGHTS A WEEK
☆ 8 DIFFERENT AUSSIE BEERS
☆ TOP LINE D.J.s
☆ LIVE GROUPS
☆ GOOD TUCKER

Bar flyer, c. 1980. Australians and New Zealanders in London have always been quick to develop their own forms of entertainment

secretarial and accountancy work. There are 'Aussie' and 'Kiwi' pubs, and Waitangi and Australia Day celebrations. However, the current recession seems to have had some effect on the pattern of work and travel among this traveller group. Although independent travel ('back-packing') is still popular, more people are reluctant to give up jobs at home and are instead taking shorter periods of leave.

Following the pattern established in the 1960s, another group of Australasians are coming to Britain for a couple of years and working in semi-permanent or permanent employment, travelling only during leave. They are keen to gain professional experience, and seem to make more effort to become involved in local London entertainment and social networks. According to a recent survey conducted by *New Zealand News*, only 12 per cent of their readers were in temporary work, and only 1 per cent considered themselves to be on holiday. The majority fitted a profile of young, professional people, seriously pursuing career goals; they were here, in the words of one New Zealander, to 'make a life'.

Are Australasians in London a community or merely an energetic group of hedonistic transients, with cultural traits obvious to outsiders? Are they comparable with more established groups who have settled in London as immigrants or refugees? Australasians certainly have little profile in the eyes of government as they make few, if any, demands on public or social services. In the case of the travellers, pubs, sporting clubs, events and activities keep this group largely distinct from Londoners. The 'community' is one that is defined by shared activities rather than by more traditional criteria. This community of travellers is not necessarily representative of all Australasians, and it may be shrinking in relation to another group, that of work- or career-oriented young people who wish to take advantage of opportunities in business, the media and the arts. There may also be a division within the Australasian community in relation to work and career: it seems that New Zealanders' motives for coming to the UK may be different from those of many Australians, being based more on a perception of economic necessity. New Zealand suffers from unemployment and a lack of development in certain professions and industries, even more seriously than Australia does. There is a historical precedent for this in the economically depressed 1970s, when so many people left New Zealand (many for Australia as well as Britain) that in one year, 1978, the population of the country actually declined.

Many Australasians are aware of and identify with their background, and to varying degrees they are aware of their difference from Londoners. The *New Zealand News* survey suggested that most intend to return home, especially to marry and raise families. The desire and motivation to fit in is not strong; on the contrary, there is a strong feeling of difference and sometimes superiority, mixed with a feeling of making the most of their desire to enjoy the experience of living in what is increasingly a foreign country.

Endnotes

For full details of publications, see Bibliography.

1 The term 'Australasian' is a useful generalis-
ation in the same way as 'North American',
or even 'British' is. As a Canadian or a Scot
will tell you, such generalisations are not
very satisfactory. 'Australasian' can easily be
elided into 'Australian', in thought and
speech, and New Zealanders justifiably feel
uneasy at its use, especially as they make up
a large proportion (42 per cent in 1991) of
Australasians living in London. The term is
used by outsiders to the group: few New
Zealanders or Australians would refer to
themselves as Australasian, nor do
'Australasians' really exist outside London,
or indeed outside the minds of the British.
Many Australians meet their first New
Zealander in London.

2 Sinclair, 1980, p329.

3 Quoted in Rick Bouwman, *Glorious Innings*,
Hutchinson Australia, Melbourne, 1987, p78.

4 Hughes, 1987, p11; *Eltham's Aborigines
and other links with Australia*, The Eltham
Society, 1988.

5 Quoted in Brett, 1992, pp135–6.

6 MacIntyre, 1986, p180.

7 Clive James's *Falling Towards England* and
May Week was in June are full of hilarious
details of this period.

8 Stephen Alomes, 'A Passage to Somewhere
Else', in *Culture and Colonials: The expat-
riation of Australian Writers to Britain*.
Proceedings of the Commonwealth
Conference, Susan Ballyn and Doriann
MacDermot (eds), University of
Barcelona, 1987.

9 These lurid descriptions come from a profile
by James Horowitz, *Time Out*, 1974 and
from Pippa Phemister, 'High Fashion SW5',
Guardian, 9 December 1966. Articles
routinely referred to Earl's Court as a
'jungle', 'labyrinth', etc.

10 Royal Borough of Kensington and Chelsea
Planning and Research Department, Earl's
Court Report, 1972, p6.

11 Rodney Burbeck, 'Life in Kangaroo Valley,
SW5', *London Life*, 1966.

The Chinese in London · Anthony Shang

Chinese sailors with a cargo of tea being unloaded from their ship, the *Louden Castle*, recently arrived from Hankow, China, in the East India Docks, 1877

Since the Second World War, Chinese migration to Britain has been the result of openings created by the popularisation of Chinese food, and the subsequent boom in the restaurant trade. Although precise figures are not available, the Chinese population in Britain has grown from less than 5000 in 1946 to an estimated 250,000 in 1993. Of these, 70,000 live in the Greater London area.

Most of the Chinese who live in Britain today came from Hong Kong, in particular from the rural New Territories. There are also small numbers of Chinese from the Caribbean, Taiwan, mainland China (People's Republic), Malaysia, Singapore and other countries in South East Asia. Regional origins aside, the Chinese are a heterogeneous community, even in terms of the dialects spoken. For example, Hong Kong Chinese tend to speak Cantonese or Hakka, while those from Malaysia and Singapore speak Hokkien or Chiu Chao. However, written Chinese forms a common means of communication between all of the groups.[1]

Today Soho is the heart of 'Chinatown' in London. However, a Chinatown existed in London's East End long before the present one, and the history of Chinese settlement goes back about 180 years. Apart from a small number of Chinese students, the earliest arrivals were mainly seamen, recruited by the East India Company[2] and other shipping firms. The opening up of Chinese ports to Western traders after China's defeat in the Opium Wars (1842–60) increased the need for Chinese seamen. Having being brought to London, they were discharged and left to their own resources until the ships were ready to sail again. Being both penniless and totally unaccustomed to English ways, many of these Chinese seamen fell prey to all forms of exploitation. So abominable was their situation that an Act was passed in 1814 compelling the East India Company to provide lodgings and basic essentials for Chinese and other Asiatic sailors. However, the cramped, barrack-like accommodation provided became the subject of a Parliamentary Inquiry and grave doubts were expressed on these sub-human conditions.[3] Not surprisingly, a number of Chinese seamen took up lodgings in public houses in Shadwell and Poplar rather than put up with life in the barracks. A Chinese quarter had developed by the 1880s in the Limehouse district. It consisted of two narrow streets, Pennyfields and Limehouse Causeway. Here the Chinese established grocery stores, laundries, restaurants and seamen's hostels, catering for the needs of the Chinese crews in port. By 1913 there were thirty Chinese shops and restaurants in these two streets, and a transient Chinese population of between three and four hundred.[4] Because it was predominantly a male population, many married English wives. It was a peaceful and orderly community, but it did not escape sensational reporting. Chinese social life was a subject of disdain; the popular press was quick to jump on stories of 'oriental fiends' taking innocent English girls as their mistresses, or on the occasional fights, gambling and opium-smoking in the lodging houses. These 'opium dens' excited the popular imagination, and were portrayed for example by Dickens in *The Mystery of Edwin Drood* (1870) with its stereotype of 'cunning and artful Chinamen'. They were widely seen as places of vice and sin; the reality, however, was less colourful.[5]

Chinese seamen, used as cheap labour, were regarded as 'scabs' by White sailors, but shipowners considered them more amenable to discipline. This led to violence in 1908, and again in 1911, when Chinese crews had to be taken under police protection back to their lodging houses. As Chinatown developed, meeting places (*fongs*) and clubs were established. The *fongs* were a safe refuge where the Chinese could shelter from the frequent verbal and physical abuse meted out to them. By 1907 several such societies had been formed. Early Chinese associations ran mutual-aid schemes that covered their members' funeral costs and offered sickness benefits; they also organised Chinese festivals. One such society was the powerful Chi Kung Tong (Chinese Masonic Hall), the earliest Triad Society in Britain. The Chi Kung Tong gained notoriety for harbouring its more violent members and provided a reference point for the community. The fear of 'coolies' developed into a moral crusade to save England from the moral contamination of the 'Yellow Peril'. Despite two official investigations exonerating the Chinese from any immoral practices they were accused of, the media continued to portray Chinese shops and lodgings as mere fronts for the vice that went on behind closed doors. Sexual jealousies were translated into sensational stories of 'oriental fiends' luring White girls into evil ends. The reality was somewhat different. The existence of an early Chinese Mission in Limehouse paints a picture of a community which gradually converted to Christianity with many of its members eventually marrying the White women they lived with.

Opium-smoking was popularly regarded as a vice peculiar to the Chinese although the drug was legally available at the chemists' until the start of the First World War. Initially introduced to China from British India in the last century to pay for imports of tea and silk, opium soon had a fashionable following among romantic writers and poets in England as a 'drug of dreams'. For the early Chinese, however, opium-smoking became a criminal offence often leading to deportation.

During the Great Depression of the 1920s, increasing numbers of Chinese were deported on drug offences and even for gambling. One such game, 'pak ap piu', (pigeon lottery), was a precursor to Bingo. Bets were placed on any combination of Chinese characters printed on a piece of paper. Secret betting booths were set up in Chinese shops and lodgings and patronised even by the local White population.

The introduction of Chinese laundries enabled the community to move away from dockland occupations. The first Chinese laundry in London opened in Poplar in 1901[6], and ten years later east London had thirty Chinese-run laundries. By 1931 there were more than 800 such laundries in Britain. The 1930s saw the gradual decline of East End Chinatown, and the slump in shipping led to many Chinese returning to China. Automatic washing machines and launderettes hastened the decline. During the Second World War, the Blitz finally disintegrated Chinatown when most of the Limehouse buildings were destroyed. Today, it is mainly elderly Chinese people who live in the Limehouse area, although there is a Chinese Sunday school off Commercial Street. These voluntary Chinese-language classes are the successors to the Chung Hua Chinese School established in Pennyfields in 1935. Funded by wealthy Chinese patrons overseas, the school catered to the growing number of Anglo-Chinese children in the East End. A few Chinese restaurants, such as the Young Friends, and street names, such as Ming Street, Pekin Street and Canton Street, are reminders of the earlier Chinese presence.

Between the wars, Chinese restaurants were few in number and patronised mainly by Chinese students. The rapid growth of the present-day Chinese population in Britain was a result of the economic boom of the 1950s, and was directly related to the boom in the Chinese restaurant trade. The relative affluence of the 1950s, changing diet and conventions of eating out increased the demand for Chinese food, and by then a number of ex-seamen had moved into catering. Starting with a few restaurants in the East End supplying fellow-countrymen, some enterprising Chinese moved to Soho to serve the theatre trade. Others with laundry shops sold their businesses in the face of competition and followed. Another group of restaurateurs were made up of former nationalist officials from the Chinese Embassy in London. When diplomatic relations between Britain and the People's Republic of China were established in 1950, many of these Mandarin-speaking former diplomats from north China opened restaurants specialising in the regional Peking cuisine. This was to be the base for the expansion of the mid-1950s.

Most of the post-war Hong Kong Chinese were from a cluster of villages in Hong Kong's rural hinterland known as the New Territories. They came largely at the behest of relatives and fellow-villagers already established in London. Mainly recruited through an informal network of chain migration, the newcomers were advanced their airfares and provided with accommodation and employment by the earlier arrivals to Britain. In many cases, kinship ties provided the link in this chain, but it was also common for fellow villagers to advance passage money to the prospective migrants. As news spread of the rich pickings abroad, even the more

conservative village elders started to encourage their sons to jump on the migration bandwagon. These contacts were a key incentive, but the motive to leave home was economic: cheaper and higher-quality rice from Thailand and Burma threatened to put the New Territories paddy-farmers out of business. In search of a new livelihood in London, these farmers soon had to adapt to being waiters and chefs. First to come were the male villagers, whose main aim was to save up for a comfortable retirement back home. Many also had families to support in the home villages. By working long hours (sometimes more than eighty hours a week) and forgoing holidays, they were able to send a portion of their earnings to relations at home. Far from severing ties with the past, the housing boom in the New Territories today is proof of the migrants' continuing stake in their native villages. With their savings, the migrants bought land and built new bungalows, or 'sterling houses' (named after the sterling remittances) thus fuelling a frenetic property boom in the once quiet rural hinterland. Even today, many of the younger catering workers return to the New Territories to find brides. Important decisions affecting the village or clan usually await the return of these migrants during the festive season such as Lunar New Year (see colour plate 12).

The Old Friends Restaurant in Limehouse, probably 1940s. The original Chinatown grew up around the docks near here to cater for the needs of Chinese sailors

It was only in the early 1960s that Soho developed into London's second Chinatown. From a mere handful of restaurants along Gerrard Street twenty years ago, Soho Chinatown (known to the Chinese as 'Imperial City') has spread eastwards to Leicester Square and northwards beyond Shaftesbury Avenue. Run-down properties on short leases were snapped up, renovated and converted into Chinese restaurants. Restaurant work is physically demanding and monotonous, involving unsociable hours. Kitchen staff have very little opportunity to socialise, and many Chinese speak only a few words of English in spite of having been in Britain for ten years or more. For most, their primary ambition is one day to own their own restaurant. This was an attainable goal in the early days, but the cost of purchasing a medium-sized restaurant in the West End today is prohibitive. Partnerships, often between relatives or fellow-villagers, have therefore become the next best choice, with managers, waiters and sometimes chefs all sharing the profits.

As Chinese food became more popular, a new market developed for Chinese restaurants and take-away shops in the suburbs and smaller towns, where premises were cheaper. Conveniently, the arrival of family dependants in the 1960s and 1970s provided the necessary labour to run such family businesses. London has many such family-run take-aways, and almost every small town and seaside resort in Britain today has a Chinese restaurant or take-away. While restaurants in Chinatown serve authentic Chinese food (mainly Cantonese), those in the suburbs have popularised an adapted form thought to be more palatable to Westerners. The term for it, chop suey, was invented by a Chinese chef in the USA to refer to a dish made of fried leftovers.

Chinatown in London is essentially a commercial marketplace made up of restaurants, supermarkets, bookshops and a plethora of other shops and businesses (see colour plate 6). Its main pedestrianised thoroughfare, Gerrard Street, has been laid out by Westminster Council to emulate other Chinatowns across the world, with lanterns, street signs in English and Chinese, and even pagoda-shaped telephone boxes. For non-Chinese it is principally a place to go for a meal or to witness the lion dances performed in celebration of the Lunar New Year, which falls between late January and mid February. For the Chinese, Chinatown is a great many other things. It is a place to buy food and other provisions, to have a meal, send money home, see a herbalist, hire a Chinese movie, seek advice, buy newspapers, or borrow books (the local library has a Chinese librarian). Apart from the restaurants where the Chinese go to *yum cha* (meet and eat snacks such as *dim sum* – 'small eats') and the video shops, the major pastime for a good many workers in Chinatown is still gambling. Soho has several exclusively Chinese gambling clubs frequented by workers during their rest hours. These clubs are controlled by secret societies, or 'Triads', whose members are said to be engaged in protection rackets, extorting payments from Chinese restaurants. The Triads' present control of vice is a far cry from their original aims in China, when they were the principal instrument for expressing the popular grievances of the poor against the Manchu rulers. Triad operations today allegedly extend to prostitution and video piracy,

Lady at the Chinese Community Centre, Gerrard Street, Soho, 1992

Chinese Community School, Euston, 1992. Many parents are keen that their children learn about Chinese culture and language

but their influence in Britain tends to be sensationalised and overstated.

One thing which Triad membership does confer is a sense of belonging for those Chinese, many of them young, who regard themselves as unwanted outsiders in an alien society, just as the early associations set up by Chinese seamen in Limehouse also gave them a sense of communal identity. As the community has grown, the Chinese have established other associations and agencies to look after the needs of the community. The post-war Chinese from Hong Kong brought with them their own communal associations, based on clan or common surname. The offices of the Pang, Man and Cheung clansmen associations are located in Soho, with activities largely confined to organising annual get-togethers and leisure trips. There are also more functional organisations, such as the Chinese Chamber of Commerce, which is made up chiefly of restaurant traders. Besides helping its members on business matters, the chamber has been in the forefront of efforts to protect the interests of Chinatown. Despite its long history in Britain and the plethora of associations, the Chinese community remains a 'silent' minority. Their continuing isolation is, in large part, due to the absence of any all-embracing association which can speak for the whole community in its dealings with the wider society. Many of the existing associations are parochial in outlook and organised along traditional lines of loyalty based on shared dialect or surname. It is still not uncommon to hear immigrants from the New Territories speaking contemptuously of Mandarin-speaking proprietors who are seen as incapable of running a restaurant.

Today, with the arrival of wives and children, even those migrants who once dreamed of retiring to their home villages have lost the urge to do so. Hong Kong's future under Chinese sovereignty from 1997 has also created uncertainty, which no doubt has influenced many of the older Chinese to remain in London. The Chinese are now a part of British society, and demographic changes since the arrival of wives and children have increased their visibility in the wider society. This has brought its own pressures, including the legacy of derogatory stereotypes, and racial harassment, which has grown with the resettlement in Britain of 20,000 'boat people' from Vietnam, many of them ethnic Chinese. The poor self-image of many young Chinese resulting from this can affect their confidence in breaking into the mainstream society. Few Chinese teenagers wish to follow their parents in the ethnic economy or the family take-away, but many are forced to do so simply to avoid the dole queue. Many others, however, have managed to break away and move into other professions, including medicine (both traditional and alternative), nursing, the law, accountancy, the media and local government.

Now, nearly half of the Chinese population in London is British-born, and many first-generation settlers express strong fears about the assimilative pressures facing their children. Nowhere has the community shown such unity of purpose as over the issue of mother-tongue teaching. For most parents, the Chinese language is the vehicle of transmitting the ancestral culture from one generation to the next, and this has led to the setting up of over seventy mother-tongue classes and supplementary schools. The Chinese Chamber of Commerce in Soho houses the largest Chinese-language school in Europe, with 900 pupils enrolled. This, together with the widespread popular interest in such aspects of Chinese culture as Taoism, ancient healing therapies and martial arts, including the health exercise Tai Chi Chuan, help London-born Chinese maintain a pride in their own distinctive cultural identity while still permitting them to participate in the other elements of London's cosmopolitan culture. Evolving a meaningful cultural identity is the key issue preoccupying the minds of London's new generation of Chinese on the eve of the twenty-first century. The young Chinese today have begun to transcend the linguistic and cultural barriers that confined their rural predecessors to a 'niche' in the wider society. One notable example is the formation of a British Chinese Artists Association with public funds offering a platform to assert and popularise the arts and culture of the community. The long-awaited launch of a Europe-wide Chinese satellite television channel in 1994 would also do much to enrich the linguistic and cultural mosaic of cosmopolitan London.[7]

Voices of experience

Abraham Lue, a leading member of the Chinese community in London, explains something of his background and early experiences in London:

I was born in Jamaica in 1939. My parents were immigrants to Jamaica from southern China, from Guandung province. My maternal grandfather had already emigrated to Jamaica in 1904 and my father left his home village to go to Jamaica in 1919. My father was a merchant ...

Education, as most Chinese parents will tell you, is almost the sole path to social betterment. It's the Confucian ethic, I suppose. My parents said to me that there was nothing they could leave me except a good education. Chinese families are used to the idea of children leaving home to improve their lot; they had done it themselves.

I lived in Tooting in digs with a landlady. There were five students staying with her, two from Hong Kong, one from Liberia and two from Malaysia. In those days there was not the tension that people talk about today about people of different racial characteristics. The people I lived with were all from overseas. In University College at the time I'm not sure there were more than half a dozen Hong Kong students.

There were very few things that I genuinely missed and I think there was only one occasion when I was genuinely homesick badly once and that was my first Christmas in this country. Everybody thought that I had somebody to look after me and in the end I had nobody. So I spent Christmas on my own and that was quite lonely.

My experience of the Chinese here was purely as a customer in a restaurant and we didn't go to restaurants very often. In those days the Chinatown was actually in Commercial Road and I remember having to save up for many weeks to go to a well-known restaurant, called Good Friends. The proprietor made no concession to Western taste.[8]

Endnotes

For full details of publications, see Bibliography.

1 See Shang, 1984a; Shang, 1991.
2 *Report on Lascar and Other Asiatic Seamen*, Parliamentary Papers, 1814–15.
3 Ibid.
4 Ng, 1968.
5 *The Times*, 25 November 1913.
6 *Evening News*, 15 January 1901.
7 Other sources for the Chinese in London include Berridge, 1978, D. Jones, 1979, Lai, 1986, May, 1978, Shang, 1984(b), Waller, 1985 and Watson, 1977. An overview of the contemporary community is available in a House of Commons Home Affairs Committee Report, *The Chinese Community in Britain*, HMSO, London, 1985.
8 Extracts from an interview taken from the Museum of London Oral History Archive.

Cypriots in London

The Cypriot community in London consists, mainly, of Greek-Cypriots and Turkish-Cypriots. The population pattern of four Greek-Cypriots to one Turkish-Cypriot is the same in London as in Cyprus. In addition, there are some Armenians and Maronites from Cyprus living here. London has always provided a place where all sections of the Cypriot community have lived and worked together.

The 1991 census showed that around 50,000 Cypriots from all communities living in London were born in Cyprus. The total number of Cypriots at present is estimated to be close to 200,000 including the second and subsequent generations.

Greek-Cypriots • Zena Theodorou and Sav Kyriacou

In 1878, Britain took over the administration of Cyprus from the Ottoman Sultan. It remained under Turkish sovereignty until the First World War, and the island was annexed by Britain. It officially became a British colony in 1925. The adverse economic conditions affecting the island in the 1920s and 1930s earned the island, otherwise renowned for its beauty, the name 'Cinderella of the Empire'. It was during these two decades that the main pre-war Greek-Cypriot migration to Britain took place. The vast majority were villagers looking for work; some townspeople arrived in the 1930s, but never in large numbers until decades later.

The Greek-Cypriots established their first main settlement in Soho. The Depression of the 1930s meant housing problems and a lack of job opportunities; even educated immigrants could find work only in the service industries. Due mainly to the plethora of restaurants in the area, and the need for low-paid, unskilled kitchen-hands, they found work as chefs and waiters, settling in what was then the most cosmopolitan area of London.

The first arrivals tended to be single men, soon followed by sisters and/or wives and fiancées. As the women started arriving, further job opportunities were sought and found in dress factories, mainly in Jewish ownership. The skills that young girls traditionally acquired in Cyprus as part of their preparation for family life were used in London to earn a living. As accommodation in Soho became more expensive, the settlers moved north to the low-rent, often slum accommodation on Euston Road and large, multi-occupancy housing in Camden Town. When hopes for a return to Cyprus became increasingly remote, an attempt to become less foreign and less noticeable became apparent in the 'Anglicising' of Christian names. Children learnt English when they entered school, and at that point their mother-tongue skills often began to decrease in their effort to assimilate in order to avoid discrimination and racism. Their parents' background was often kept secret from schoolmates and the children frequently had to act as interpreters for them.

Men usually acquired sufficient command of English to 'get by', but the women's knowledge often did not extend even to the bare essentials needed for survival in the days before self-service shops and community self-sufficiency. It is no wonder the Greek-Cypriot community was slow to integrate; these two oral testimonies point out the difficulties involved:

> As I could not understand the language, my only contact was with Greek-Cypriots. In the beginning it was very lonely, work, home, then from home to work again. (Athanasios)[1]

> I had some difficulties because of the language, at work, shopping, and so forth. When I used to go to the doctor, I used to take my husband with me. When our children grew up, I was able to learn English from them. (Xristalla)[2]

After the War, Camden Town remained the principal magnet for new settlers. Any immigrant will always look for friends or relatives to stay with, and will then be helped by them with accommodation, finding work and coping without the language of the host community. The first sizeable influx of Greek-Cypriots in the late 1940s and early 1950s naturally looked to Camden for its base:

Cypriot men outside the Atlantis restaurant, Soho, 1930s

> In May 1949, at the age of twenty, I arrived in London and stayed with my auntie and uncle in Camden Town, which was the base of Greek-Cypriots at that time. They rented a small flat of three rooms and a kitchen over a garage. In the flat was my uncle, his wife, their twelve-year-old son and their twenty-six-year-old nephew, so when I arrived I had to sleep in the same room as their nephew. I did wonder how we would manage in such a small flat. (Athanasios)[3]

There have, of course, been other settlements of Greek-Cypriots in London, in areas such as Fulham and Camberwell. Fulham, for instance, has followed similar patterns to north London. Many Cypriots moved to Fulham from north London in the 1950s because the area offered very cheap rented accommodation. With relatives arriving from Cyprus, by the mid-1960s the Greek-Cypriot community in Fulham was sizeable and established. As well as shops and businesses, a Greek

A home-worker in
Camden, 1957. Many
Cypriot women worked
and continue to work at
home on piece-rates in
London's clothing
industry

Orthodox church and a Greek-language school were established locally. More
recently, like the north Londoners, much of the old community has moved further
out, in this case to the suburbs of Kingston.

By the 1950s more Greek-Cypriots had begun to set themselves up in business.
This provided opportunities for the latest arrivals:

> In a few days I had found a job as a shoe machinist in a small workshop, a
> basement in Hanson Street, W1. The owner was a Greek-Cypriot and
> another young man from my village was working there, making three of us
> in all. (Athanasios)[4]

Without the support and job opportunities given by the Greek-Cypriot
community, life was often more difficult:

> My first job was as a plasterer for the railways. After six months I lost my
> first job because I could not communicate with my colleagues properly due
> to our language differences. (George)[5]

This second wave of immigrants consisted mostly of young families, often joined subsequently by their parents. Immigration from Cyprus reached its peak between 1960, the year Cyprus became independent and 1961, with approximately 25,000 Cypriots entering Britain in those two years alone. Levels subsequently fell back to the 1950s figures of 4000 a year and continued to decline as conditions and prospects in Cyprus began to improve and immigration regulations in Britain changed. Relatives, of course, never ceased to arrive, either as immigrants joining their families or wishing to seize the opportunity to further their education. For many of these people, life was spent among their own community. Working in Greek-Cypriot businesses or for Greek-Cypriots at home, as many machinists did, became the norm. Accommodation was either a rented room in a Greek-Cypriot household, sharing a flat with another family or being put up for a while:

Our family was upstairs and we also had, during the years, aunts and uncles and cousins and all sorts of relations staying with us, because as they came over from Cyprus they didn't know anyone, and they stayed with us for a while until they sorted themselves out. (Argiri)[6]

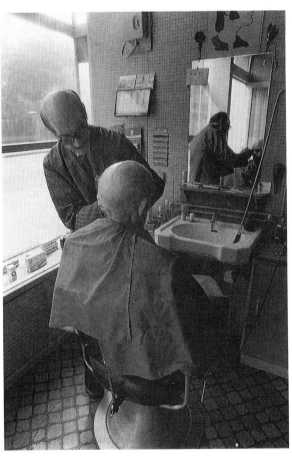

A barber's shop run by a father and son, mid-1980s

Many of the Greek-Cypriot businesses in Camden began to flourish, as they were now serving a sizeable community. It was not only that people were able to buy familiar goods, they could buy them from shopkeepers who spoke their own language. It was no longer necessary to point to items, and then to hold out a handful of change! The presence of Greek-Cypriot travel agents also made it much easier to book flights to Cyprus.

The Greek-Cypriots, traditionally accustomed to self-employment, pursued their desire to work independently. They continued in the pattern of entering the retail business and made inroads into the 'rag trade', expanding into fashion design and 'ready-to-wear' clothes. Skills such as shoe- and jewellery-making and repairs sustained thriving businesses, and Greek restaurants, fish-and-chip shops and grocers appeared alongside travel agencies, barbers and hairdressers. At the same time, as the community began to acquire a sense of itself, opportunities for leisure activities were sought and developed:

In our free time, and for rest and leisure, we used to go to the cinema to see Greek films in the West End; we would also visit each other and go to the Greek church in Camden Town. More or less, this was how we were spending our free time. (Loukia)[7]

Women shopping, Green
Lanes, Haringey, 1980s

As Greek-Cypriots raised enough money for a deposit on a house, they looked to buy in quieter, residential districts. With children being born, the flats they had been renting in Camden had become too small. Thus began the move north to Haringey and the leapfrogging up Green Lanes to Turnpike Lane, Wood Green and Palmers Green. By 1971 Haringey had taken over from Camden and Islington as the borough with the highest concentration of Cypriots. Businesses quickly expanded and new ones were established all over Haringey and Wood Green (see colour plate 6). Businesses, as well as churches, still exist in Camden and cater for the few Greek-Cypriots remaining there, now mostly pensioners in council accommodation. There is a regular traffic along the 29 bus route: Camdenites going to Haringey for the specialist shops, people from Wood Green going to the long-established travel agents in Camden, and everybody going to Fonthill Road on a Saturday morning for the cut-price fashions produced by the many Greek-Cypriot dress manufacturers based there.

In 1974, as the Greek-Cypriot community was about to take a deep breath and sit back to enjoy the fruits of years of hard struggle and sacrifice, and perhaps to contemplate a more conscious and willing opening out to the host community, a horrific tragedy struck their island. A military coup ousted Archbishop Makarios from power on 15 July. Five days later, Turkish forces landed and by the time a ceasefire was agreed they controlled over a third of the island. This area was declared an independent 'state' in November 1983, but has not been recognised by any country other than Turkey. These events affected not only Cyprus but also the community in London. 'British Cypriots' were joined by thousands of homeless relatives, and Haringey was, as a matter of course, the borough that absorbed most of the incoming refugees. Leaving aside the immeasurable despair, suffering and loss that the catastrophe caused to Cypriots throughout the world, these events had an immense consequence on the community in London: a stronger than ever sense of identity for what was by then predominantly a second-generation Greek-Cypriot community, and an acute and sensitised awareness of their roots, origins and emotional loyalties. As the struggle for aid relief and political lobbying to help Cyprus intensified, the bond with Cyprus became solidified as a sacred duty to every Greek-Cypriot, regardless of age or background.

Immigrant families who had been on the point of returning to their homeland had to abandon their plans, often at huge financial cost. Many of those who did return found themselves forced to endure yet again the difficulties of migration, doubled by the burden of their refugee status. For Greek-Cypriots in their thousands, dreams of return were shattered as the Turkish occupation of a large part of the island made this an impossibility.

Two aspects in the life of the Greek-Cypriot community in London seem to have played a vital role in the formation and maintenance of its identity. These primary resources are the community's social life and mother-tongue classes. A common link between the two is the Church, whose towering role still seems to dominate the life-cycle of Greek-Cypriots in London. There are, at the moment, thirty-two

Greek Orthodox churches in London and its suburbs.

Alongside the weekly Sunday services, all rituals of Orthodoxy are faithfully followed, culminating in the celebration of the Greek Easter foremost in traditional symbolism for every Greek Orthodox Christian. Dedicated participation throughout the Holy Week in Christ's suffering and resurrection has always held a tremendous appeal to Greek Orthodox people, regardless of age and degree of religious belief. Among the many customs that characterise the Greek Easter are the *Epitaphios*, the torrent of flowers that accompanies Christ's body to burial on Good Friday and the laments of the women, covered in black, who follow it; the glorious fire where the traitor Judas is burned; the theatrically majestic victory of the Cross over all evil; and the journeying home through the streets of London to carry the blessing of thousands of candles lit with the Holy Light. All these are compulsive spectacles, even to the unconverted.

Marriage is a central event, celebrated in the grandest manner possible. Nowadays, the institutions of dowry and arranged marriages have become less customary. Parents (the obligation being stronger for the bride's family) provide support in the form of property or money, to give the couple a good start in life. As for the traditional *proxenia*, the primary step in the process of arranging a marriage, it seems today to retain only its initial social function. (*Proxenia* literally means the introduction of two people to each other with the purpose of bringing them closer together.) Most young people still opt for the safety and security this kind of marriage is perceived to provide, and the vast majority of second- and third-generation Greek-Cypriots still prefer to marry someone of their own ethnic group. Marriage in church is a 'must', since the Greek-Cypriot community will not regard a couple as truly married if 'they have only been to the registry'. During the ceremony, friends and relatives queue in their dozens to become the bridesmaids and the groom's best men. A reception invariably follows, to which a large number of people are invited.

The Greek schools, with evening and/or Saturday classes, feature prominently in the community's activities. They are run by various voluntary and independent bodies, including parents' associations and the Church. As most Greek-Cypriots do not accept assimilation, their aim is to use the schools as places where their children's identity is developed. The curriculum does not simply include language-teaching; Greek and Cypriot music and dancing are also taught, and are very popular with the youngsters. Premises are usually provided by local councils and some of the teachers are paid by the Greek and Cypriot governments, but parents' associations have to organise regular fundraising dinner-dances to keep the schools going. Similar dinner-dances, again featuring high in the community's social life, are traditionally organised by village associations. Loyalty to one's village is paramount. In terms of identity and sense of belonging, for the first-generation Greek-Cypriot immigrants their village comes second only to their families. The natural progression is family, village and then island.

The conditions of life of Greek-Cypriot immigrants have, beyond any doubt, improved tremendously. This is largely due to their traditional spirit of enterprise and hard work. Successful business families continue to move further north, and are now settling in the suburban areas of Southgate, Winchmore Hill and Enfield Town. Significant improvements and achievements have been made by first and second generations, and by the many educated and experienced refugees who settled after 1974. Many Greek-Cypriots have moved into the professions and others have made contributions to the arts and sciences. In one sense the Greek-Cypriot community seems today to be standing close to where it was just before the tragedy of 1974. More and more people are planning to return to Cyprus, including equal numbers of enthusiastic first-, second- or even third-generation Cypriots; to some, these numbers indicate an 'exodus'. Undoubtedly, if a just and stable solution were to be found to the Cyprus problem, the exodus would become a reality, confounding the 'myth of return' theory so popular in immigration studies.

The Greek-Cypriot community survived the process of immigration largely because of the strength of its values and its internal network. In London it is estimated that the community is now about 160,000 strong. It has now acquired, especially after the experience of 1974, a stronger than ever sense of ethnic identity. Its beliefs, traditions, values, social customs and institutions continue to thrive in the new generations. Η παροικια μας ('our own colony, our outpost'), as it is affectionately referred to both here and back home, will continue to thrive as a source of ethnic pride and as an inspiration for achievement and progress to all Greek-Cypriots.[8]

Card games in a Greek-Cypriot social centre

Turkish-Cypriots • Rozina Visram[9]

After 1878, when Cyprus was placed under British administration, Turkish-Cypriots began to arrive in Britain as students and some married and settled here. Others came to escape the difficult economic and political life in Cyprus. The main period of migration took place after the Second World War. Between 1945 and 1955 many Turkish-Cypriot males migrated to Britain. Most of them married non-Turkish women and although some of them gave their children Turkish names, their connection with Turkish culture and traditions was minimal. However, from the mid-1950s whole Turkish-Cypriot families began to arrive as a result of the political upheaval on the island and this helped those immigrants who followed to preserve and develop their traditions and family customs. In 1951 the Cyprus Turkish Association was established to cater for the welfare of the Turkish-Cypriot community in London.

Another group of Turkish-Cypriots arrived after Cyprus became independent in 1960. The modicum of prosperity brought by the Second World War had not lasted and the young and the enterprising, disillusioned to find that the fruits of liberty accrued mostly to the Greek-Cypriots, and frustrated that their ambitions could not be fulfilled in Cyprus, wanted to leave. Britain offered good business prospects for small-scale entrepreneurs and better education, and many Turkish-Cypriots migrated to Britain during the years 1960 to 1963. The deterioration in the political

Turkish-Cypriot worker in a Stoke Newington clothing factory, 1989

Turkish-Cypriot shop in Green Lanes, Haringey, 1993

situation on the island arising from the Greek-Cypriot agitation for *enosis* (the union of Cyprus with Greece) was a further reason for the Turkish-Cypriot exodus. When Cyprus gained independence in 1960, the withdrawal of much of the British administration led to the loss of lucrative jobs, and among those who left the island were many who had compromised themselves by helping the British in their fight against the *EOKA* (National Organisation of the Cypriot Struggle for the Furthering of the Greek cause in Cyprus).

The 1960s emigrants were mostly families, rather than single men; elderly parents followed as soon as their children were settled. By 1971 economic growth in Cyprus had reduced the number of Greek-Cypriot emigrants to a trickle, but this did not affect the Turkish-Cypriots who by then were living in a state of siege on the island after the intercommunal conflict of 1963. The final and most dramatic exodus followed the events of 1974. In July 1974 the regime of the colonels in Greece attempted to overthrow the Government of Archbishop Makarios on the island, and Turkey intervened militarily. Over a third of the island is now under Turkish administration. Since those events and the political uncertainty which ensued, many Turkish-Cypriots came to Britain as refugees.

Today Turkish-Cypriots in London live mostly in the boroughs of Haringey, Islington, Hackney, Lewisham and Southwark, with a few in Enfield, Barnet, Camden Town and Tower Hamlets. The majority are working-class people, originally from rural areas. They have a variety of occupations. A large number work in factories; others are self-employed, running their own corner shops, restaurants and butchers' shops. Turkish-Cypriots also work in catering, dressmaking, hairdressing, shoemaking, the rag trade and various service industries, or as artisans, for example, builders, plumbers and electricians. Some are successful businessmen and there are many UK-trained Turkish-Cypriot professionals: teachers, lawyers, economists, accountants, doctors, dentists, engineers and scientists. Many Turkish-Cypriot women go out to work. They are usually employed in dressmaking and tailoring, in Turkish-run establishments, or in restaurant kitchens. One of the better-known members of the Turkish-Cypriot community in London until his recent departure, was Asil Nadir, former head of the Polly Peck business empire.

The older generation still think of Cyprus, but Turkish-Cypriot children born in Britain identify themselves more closely with this country. To them Cyprus is a distant land for holidays with their relatives. The Turkish-Cypriots have forged a new identity in England, by adapting and developing a new version of their Turkish-Cypriot culture into a British-Turkish culture that has its own identity.

Turkish-Cypriot sisters, Brockley, 1992

Voices of experience

Salih Adalier, born in northern Cyprus in 1931, came to London almost by accident:

> I was preparing myself at that time to go to Turkey. Turkey had joined NATO and I could be earning good money to be interpreter in the NATO bases there,

Turkish interpreter, Turkish–English; I knew Greek as well. But before I left for Turkey some friends of mine came back from London and they said it will be better for you if you go to London; at least you can work anywhere and you can continue evening classes. And that's how I changed my mind.

There were two ways of coming to London. One was you have to have a guarantor here to find you shelter and a job, and with that document you could get a passport easily. And there was another way, getting a passport that you were going to travel and then being British subject you can come here and take work, and that's how I did, because I didn't know anybody to be my guarantor.

You don't think how long you are going to stay. I came to England in 1953.[10]

Endnotes

For full details of publications, see Bibliography

1 Ethnic Communities Oral History Project,
   Xeni – Greek Cypriots in London, 1990, p8.
2 Ibid, p23.
3 Ibid, p8.
4 Ibid, p8.
5 Ibid, p25.
6 Ibid, p27.
7 Ibid, p18.
8 Other sources on Greek-Cypriots in
   London include: Fuat Alkan and Susie
   Constantinides, *Cypriots in Haringey*, Borough
   of Haringey, London, 1986; Aloneftis, 1984;
   John Charalambous et al (eds), *Business and
   the UK Cypriot Community*, PNL Press,
   London, 1991; John Charalambous, George
   Hadjifanis and Litsa Kilonis (eds), *The Cypriot
   Community of the UK: Issues of Identity*, PNL
   Press, London, 1988; Constantinides, 1977;
   and Haris Pellapaisiotis, *Laying the
   Foundations*, Theatro Technic Project,
   Centurion Press, London, n.d.
9 This piece has been compiled by Rozina
   Visram and is based, with his kind perm-
   ission, on information contained in Salahi
   Ramadan Sonyel's *The Silent Minority: Turkish
   Muslim Children in British Schools*, Islamic
   Academy, Cambridge, 1988.
10 Taken from the Museum of London's Oral
   History Archive.

Germans in London · Panikos Panayi

The German community is one of the oldest in London. From the German soldiers serving in the Roman army and the Anglo-Saxon settlers of the fifth century, to the Hanseatic merchants of the Middle Ages, Germans made a significant impact on London's early development, as Nick Merriman has shown earlier in this volume.

From the middle of the sixteenth century, however, a distinct new group of Germans began to enter London. These were Protestant refugees from religious persecution after the changes and instability caused by the Reformation. Together with exiles from all over Europe, they worshipped in the Austin Friars Church, and the Germans also established a Sunday school. These German worshippers were mostly emigrants from the Netherlands and Westphalia, and the congregation continued until the seventeenth century.[1]

The late seventeenth century represents a major milestone in the history of Germans in Britain because a number of churches were established which, in some cases, have lasted until the present. The nucleus of the German community was businessmen, many from Hamburg, and sugar-refiners. The first church, the Hamburg Lutheran, was established in 1673 and between 1686 and 1713 it carried out 300 baptisms. By 1700, after the Toleration Act of 1689 allowed foreign congregations to worship in Britain without the granting of a charter, there were three more German churches: St Mary's, in the Savoy Palace; St Paul's Evangelical Reformed Church, which also held services in the Savoy Palace; and the Royal Chapel in St James's Palace, primarily established for Prince George, the husband of Queen Anne.[2] By the end of the seventeenth century the first Ashkenazi synagogue, for Jews from Germany, Poland and Holland, had been established in Duke's Place, following the readmission of Jews into Britain in 1656.[3]

During the eighteenth century, the German population of Britain began to increase as a consequence of the growth in emigration from central Europe. A major influx into London occurred between 1708 and 1709 from the Palatine, partly on the instigation of Queen Anne, who offered to send the immigrants to the British colony in Carolina, and also because of the long-term reduction in the size of land-plots inherited, short-term religious persecution and economic crisis. Eventually between 13,000 and 15,000 Palatines arrived destitute in London, and were housed in insanitary conditions in warehouses in Southwark and in the Archbishop of Canterbury's granaries in Lambeth, before being settled in North

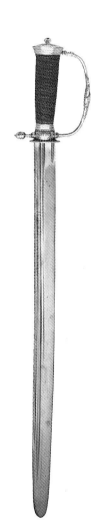

Cutlass made by Johan Kinndt at Hounslow, 1634. Several German blade-smiths from Solingen came to England when the Hounslow sword factory was set up

America and southern Ireland.[4]

With the accession of George Ludwig, Elector of Hanover, to the English throne in 1714, a German dynasty was established. George I himself remained firmly German and surrounded himself with German advisers. Apart from the king, perhaps the most prominent German in London was the composer George Frederick Handel (1685–1759).

The eighteenth century saw the beginning of future patterns of German migration to Britain. We can identify three groups: merchants, who moved to Britain for a variety of reasons, including the opportunities offered by industrialisation;[5] transmigrants, travelling through Britain on their way to North America;[6] and craftsmen, who wanted to remain. In the last group we can include sugar-bakers, who worked in London from the mid-eighteenth century and whose numbers increased during the Napoleonic Wars. They mainly settled where they worked, in east London.[7] In addition to these three groups, there was also the expansion of the eighteenth-century German-Jewish community.[8]

The growth of the German population in London during the eighteenth century led to the foundation of a new church, St George's in Little Alie Street, Whitechapel, which still exists, and another in Ludgate Hill.[9] Later, in 1809, a German Catholic congregation was established.[10] At the beginning of the nineteenth century the Society of Friends of Foreigners in Distress, an essentially German charity, had also been founded.[11] St Mary's had a school connected to it from 1708, as did St George's from 1805.[12] The Ashkenazi Jewish community had also developed its own institutions by the early nineteenth century, including a hospital, a free school and a ladies' benevolent society.[13]

Any attempt to estimate the number of Germans in London before the mid-nineteenth century remains pure speculation. After this date, however, we can speak with some confidence because censuses recorded the numbers of people of non-British birth. Figures taken from the census statistics reveal that throughout the period 1861 until 1911 about 50 per cent of all Germans in Britain lived in the capital. The numbers rose from 16,082 out of a total German population of 28,644 in 1861 to 26,920 out of a total of 50,599 in 1911, the peak of the German immigrant population before the First World War. In the capital the German community was centred on specific areas, the most important being the East End, and especially Whitechapel, although this area declined in importance during the course of the nineteenth century, when there was a movement to Canning Town, Silvertown and East and West Ham as industries developed there. A second major area of settlement, especially by the end of the nineteenth century, lay in St Pancras, west of Tottenham Court Road. There was also a middle-class German community in Sydenham and Forest Hill.[14]

Forming, shaping and wrapping sugar loaves, 1843. In the early 19th century, many sugar bakeries run by Germans were located to the east of the City, in Whitechapel and East Smithfield

Before examining nineteenth-century German London, we need briefly to consider the reasons for its growth. The background factors within Germany included, in particular, a large population increase, and less significant, non-economic factors such as repressive measures pursued by successive governments.

These factors, overwhelmingly economic, meant that 4.8 million Germans emigrated between the years 1815 and 1930.[15] The vast majority made their way to the US, so what attracted the small numbers who entered Britain? First, there were greater economic opportunities, as Britain had industrialised earlier. Some Germans who found themselves in Britain were on their way to the US, travelling from an east- to a west-coast port, but decided to remain either because they ran out of money or because they obtained a job.[16] In addition, a small number of political refugees made their way to Britain because it offered greater freedom than any other European country.[17]

German society in nineteenth-century London mirrored British society, including every strand from destitutes to millionaires. At the lowest level were the homeless and prostitutes; slightly higher up was a working class. In the first half of the nineteenth century, the most important occupation for German immigrants continued to be sugar-baking, centred on Whitechapel.[18] By the 1880s this had lost its importance, as Germans moved into other employment, working as waiters, bakers, butchers and hairdressers. In the last three of these occupations, many Germans established themselves as small shopkeepers, forming a petty bourgeoisie which also included clerks and governesses. Higher up the social scale we can count wealthy businessmen involved in a variety of fields, notably banking,[19] and industrialists who imported expertise to develop firms involved with engineering, and the chemical, dyeing and paint industries.

Sometimes settlers anglicised their names. For example, Camerer Kuss & Company, clockmakers of New Oxford Street, changed the German name Kuss to Cuss

Left: A German butcher's shop in East Ham, 1911

The German Church, Forest
Hill, *c.* 1900

Forest Hill   German Church   London

These class divisions affected the social activities of Germans in nineteenth-
century London, as did their religious and political affiliations. Religion played the
most important role in maintaining a German identity. A survey of religious life in
London, published in 1905, identified fifteen places which conducted services in
German,[20] although it excluded some churches such as the Catholic St Bonifatius.
German churches also provided other activities, such as education and provision
for the German poor. Purely social clubs also existed, and these fundamentally
maintained the class structure of German London. They varied from the exclusive
Athenaeum and Turnverein to clubs which met at a local level. By the late nineteenth century many of the working-class clubs had connections either with trade
unions or anarchist organisations.[21]

   At the outbreak of the First World War, German London had a wide variety of
institutions, and a rich cultural life. The events of the War, when Britain became
gripped with Germanophobia, destroyed virtually all aspects of German life in
Britain. The attack came from both the government and public opinion. The Aliens
Restriction Act, passed in August 1914, dictated all future legislation for Germans.
As well as restricting their movement, it closed down German newspapers and
clubs. The government also used Trading with the Enemy Acts to confiscate all
enemy alien businesses. It is interesting to note that at this time the British royal
family, with its German ancestry, changed its name from Saxe-Coburg-Gotha to

Windsor, and the Battenburgs changed their name to Mountbatten. The introduction of a policy of wholesale internment (and subsequent repatriation) meant that the German population of Britain had shrunk to less than 23,000 by 1919. A large number of sites were used to house German males during the War, including Alexandra Palace.

Hostile public opinion assisted the government in the introduction of such measures. The belief circulated that all Germans were spies, and organisations of every description, from the Stock Exchange to trade unions, boycotted Germans. Anti-German political parties developed and, worst of all, there were anti-German riots in London. These broke out on five occasions, most notably in May 1915 following the sinking of the passenger liner *Lusitania* by a German submarine, with the loss of over 1000 lives. The disturbances of that month resulted in damage to over 2000 properties at a cost of £200,000, leading to 866 arrests.[22]

Despite the events of the First World War, some Germans remained in London into the 1920s. Restrictive immigration policies prevented a further influx until the 1930s, when the newcomers essentially consisted of Jews fleeing from Nazism. They began to arrive from 1933 but not until 1938, when the government relaxed its immigration policies, did large numbers enter Britain. Consequently the 11,000

Shop owned by a German Londoner being smashed and looted in East London in a wave of anti-German feeling following the sinking of the *Lusitania* in 1915

admitted before November 1938 had increased to 55,000 by the outbreak of the Second World War.[23]

The events of the Second World War led, in the spring of 1940, to the introduction of a policy of wholesale internment, affecting 30,000 people. The policy was supported by Winston Churchill's government, the security services and public opinion. However, in contrast to policy during the First World War, the government did not carry out a vindictive policy designed to destroy the German population of London, perhaps because the newcomers had fled Nazi oppression. All internees were free by the end of 1943.[24] After the War, they again developed ethnic communities reminiscent of those which had existed in the nineteenth century, but not as widespread.[25] Many German Jews progressed through British society in a variety of fields, including academic and business life.[26]

New influxes of Germans made their way to Britain after 1945. Some German prisoners of war decided to remain, and over 10,000 German women arrived as part of the government's schemes to rebuild industry in the post-War period.[27] One estimate from 1976 was that approximately 30,000 Germans were living in London, including 'businessmen and journalists, technicians and students, chefs in hotels and workers in factories, wives and children of British husbands and fathers'.[28] In contrast to previous German populations in London, that of the present day does not congregate in any particular area, but German institutions still exist within the capital, including some of the churches and charities founded in the seventeenth to the nineteenth centuries.[29] The existence of societies, such as the Anglo-German Family History Society, which trace family histories between the two countries, serves to emphasise the point that Germans have always formed a significant part of the mosaic of identities that make up 'Londoners'.[30]

Endnotes

For full details of publications, see Bibliography.

1 Rieger, 1942, pp101–2; Schöll, 1852, pp1–6.
2 Rieger, 1942, pp104–5; Schöll, 1852, pp1–6.
3 Roth, 1950. See also Kershen, this volume.
4 Knittle, 1936.
5 Chapman, 1980.
6 Engelsing, 1961, pp14–15; von Archenholtz, 1797, pp52–6.
7 Towey, 1988, pp3–5; Stern, 1954, pp29–31; Burckhardt, 1798, pp16–17, 19–21.
8 Endelman, 1979; George, 1925, pp131–8.
9 Burckhardt, 1798.
10 Timpe, 1909.
11 Society of Friends of Foreigners in Distress, 1814.
12 'Geschichte der deutschen evangelischen St Marien Schule', Bundesarchiv, Potsdam, 38989; 'Jubiläeums-Bericht der deutschen und englischen St Georg's Schule, 1. Juli 1905', Tower Hamlets Local History Collection.
13 Finestein, 1957, p73; Margoliouth, 1852, vol. ii.
14 Census, 1861, vol. ii, plxxv; Census, 1911, pxviii.
15 Baines, 1991, p9; Walker, 1964.
16 Engelsing, 1961.
17 Ashton, 1986.
18 Greenwood, 1874, pp264–70.
19 Brand, 1902.
20 Mudie-Smith, 1905.
21 Dorgeel, 1881; Katscher, 1887; Anglo-German Publishing Company, 1913.
22 Panayi, 1991.
23 See contributions to Hirschfeld, 1984.
24 Gillman & Gillman, 1980.
25 Berghahn, 1987.
26 See contributions to Mosse et al, 1991. See also Kershen, this volume.
27 C. Holmes, 1988, p213.
28 Breitenstein & Hommerich, 1976, pvi.
29 Breitenstein & Hommerich, 1976.
30 Other sources on Germans in London include Anderson, 1980; Aronsfeld, 1985; Farrel, 1990; Kellenbenz, 1978; McKellar, 1991; Panayi, 1989; Schaible, 1885; Schönberger, 1937; Specht, 1989; and Ward, 1899.

The Irish in London · Seán Hutton

An Irish tailor was the victim, in 1288, of the first recorded murder in Fleet Street and in 1485, London had an Irish mayor, indicating a continuing Irish presence in the capital in these early years.

Henry II was formally installed as Lord of Ireland in 1171, and between 1541 and 1800 the country was ruled as a subordinate kingdom by the British sovereign. After the Act of Union in 1800, the Kingdoms of Great Britain and Ireland were united, but this situation was partially altered in 1922 with the creation of the Irish Free State (now the Republic of Ireland). Northern Ireland continued to be part of the United Kingdom, and until 1949 the independent Irish state was a member of the British Commonwealth. Even after the declaration of a republic and withdrawal from the Commonwealth, Irish citizens continued to have unrestricted entry to Britain.

From the second half of the eighteenth century onwards, population increase, the transformation and relocation of manufacturing and agricultural change encouraged more people to leave Ireland; improved and cheaper travel facilities assisted this process. The Great Famine (1845–50) accelerated these more gradual developments. Continuing agricultural change, and the failure of nationalist hopes that the Irish state would build an industrial economy with the capacity to sustain its population, have meant that emigration has continued down to the present day.

While the identity of migrants was itself modified by the development of Irish nationalism in the nineteenth century, and by reactions to it, until 1922 those Irish who migrated to Britain were moving to a sister kingdom or within a united kingdom. Members of (or aspirants to) the professions and those with crafts or trades often regarded the two islands as one labour market, and for the Anglicised there were many common cultural aspects. However, similarities existed side by side with differences. The latter were particularly marked for the rural and small-town poor, as well as many of those pushed off the land, down to the 1950s. It was the extension of access to secondary and tertiary-level education in the Republic of Ireland, in the 1960s, and the spread of elements of a transnational popular culture among Irish (and British) youth, which served to bridge the gap for most migrants.

Significant Irish settlement in London began in the eighteenth century. The Irish were mostly part of the unskilled, casual labour force of the metropolis, finding employment as builders' labourers, chairmen, porters, coal-heavers, ballast men,

weavers, milk-sellers, street hawkers, publicans, lodging-house keepers and professional beggars. They lived in all areas of London, but the census of 1851 shows
most concentrated settlement in the parishes of St Giles, Whitechapel and
Southwark. Particular areas, like 'Little Dublin' in St Giles, had streets and courts
with exceptionally high numbers of Irish. A mid-nineteenth-century description of
the St Giles 'rookery' reinforces a widely perceived connection between Irishness
and poverty:

> Rows of crumbling houses flanked by courts and
> alleys ... You seem ... to leave ... the habits of
> your fellow-creatures behind you ... squalid chil-
> dren, haggard men with long uncombed hair, in
> rags, with a short pipe in their mouths, many
> speaking Irish, women without shoes or stockings
> – a babe ... at the breast ... ; wolfish-looking dogs;
> decayed vegetables strewing the pavement, low
> public houses, linen hanging across the street to
> dry ... [1]

Lynn Hollen Lees' *Exiles of Erin: Irish Migrants in Victorian
London* shows that Irish settlement in St Giles reflects
the complex pattern of Irish settlement in other British
cities at this time. For instance, the more respectable
northern part of the parish contained some Irish
professionals and artisans and many Irish domestic
servants, while in other parts of the south of the parish
Irish settlement was less concentrated.[2] However, the fact
that concentration of Irish settlement was greatest among
the poorest meant that it was the Irish poor who were
most visible in London.

The 1851 census shows an Irish community which was
also complex in its social structure. The majority of Irish-born male workers were
labourers, and Henry Mayhew noted the presence of the Irish men, women and
children in residual casual occupations; he calculated that in 1861 they formed just
over one-third of the costermongers of the capital.[3] However, about 20 per cent
had crafts or trades, and there was also a small professional category.

The number of Irish-born recorded for London had reached a peak in 1851,[4]
thereafter declining for the rest of the century. The second major wave of Irish
immigration, beginning in the 1920s, reached its peak in the 1950s. It was in this
period that Britain replaced the United States as the chief destination for Irish
migrants. In the 1930s, and during and after the Second World War, government
agencies and private employers actively recruited Irish labour. An increasing
proportion of the Irish were employed in skilled, administrative, commercial

The 'Rookery', c. 1820.
Many Irish immigrants
lived in the Rookery,
in the parish of St Giles-
in-the-Field, the site of
present day New Oxford
Street

Irish nurses singing carols
to raise money for
St Andrew's Hospital,
Neasden, 1957. Many
young Irish women have
come to London to work
in the health service

and professional occupations. Nevertheless a major area of employment for Irish men continues to be the construction industry, and for Irish women it was domestic service, in the first half of the twentieth century, followed by nursing after the Second World War. While there has undoubtedly been upward mobility within the Irish community, the Irish continue to be under-represented in higher employment and over-represented in lower.

As J. A. Jackson states in *The Irish in Britain*, 'In both the main periods of heavy Irish immigration to Britain the labour force which the Irish have provided has corresponded closely to the needs of an expanding economy.'[5] Irish labour helped build the canals, docks and railways of London's nineteenth-century infrastructure, and by the end of the nineteenth century Irish migrants and their children had established their position within the dock labour force (see colour plate 13). A conversation among Irish labourers of the 1950s concerning work opportunities, in Dónall Mac Amhlaigh's *Schnitzer O'Shea*, indicates the continuing draw of London as a source of employment:

'Is it London sonny? What in the name of God is bringing you to London?'
…
'Sure all the work in London is done, now!'

'All the big buildings are built!'
'All the new gas mains are laid!'
'All the electric cables, too!'[6]

The presence of the employees and the equipment of John Murphy & Co. and McNicholas Engineering at many sites of excavation and improvement today is further evidence of the contribution of Irish labour to the maintenance of London's infrastructure – as well as of Irish entrepreneurial skill. A number of public services, such as the National Health Service, have been heavily dependent on Irish and other immigrant labour.

The Irish presence is visible in the fabric of London in other ways. For instance, the work of a number of Irish sculptors can be seen on the Albert Memorial: the figures of Prince Albert himself and 'Asia' were sculpted by John Henry Foley, that of 'Europe' by Patrick Macdowell, and that of 'Engineering' by John Lawlor. This fact reminds us that, from the seventeenth century onwards, London was a magnet for many in Ireland who hoped to further their careers in literature, journalism, theatre, the arts and certain of the professions. In *Ireland in London* (1889), two young Irish expatriates, Francis A. Fahy and D. J. O'Donoghue, engage in a process of cultural retrieval, reclaiming such figures as Nahum Tate, Sir Richard Steele, Sir Hans Sloane, Richard Brinsley Sheridan, Oliver Goldsmith, Edmund Burke and George Canning for Ireland. They also draw attention to personalities like Christian Davies, the female soldier, and the many female Irish singers and actors who made their careers on the London stage. Indeed, two of their own Irish contemporaries, Oscar Wilde and George Bernard Shaw, were to make their mark as dramatists in the metropolis. Wilde's plays are now classics of the 'English' comedy of manners,

Irish paviours sketched by John Nixon in Lothbury near Bank, in 1810. The Irish have a long association with London's construction industry

to the development of which Irish-born writers in London had already made such a contribution.[7] Shaw, who had already established his reputation as a music and drama critic and as a leading Fabian socialist, would quickly gain international fame as a dramatist in the early 1900s.

In the 1890s the Irish Literary and Irish Texts Societies were formed in London, manifestations of that cultural nationalism which was reshaping Irish identities; and at the beginning of the new century the London branch of the Gaelic League was not only the largest but also one of the most important in that Irish-based organisation. It was a particularly vigorous manifestation of the Irish presence in London, with its programme of Irish language and Irish dancing classes, its summer outings and festivals, its Irish-language plays, its annual fair to promote the sale of Irish products, and its St Patrick's Day concerts at prime London venues attended by up to 3000 people. Among its members at this time were Michael Collins, an architect of the independent Irish state, who worked as a Post Office clerk in London, and Pádraic ó Conaire, one of the most important writers of the first phase of the Irish-language literary revival. Sections of the expatriate Irish in London now contributed to cultural and political developments in Ireland itself, and many would return to play an active part in the development of the new Irish state. In London too, the Irish impact on political activity was considerable. At the time of the campaign for the repeal of the Act of Union in the 1840s, it was claimed that there were 80,000 repealers in London. Feargus O'Connor was a leading figure in the Chartist movement, which was supported by Irish Confederate clubs in London. After the First World War, the Irish tended to support and become involved in the Labour Party, an association signalled by such Irish names as Callaghan and Healey in its recent leadership.

Until the arrival of Jews from Eastern Europe at the end of the century, the Irish were the largest and most visible group of migrants in London. Attitudes towards them were affected by the rapid increase in the Irish population of the capital between 1841 and 1851, against the background of famine and disease in Ireland and a preoccupation with what was perceived as a state of urban crisis in Britain. They were stereotyped and regarded as both different and as a source of amusement. Michael Doheny, an Irish barrister, experienced this when he arrived in London in 1848 disguised as an Irish labourer, 'on the run' following the failure of the attempted insurrection in Ireland:

> My costume attracted universal attention ... I was soon followed by an uproarious crowd of most incorrigible young rascals ... They peered at me round lamp-posts, and occasionally, 'Teigue', and 'Phelim', pronounced in a broad English accent, grated on my ear ... [8]

The 'Irish joke', the nub of which is the incorrigible stupidity of the Irish 'Paddy', is the residual manifestation of this attitude. Its last major manifestation coincided with the Provisional IRA's bombing campaign of the 1970s and 1980s.

The activities of the Fenians[9] in England, and of the Land League in Ireland, were major causes of virulent stereotyping of the Irish in the 1860s, 1870s and 1880s. The fear that cheap Irish labour would lower general conditions of labour could also stir up anti-Irish feeling, as in the Spitalfield riots of 1736; and at the end of the nineteenth century, the dockers' leader Ben Tillett (whose own mother was Irish) was complaining about the effect of Irish ex-agricultural labourers on employment in the London docks. However, the arrival of subsequent waves of non-Irish migrants took some of the pressure off the Irish in this respect, as these became the targets for such feelings.

The vast majority of nineteenth- and twentieth-century Irish migrants were Catholics. Their presence was one of the most important factors in the Catholic revival, introducing a substantial Irish poor and working-class element at a time when the Church was being restructured under the leadership of Wiseman and Manning, successive archbishops of Westminster. A programme of church-building, partly paid for by the contributions of the Irish poor, to meet the needs of growing congregations, helped to develop the identity of local congregations. This sense of pride was expressed by Father William Kelly of SS Mary and Michael in Commercial Road: 'This splendid new church ... beats hollow in beauty the finest of the [gin] palaces ... and has, in the eyes of our Protestant neighbours, raised this poor congregation at least fifty years in social position and consideration.'[10]

Restructuring also made available to congregations a rich parochial life, including a system of elementary schools and a wide range of social activities. In the twentieth century, the Catholic Church has continued to fulfil an important social role: 'The Church was like a lamp to moths ... [It] was a place for meeting.'[11]

The stories of twentieth-century migrants prior to the 1960s suggest lack of economic and social opportunity as the main motives for leaving Ireland. A number of male migrants stress the dignity to be achieved in an expanding economy. Eamonn Smullen, a shop steward on the Shell site on London's South Bank in the 1950s, writes: 'In England I met men that I had known in the building industry in Ireland, men ... who used to walk about with fear in their eyes. In England, in the conditions of full employment at that time, the fear was gone.'[12]

A number of women's accounts focus on the social environment of their work. Molly Allsop, in service in London at the end of the 1920s, got into trouble for her friendliness with the milkman and Irish labourers. Apart from the intensity of the work ('I was up from six in the morning until twelve at night'), it was the loneliness which she remembers.[13] Others, like Hannah Raynor, preferred to work for Jewish families because of the more homely atmosphere. Speaking of her Jewish employers, she says, 'They took a great interest in me, and they acted as a mother and father to me.'[14] The companionship of live-in hotel and hospital work were important for young, unmarried Irish women like Maria Curran: 'We all went out together, all the nurses. We used to walk along with our arms around one another, down the road, singing and shouting.'[15] For young male immigrants of the 1940s and 1950s, the pub and the dancehall were important social centres: 'I used to ... get

First Holy Communion,
Sacred Heart Church,
Camberwell, 1992

drunk in the Black Horse, then go to the Pride of Erin club … You went to the dance-halls to meet people, to talk to girls.'[16] Explaining the attraction of the pub, Paddy Fahey commented: '… today you have every possible luxury in your homes. In those days I had a tiny room with a bed and a table and a chair … When I finished work at night I only had the four bare walls to look at.'[17]

The pattern of life for young married couples, especially those who had started families, was different. Dónall Mac Amhlaigh recorded in his diary:

> To mass at Highbury this morning. I didn't get anything like the same satisfaction from it as I would get in Camden Town, somehow. It's mainly married couples who attend mass here and there was no crowd gathered outside the church like you would see in other places [translated from the Irish].'[18]

Yvonne Hayes, who grew up in London in the 1970s, remembers that a visit to the Catholic social club after mass on a Sunday was her mother's main social outing when the children were small.[19]

In the twentieth century attitudes to the Irish often reflect the current state of Anglo-Irish relations. The experiences of individuals in these circumstances have varied and, as Gearóid ó Tuathaigh has pointed out, the repercussions affect mainly the working-class Irish.[20] Teresa Burke recalls 'No Irish Need Apply' notices in the shops in south London in the 1930s. Her husband, Pat Burke, was told by a fellow-worker: 'Get out of it, you Irish bastard. Why don't you go back home?'[21] Margaret Ridgeway came to London in 1928 and worked as a chambermaid and linen-keeper, learning bookkeeping and typing in her free time and entering the civil service during the Second World War. She experienced little prejudice, but for many years she shared the view of her London-based relatives that it was better not to get involved in Irish life in the capital, 'because there was still the political background all the time … [and] if anything crops up … you might be deported or something like this'.[22] Yvonne Hayes remembers how, in the 1970s, her parents 'just tried to keep their heads down and not get into trouble'. Her story also reveals how vulnerable children from minority cultures can be to prejudice or insensitivity in the school situation.[23]

The influence of the Catholic Church is important for many, especially in their youth, as are the influences of home and family. However, the identity of second- and subsequent-generation Irish, growing up in a multi-cultural situation, can be quite complex. Jenneba Sie Jalloh describes herself as 'part Irish, part African … and a Londoner'. London-born Yvonne Hayes has settled for an Irish identity, yet she sees that identity as different from her parents' – 'more than just going to church and knowing Irish people'.[24] For many second-generation Irish born in London since the late 1930s, the periodic visits 'home' to Ireland became part of the childhood ritual and are embedded in memories of childhood.

London-Irish 'pioneers' of the Church of the Sacred Heart, Kilburn, returning from a coach trip to Clacton, 1961

Many Irish migrants did not intend to emigrate permanently; and many did return in the 1970s, during a period of growth in Ireland. However, Mary Galvin from Battersea describes the process by which immigrants become settled:

> I don't go back to Ireland since I lost my father and mother. I used to go home twice a year ... I never felt that I wanted to go back and live in Ireland ... Because my family were over here ... and I like to have my family.[25]

The last twenty years have seen the strengthening of Irish communal identity, partly due to campaigns around issues arising from the crisis in Northern Ireland. The impetus given to community politics by the Greater London Council between 1981 and 1985 was also important, encouraging demands connected with such issues as health and housing, on the basis that the Irish are disadvantaged in these areas. London Irish Women's Conferences have been held since 1984, and the rights and needs of Irish Travellers in the London area have been raised. Latterly Irish lesbian and gay networks have been set up in London, as well as a referral service for Irish people affected by HIV/AIDS.

The period is also one which has seen the Irish government and more established bodies, like the Catholic Chaplaincy and the Federation of Irish Societies, becoming more high-profile in the pursuit of the interests of the Irish community, especially since the signing of the Anglo-Irish Agreement in 1985. Among the London-based organisations currently affiliated to the Federation of Irish Societies, for example, are the Cara Irish Homeless Project, the Irish Support and Advice Centre, Hammersmith, the London Irish Pensioners Action Group, and the Safe Start Foundation (which exists specifically to help young Irish people arriving in London).

Equally, the Irish within the business community have adopted a higher profile, participating in philanthropic initiatives concerned with the welfare of the Irish. These not only involve Irish people occupying leading positions with British firms, but representatives of British-based firms founded on Irish enterprise; as well as representatives of Irish businesses adopting an active role in the British market.

Since the 1960s an increasing proportion of Irish emigration has been directed to London. Those leaving the Republic of Ireland in the 1980s have been much better qualified than those leaving in previous periods, and there has been a rise in the proportions of Irish migrants employed in administrative, professional and managerial occupations.[26] It is no surprise that Irish graduate associations are extending their activities and that new associations like the London Irish Society – an organisation for young Irish professionals in London – are being set up alongside the older associations of the middle class. Many of the businesspeople and young professionals who have come to London are attuned to living across cultures and regard migration as opportunity rather than as loss.

Since 1971 the London-based *Irish Post* has played an important role in seeking to draw together the various elements in the Irish community and to promote positive images of the Irish in Britain. Its annual awards have highlighted the Irish contribution to life in Britain, through service to the community or cultural or sporting achievement. And, of course, it is through social events organised by county associations, pub sessions and concerts, Irish dancing competitions, golf, rugby and Gaelic Athletic Association fixtures, and annual events like the St Patrick's Day celebrations, the London *Fleadh* or a host of Irish festivals, that the Irish community's collective identity in London is chiefly expressed. In 1957, Dónall Mac Amhlaigh noted in his diary: *'Is Gaelaí go mór an baile seo ná bunáite na n-áiteanna sa bhaile'* [This town is more Irish than most of the places at home].[27] The Irish community still forms the largest single migrant group in London,[28] and after centuries of settlement and generations of London-born Irish integrating and assimilating into the city's population, Irish influence is inextricably woven into the fabric of London life. [29]

The *Fleadh* Irish music festival, Finsbury Park, 1993

Endnotes

For full details of publications, see Bibliography.

1 Montague Gore, *On the Dwellings of the Poor in London and the Means of Improving Them*, James Ridgway, London, 1851, ppvii–viii.

2 Lees, 1979, pp66–7.

3 Henry Mayhew, *London Labour and the London Poor*, Griffin, Bohn & Company, London, 1861, vol. 1, p104.

4 In 1841 the Irish-*born* made up 3.9 per cent of the population of London, and 4.6 per cent in 1851. By 1861 this had decreased to 3.8 per cent and by 1891 it stood at 1.6 per cent. In 1981 the Irish population of the Greater London area (including those born in Northern Ireland and the children of heads of households born in Ireland) was calculated at 5.3 per cent. However, this population was never evenly distributed throughout London. Nineteenth-century concentration of population is mentioned in the text. In 1981 the highest concentrations were in Brent, Camden, Islington and Hammersmith. Lynn Hollen Lees's calculations for the mid-nineteenth century, which include the English-born children of Irish parents, lead her to give *minimum* figures of 156,000 and 178,000 respectively for the Irish population of London in 1851 and 1861 (as compared to census figures of 109,000 and 107,000 Irish *born*). (Lees, 1979, pp46–8, table 1.1, p47; Connor, 1987, pp25–6, 27)

5 Jackson, 1963, p109

6 Dónall Mac Amhlaigh, *Schnitzer O'Shea*, Brandon, Dingle, 1987, p31.

7 Seamus Deane, *A Short History of Irish Literature*, Hutchinson, London, 1986, pp118–39.

8 Michael Doheny, *The Felon's Track*, M.H. Gill & Son, Dublin, 1943, pp274-5.

9 'Fenians' is the name by which members of the Irish Republican Brotherhood were known. This secret revolutionary organisation had been set up in 1858. It existed not only in Ireland, but also in the United States and Britain. It is estimated that there were some 18,000 members in Britain in the mid-1860s. An explosion at Clerkenwell prison in 1867, in an attempt to free Fenian prisoners, resulted in the deaths of a number of people living near the prison. See Quinlivan & Rose, 1982.

10 *The Tablet*, 6 January 1844, quoted in Lees, 1979, pp175–6.

11 Fahey, 1991, pp30, 33.

12 Eamonn Smullen, 'What We Do Over There', in Clancy *et al.*, 1991, p113.

13 Schweitzer, 1989, pp5–6.

14 Ibid, p155.

15 Ibid, p60.

16 Fahey, 1991, pp25, 30.

17 Ibid, p33.

18 Dónall Mac Amhlaigh, *Dialann Deoraí*, An Clóchomhar, Dublin, 1960, p118. (Translated by Valentin Iremonger as *The Diary of an Exile*, Routledge & Kegan Paul, London, 1964.)

19 Lennon *et al.*, 1988, p220.

20 Ó Tuathaigh, in Clancy *et al.*, p23.

21 Schweitzer, 1989, p27, 38.

22 Lennon *et al.*, 1988, p50.

23 Ibid, pp219, 220.

24 Ibid, pp217, 220.

25 Schweitzer, 1989, p73.

26 Hazelkorn, 1990, pp22–5, 31–3.

27 Dónall Mac Amhlaigh, *Dialann Deoraí*, p109.

28 In the 1981 census those of Irish origin formed 5.3 per cent (4.6 per cent Republic of Ireland; 0.7 per cent Northern Ireland); New Commonwealth Caribbean formed 4.7 per cent; and New Commonwealth Indian formed 3.4 per cent (Connor, 1987, p26).

29 Further information on the Irish in London can be found in Bennett, 1991; Curtis, 1971; Curtis, 1984; Davis, 1991; Garratt, 1853; George, 1925; Gilley, 1969, 1971, 1973; Goodway, 1982; Lovell, 1977; Lunn, 1992; Marks, 1990; O'Connell, 1993; Ó Súilleabháin, 1989; Rossiter, 1991; Ryan, 1894; Swift & Gilley, 1985, 1989 and Walter, 1989.

Italians in London · Lucio Sponza

A real Italian community in London has existed only from the early nineteenth century, but people from the Italian peninsula have settled in the capital for centuries (see Nick Merriman, this volume). The break with the Church of Rome under Henry VIII and the economic decline of the Italian peninsula did not interrupt the flow of migrants. Renaissance Italy became a model which could best be imitated by inviting scholars, artists, musicians and craftsmen to come and work in Britain, particularly London. This tradition was strengthened during the eighteenth century, when Palladian villas became fashionable among the wealthy. Italian architects were accompanied by painters, sculptors, decorators and other craftsmen (see colour plate 8). One of the best-known Italian artists to live in London was Canaletto (see colour plate 3), whose paintings now hang in the National Gallery, Buckingham Palace and Windsor Castle. Sometimes Italian artists worked together as, for example, when Cipriani, a draughtsman, carver and decorator, and Capezzuolo, a sculptor, designed the Lord Mayor's coach, now on display at the Museum of London. Italian musicians and opera singers were also in great demand in London and some made it their home, including Clementi, a piano manufacturer considered to be the first genuine composer for pianoforte. In a different sphere of the arts, Joseph Grimaldi, the London-born son of an Italian ballet master, became the 'king of clowns'. Grimaldi lived in Clerkenwell (Holborn) in the early nineteenth century, when the district was becoming the centre of an Italian colony.

At the end of the Napoleonic Wars, the worsening economic conditions in mountain villages in northern Italy, which already had a tradition of seasonal emigration, forced young peasants to seek a living abroad. Paris was a favourite destination and the more adventurous proceeded to London. They settled in the warren-like streets around Hatton Garden and Saffron Hill, in Holborn, where low-grade lodging houses provided cheap accommodation. Charles Dickens, who knew the area well, chose it as the location for the thieves' den in *Oliver Twist*, and an article in *The Times* complained:

> The public have of late been exceedingly annoyed by the appearance of a number of Italian boys with monkeys and mice wandering about the streets, exciting the compassion of the benevolent ... There are no less than twenty boys now in London under similar circumstances.[1]

'Les Savoyards' by George Cruikshank, 1818. The first street musicians from Italy came to London in the early 19th century. The vocalist and violinist came from the Savoy region between France and Italy, and the organist from Parma

Undeterred by such remarks, Italian street performers and musicians became a ubiquitous feature of London streets; their numbers increased throughout the nineteenth century, reaching about a thousand. Other Italians at this time were vendors of plaster figures or craftsmen making such things as looking glasses, picture frames and precision instruments. Two such artisans, Negretti and Zambra, set up a highly successful firm famous for its barometers. These craftsmen lived in the Italian quarter, in larger houses which doubled as their workshops. The more successful eventually moved out of the Italian quarter and dispersed, their integration into the host society facilitated by marriage to English women. In the poorer section of the community, men married women from the same villages; however, the majority of the male immigrants were single and returned to Italy after a few years.

The pattern of occupation had a strong regional flavour. In the main, street musicians were from the Apennine area around Parma; statuette-makers and pedlars were from a few villages in the mountains near Lucca; and skilled artisans were from the Alpine valleys near Como. The regional link was reinforced by a recruitment system based on kinship and village ties. These Italians spoke dialects which would be fairly intelligible to other Italians, but emphasised their cultural differences.

An altogether separate category of Italians also came to London during the first half of the nineteenth century. They spoke good Italian and were often highly educated. These were political refugees, welcomed to Britain as the romantic victims of the petty tyrannical rulers who resisted the unification of Italy. Some exiles were men of letters and scholars, including Gabriele Rossetti (the father of Christina and Dante Gabriel) and Antonio Panizzi, who became Chief Librarian at the British Museum and designed its famous domed Reading Room. The most famous Italian political refugee was Giuseppe Mazzini, the nationalist visionary and restless conspirator, who lived in London for many years and was actively involved in the life of the Italian community. In 1841 he established a free school for destitute Italian children in Greville Street, Hatton Garden, but ran up against the hostility of the Italian priests of the Sardinian Chapel, who had more orthodox views. The desire to maintain religious traditions resulted in the building of St Peter's, the 'Italian church', in Clerkenwell in 1864, at which time the Italian population in London numbered about 2000. Mazzini and his friends also tried to rescue many children from wicked masters who had brought them over from Italy, and the plight of the little Italian organ-grinders contributed to the passing of the Children Protection Act in 1889. The Bill was introduced in parliament by Anthony J. Mundella, the son of an Italian political refugee.

The Italians were often the subject of complaints, which must be seen in the context of major changes in the social life of London. For instance, while organ-grinders were welcomed by children in slum areas, they were a nuisance to the professional class which was growing in numbers and status by the middle of the century.[2] *Punch* magazine launched a crusade against the organ-grinders and a law was passed in 1864 to curb street music, but without effect. Only the subsequent movement of the middle class to suburban London delivered them from this torment.

Street musician in King William Walk, Greenwich, 1885

The 1880s and 1890s represent a crucial period for the Italians in London. Their numbers trebled, from 3500 in 1881 to 11,000 in 1901, but remained a tiny proportion of the overall population of around 4.5 million. Street music continued to be the main occupation, but a change took place in the community, with the growing importance of such employment as board-and-lodging, dealing in food and, in particular, the itinerant ice-cream trade. Small family-based businesses were the norm, but in a few instances they developed into large enterprises. This was so in the case of Carlo Gatti, a Swiss-Italian immigrant who began as a pedlar of roast chestnuts, then exploited the Victorian craze for ice-cream. At first he sold it in the streets of London and then became a wholesale importer of ice from Norway, employing a small colony of Italians at his ice wharf in East London. Gatti also became the proprietor of one of the most famous London music halls, and died a millionaire in the late 1870s.[3] In these years the foundations were laid for the stereotypical connection between Italians and catering, still with us today. Many Italians opened their own cafés, wineshops, restaurants and food shops supplying the Italian and local community. A good number still exist, such as Terroni & Sons in the Clerkenwell Road (established 1890) and G. Gazzano & Son in the Farringdon Road (established 1901). Not all Italians worked in catering, however. Many men worked as road-paviours, mosaicists, barbers and knife-grinders. Women particularly worked as domestic servants, and worked within the home, taking in laundry, making lace, and manufacturing pasta.

This expansion and transformation was caused by changes taking place in Italy and in London. In Italy, demographic pressure and the agrarian crisis induced a massive exodus of poorer peasants, most of them to North and South America. The established pattern of regional provenance in the London community was now broadened by the arrival of people from the Liri Valley (between Rome and Naples), who were mainly absorbed into the ice-cream trade. They were regarded as 'Southerners' by other Italians, and looked upon with suspicion because of their different habits and near-unintelligible language.

As London grew in the late nineteenth century, the Italian community of peasants broadened its niche. Its clustering in the narrow streets and dark courts around Saffron Hill aroused concern. The Italian quarter had frequently been singled out as a health hazard, and the Royal Commission on Housing of the Working Classes (1884–5) confirmed the serious state of overcrowding. The government's policy of 'slum clearance' was intensified, and between the late 1870s and the early 1890s the quarter was cut through by two new roads: Clerkenwell Road and Rosebery Avenue. *St James's Gazette* expressed the hope that 'the Clerkenwell [Italian] colony will be swept away in due time'.[4] Ironically, while the slum clearance contributed to the dispersal of Italians, it also created new job opportunities for them in road-building, especially the unpleasant task of asphalting.[5] The old colony was not entirely swept away, but Italians gradually moved to neighbouring districts: St Pancras, Finsbury, Islington and, above all, Westminster, where a second 'Little Italy' developed, in and around Soho. Some streets became 'almost exclusively occupied by Italians who worked as cooks or waiters in the West End's numerous restaurants and hotels'.[6]

As their numbers continued to increase, various clubs were set up in Clerkenwell and Soho where Italian men could socialise after work. There they would drink, play cards and dance (with English and Irish women). Some of the clubs acquired a bad reputation and it was said, with much exaggeration, that they fostered vice and subversion. At the end of the nineteenth century, anarchist and socialist militants from all over the Continent found sanctuary in London. Some came from Italy, but they did not become part of the Italian community proper, where political debate was absent. An Italian Society of Mutual Aid and Employment among Hotel and Restaurant Employees was set up in 1886 in Gerrard Street; it prospered at first and ten years later moved to larger premises in Soho Square, but later collapsed because of internal squabbles. More lasting was the establishment of the Italian Hospital in 1884 by a successful merchant, Giovambattista Ortelli, who transformed one of his houses in Queen Square to provide medical aid for his compatriots. It was conveniently located halfway between Soho and the old quarter. Unfortunately, after a century of service it closed in 1989 due to lack of financial resources.

Procession of the Madonna del Carmine, Clerkenwell, 1930s. The parade, from St Peter's Church, first took place in 1883

With the growth of the community, and the higher proportion of women and children, the religious, educational and leisure activities provided by St Peter's church became increasingly important. The great religious event of the year was the Festival of Our Lady of Mount Carmel, celebrated in mid-July, when hundreds of Italians flocked to Clerkenwell to walk in procession behind the statue of the Madonna. When it began, in 1883, it was 'the first attempt made by Roman Catholics at any parade or open-air demonstration in London since the pre-Reformation days'.[7] The festival is still held today, although in a less glamorous fashion.

At the turn of the century, liberal attitudes towards immigration to Britain were under strain. The 1905 Aliens Act aimed at excluding 'undesirable and destitute' foreigners. The main target was the large influx of Jews from Russia and Poland, fleeing from discrimination and persecution. Some people also regarded the Italians as undesirables, but they could not be said to undercut wages, since most of the work they were engaged in was not pursued by British labour. By then, in any case, 'Little Italy' was accepted as an exotic dimension of London's life:

> If it is a fine sunny day you will see the men sitting on the doorsteps or along the walls, their knees closely bent against their stomachs in Oriental fashion, smoking curved reed pipes, and nursing their limbs with folded hands. On the shady side are the women and girls on stools and chairs knitting and sewing. Some are standing in little groups in characteristic attitudes; they are discussing domestic affairs. Further up the street men in shirt sleeves are churning ice-cream, loading barrows, tinkering potato ovens; while in the courts and alleys, where no one intrudes, girls are washing and ironing and cooking al fresco in true Italian fashion.[8]

Italian ice-cream seller at the foot of Stockwell Street, Greenwich, 1884. Italians exploited the Victorian craze for ice-cream from the 1850s

Then came the Great War and its aftermath. The worldwide economic uncertainties and the protectionist policies adopted by governments in the inter-war years resulted in a marked decline in migratory movement. From nearly 12,000 in 1911, the Italian-born population in London was reduced by 1921 to 11,000 (a more notable decline occurred in the rest of the country) and remained at that level for the next twenty years. The old itinerant occupations virtually disappeared, with the exception of ice-cream selling. In fact, this was a period of consolidation within the catering and food-dealing sectors. Fashionable Italian restaurants were established in Soho and Mayfair, such as Leoni's Quo Vadis, Bertorelli's and Quaglino's. Modest businesses mushroomed and spread outside Clerkenwell and Soho: snack bars, ice-cream parlours and café-restaurants. Colonies of London Italians could now be found in Islington, Marylebone, Kensington and Lambeth. On Sunday mornings, after attending mass at St Peter's, St Patrick's (Soho) or St George's (Southwark), Italians would meet for a gossip in compatriots' cafés nearby.

A powerful new factor in Italian national identity was the 'Fascio di Londra', the first Fascist section set up abroad. The founders, officials and well-off members of the London community had difficulty in recruiting members at first, due to an atavistic suspicion of officialdom and of grandiloquence. In the end, however, most Italians accepted and even welcomed the Fascio's leadership since, for the first time, it appeared that the Italian authorities in Rome and London really cared about them; in addition, until 1935 Mussolini was highly praised by the British and by the Catholic priests. The Fascio's grand headquarters in Charing Cross Road was a dynamic centre for social activities and acted as a welfare agency, giving special attention to children. An Italian school was opened in Hyde Park Gate, and free holidays as far away as Italy were organised for the children.

All this activity was shattered in June 1940 when Mussolini declared war on Britain. Some Italian shops had their windows smashed by angry crowds, particularly in Soho. Italians became the target of abuse, although there were also signs of sympathy. Officially, they were now 'enemy aliens' and many Italian-born men were interned. Family life, the centre of their world, was disrupted as thousands of husbands and sons were confined to the Isle of Man. In the rushed operation even Italian Jewish refugees and known anti-Fascists were rounded up and interned. The process of releasing the internees was frustratingly slow. Worse was soon to come when the liner *Arandora Star*, carrying over 700 Italians and other deportees to Canada, was sunk. Of the 450 Italians who drowned, 230 were from London – harmless waiters, cooks, shopkeepers and restaurant managers. It was a devastating blow, but when those Italians still at liberty were offered the opportunity to be sent back to Italy only a few accepted. This operation came to nothing in the end, but the London Italians' response was significant: they belonged in London, they were part of it and they could see no alternative other than remaining, for better or for worse.

The tragedy of the *Arandora Star* is still vivid in the memory of the older generation of London Italians, and is commemorated by a plaque outside St Peter's. Yet it has left little resentment in a community which endures misfortunes with a combination of courage and fatalism. Bitterness and self-pity had no place among a people intent on achieving respect and well-being through hard work. In the early 1940s, many thousands of Italian prisoners of war were brought to Britain, mainly to work in agriculture. Some camps were located around London and when a degree of freedom was granted to the prisoners (after Italy's armistice with the Allies in 1943), they were often introduced to Italian families. Several hundreds of them were eventually allowed to stay, thus contributing to the expansion of the Italian population in London.

Labour shortages at the end of the war induced the British government to recruit workers from southern Italy, among other places. The newcomers were mainly directed to industries and services in the provinces, but some came to, or later settled in, London. Almost 10,000 Italians were living in London by 1951, mostly around their traditional haunts of Islington, St Pancras, Westminster, Kensington and Lambeth. Twenty years later, at the peak of the Italian presence, there were nearly 33,000, many now living as far afield as Enfield, Hounslow and Bromley. Their occupations were also more varied, although catering remained their principal activity. Small owner-operated businesses of the coffee- or sandwich-bar variety were set up, in what was 'the first attempt to sell "Italianness", in the form of new concepts imported from Italy, to the population at large'.[9] Coffee machines serving espresso and cappuccino, and menus including spaghetti bolognese, lasagne al forno and pizza, became commonplace. The espresso bars of Soho became the focus for London's developing youth culture. Some, such as Bar Italia in Frith Street, are still a lively focus for all things Italian. Italian fashions became all the rage, particularly among the 'mods' of the early 1960s.

By the beginning of the 1970s, the Italian community in London (and elsewhere in Britain) began to decline and change in character. In 1991 it included some 30,000 people, although if the London-born of Italian origin are added the estimate is probably close to 100,000. Elderly people returned to Italy to retire and the newcomers, fewer in number, were not the traditional Italian immigrants. They were students, particularly those in London to learn English, professionals, businesspeople and managers, reflecting Italy's standard of living now equal to that of Britain, and its transformation into a country of immigration rather than emigration.

Twenty years after Britain's entry into the Common Market, the Italian community in London can be said to consist of three distinct elements: the descendants of the old, pre-war arrivals, indistinguishable from the rest of society; the emigrant flow of the 1950s and early 1960s, generally assimilated; and the more recent educated arrivals, who immediately became part of English life and culture. Thus the Italians contribute to London's cosmopolitan tapestry.[10]

Interior of Porselli's ballet shoe workshop, Cambridge Circus, 1986. Colombano Porselli came to London from Milan in 1927. His customers included the ballerina Anna Pavlova

Endnotes

For full details of publications, see Bibliography.

1 *The Times*, 20 March 1820.
2 It was said that organ-grinders deliberately played out of tune to 'extract money in return for silence on their departure'. Ben Weinreb and Christopher Hibbert (eds), *The London Encyclopaedia*, Macmillan, London, 1983, p839.
3 Kinross, 1991.
4 'Foreign Colonies in London – Italians (1)', *St James's Gazette*, 22 June 1891, p5.
5 'It is only the actual work of laying the powder (of asphalt) which is performed by the Italians. The English man apparently cannot be induced to undertake this work, alleging, no doubt truthfully, that the heat brings the skin off his feet.' See Charles Booth, *Life and Labour of the People in London*, vol. iv, Macmillan, London, third edition, 1903, p35.
6 Judith Summers, *Soho: A History of London's Most Colourful Neighbourhood*, Bloomsbury, London 1989, p160.
7 'Roman Catholics in Holborn', *Holborn and Finsbury Guardian*, 21 July 1894.
8 Count E. Armfelt, 'Italy in London', in G. R. Sims (ed.), *Living London*, vol. i, Cassell, London, 1906, p185.
9 Colpi, 1991a.
10 Other sources on London's Italian community include Colpi, 1991b; Leoni, 1966; Salvoni, 1990; and Sponza, 1988.

The Jewish Community in London · Anne Kershen

Children returning home after a Purim party, Golders Green, 1968

In 1992 the Jewish community of London was estimated to number 210,000, less than 3 per cent of the capital's population.[1] To many outsiders, London's Jews appear as a compact ethnic minority, yet in religious background and observance they are anything but homogenous. They manifest theological and ideological differences which can be traced back to their cultural and geographic roots.

In 1290, Edward I expelled the small Jewish community which had been established in England following the arrival of William the Conqueror. For 366 years the practice of Judaism in England was forbidden. In 1655, a Sephardi Rabbi,[2] Menasseh Ben Israel, travelled to England from Amsterdam to plead with Oliver Cromwell to 'tolerate a Jewish presence'. Cromwell was receptive to the Rabbi's appeal for both religious and economic reasons. There was a prevailing Puritan belief that once Jews 'inhabited *all* parts of the earth' the final Redemption could begin. But financial matters were primary. The pragmatist Cromwell recognised that Jewish merchants, with their international trading links, could only benefit an English economy in competition with Spain and France. Following heated debates by the Council of State, in June 1656 Oliver Cromwell announced that the practice of Judaism would, once again, be permitted in England. The present-day Jewish people of London are thus descendants of those readmitted in 1656 and those who came after.

The earliest Jewish community of the Readmission was affluent and cultured; composed of bullion dealers, merchants, bankers, gem importers and traders, by 1660 it numbered between thirty and forty Sephardi families. Unlike those of Central and Eastern European countries, the government and Crown of England imposed no direct controls over the practice of Judaism or on its practitioners. The Jews of the Readmission were self-governing and answerable to no one in their communal organisation. The disabilities that existed were imposed on all religious dissenters and those born overseas. The City of London maintained its own code of practice and determined who could live and work within its walls. This explains why the earliest Jewish settlement in Spitalfields developed to the east of the city boundaries.

By the end of the seventeenth century the Sephardim had acquired a house of worship and a burial ground. One of their number had been admitted to the London Exchange and another, Samuel de Veiga, endenizened in 1661, was appointed a Freeman of the City in 1663. The community's first synagogue, established in a house in Creechurch Lane, had been honoured by a visit from the future Queen of England and one of its religious festival services had been attended and recorded by diarist Samuel Pepys. In the wake of the wealthy arrivals came their poorer brethren, and by the end of the century the necessity to provide for poverty-stricken Jewish pedlars, second-hand clothes dealers and hawkers led to the foundation of what became a network of charitable institutions. London, with its lack of legal and religious restraints, acted as a beacon for the poor Jews of Central and Eastern Europe for more than two centuries to come. However, in spite of the presence of a significant number of poor, the eighteenth-century Sephardi stereotype was that of the affluent merchant or broker, not his less fortunate brother. Meanwhile, the community burgeoned and increased its wealth. In 1701, a purpose-built synagogue, which could accommodate 400 men and 160 women, was consecrated in Bevis Marks at the edge of the City of London. It stands to this day and retains the liturgy brought from Spain and Portugal.

The eighteenth century was a golden age for the Sephardim. As commercial contact with the host community increased, so did the processes of acculturation and Anglicisation. Increased wealth facilitated the purchase of country homes and enabled Jewish support for the Bank of England when its liquidity was threatened in 1745.[3] Lower down the scale, there was entry into a diversity of trades, including engraving, watchmaking, pen-making and glass-cutting. It was as a twelve-year-old apprentice glass-cutter that one of the most famous eighteenth-century boxers, Daniel Mendoza, credited with introducing 'fitness and agility' to boxing in England, began his working life. In 1787, the renowned Sephardi prize-fighter set up a school of boxing in order to teach the sport 'scientifically'. The school attracted a number of young Jewish lads, who soon became expert at a sport which retained its Jewish association in the centuries ahead.

As the terrors of the Inquisition faded, so did the flow of Sephardi newcomers. Those Sephardim who now made their homes in London did so largely for commercial reasons, joining families such as the Moccattas and Henriques. The Montefiore brothers from Italy arrived early in the eighteenth century and soon prospered. Another Italian arrival was Benjamin d'Israeli. As a result of his son Isaac's dispute with the Elders of Bevis Marks, and subsequent departure from

Mug depicting a boxing match between Daniel Mendoza and Richard Humphries, 1788. Mendoza was born and brought up in the Portuguese-Jewish community in London

Judaism, his grandson, the young Benjamin, was baptised as a Christian. This made it possible for the future Earl of Beaconsfield to become leader of the Tories and Prime Minister of his country.[4] During the twentieth century, the two world wars, the establishment of the State of Israel and the subsequent Arab/Israeli confrontations resulted in the arrival of fresh waves of Sephardi immigrants and refugees. At the time of writing, the Sephardi community remains small, no more than 2400 families. Some can trace their lineage directly back to 1656 and the first resettlement community, while others have arrived as recently as the 1960s and 1970s.

Following rapidly on the heels of the earliest Sephardi settlers were the Ashkenazim,[5] immigrants from Central and Eastern Europe steeped in Orthodox tradition. Their liturgy differed from that of the Sephardim, as did their Hebrew pronunciation and certain of their dietary laws. With a few exceptions, the Ashkenazi immigrants were poorer and less cultured than their Western European co-religionists. They were pedlars, tailors and shoemakers, artisans and peasants from the lower levels of society. They brought with them the trades and ways of the ghetto and the more traditional practices of Central and Eastern Europe. After the first few tentative arrivals, numbers grew as knowledge of the absence of religious intolerance and the presence of economic opportunity spread. By the close of the seventeenth century an Ashkenazi synagogue had been established at the eastern edge of the City of London (see colour plate 14) and an Ashkenazi burial ground had been acquired in the East End.

For the Jewish population of London, the eighteenth century was a combination of wealth and poverty, of country gentleman and town beggar, of banker and hawker, of acculturation and Anglicisation. By mid-century the Ashkenazim outnumbered their Sephardi brethren by approximately four to one in a community which had grown to one of between seven and eight thousand. The balance was not reflected in matters of communal representation, and in 1760 it was decided that a joint body, the London Committee of Deputies of British Jews, be established to represent all of London Jewry. In its earliest stages, it did little more than present loyal addresses to the monarchy. In the nineteenth century, a formal constitution was adopted, representation was extended to provincial communities and the title was changed to the Board of Deputies of British Jews. The board now acts as the representative of British Jewry on political and legislative matters, as well as liaising and advising on security, anti-Semitism and racist activities.

Although the Jews of London did not suffer directly from legislation, they were disabled by certain legal restraints. Foreign-born persons were unable to own land, a ruling which hardly affected the lower levels of Jewish society but frustrated the wealthier members of the Jewish community. Attempts were made to pass an Act of Parliament which would facilitate the acquisition of English nationality without taking the Sacrament. The 'Jew Bill' was put before Parliament in 1753, but an outburst of anti-Jewish sentiment led to its failure and it was shelved until 1825, when it was passed almost without notice.[6]

During the Napoleonic Wars, immigration came to a virtual standstill. When peace came, in 1815, the Jewish population of London numbered around 25,000. The majority were of English birth, and included notables such as the Goldsmid family, whose ancestors had settled in London in 1725, and the more recently arrived international banker Nathan de Rothschild, whose financial help proved invaluable to the British government during the conflict with France. During the nineteenth century, the movement from east to west of the capital, begun in the latter half of the previous century, continued. As integration accelerated, requests for religious reforms were made by members of both the Sephardi and Ashkenazi communities. Demands were for improvements in decorum, synagogues that were located nearer their residences and reforms of ritual and liturgy that would bring Judaism in line with modernity. In 1840, nineteen Ashkenazim and five Sephardim, frustrated by the intransigence of their religious and lay leaders, declared their intention to establish a 'united congregation under the denomination of British Jews'.

The foundation of the West London Synagogue of British Jews heralded a new phase in the history of the Jews of London. It was a positive move away from foreign roots to a form of religious worship which was in accord with the times. It was a statement of English citizenship by men whose religion was Judaism. But it was an exclusive group, and the West London Synagogue of British Jews remained the sole representative of Reform Judaism in London until the 1930s (in Manchester and Bradford sister synagogues were established in the second half of the nine-teenth century) when migration to the suburbs encouraged the establishment of new congregations. In 1942, the six extant Reform communities came together as the Associated British Synagogues and, in 1958, with a greatly enlarged member-ship, it became the Reform Synagogues of Great Britain.[7]

The creation of the first Reform Synagogue in 1840 parallels the fight for Jewish emancipation. By the middle of the century, Jews were well represented in the civic and professional arenas. In 1835, Francis Goldsmid became the first Jewish barris-ter; in that same year David Salomon, co-founder of the Westminster Bank, was appointed a Sheriff of the City of London and in 1855 became Lord Mayor. From 1837, Jews were free to graduate from London University and in the same year Moses Montefiore, the colossus of nineteenth-century Anglo-Jewry, was knighted by Queen Victoria, although it was not until the 1880s that she could be persuaded to overcome her lingering prejudices and agree to the elevation of Jews to the peerage. In spite of these freedoms, a Jew could not take his elected seat in the House of Commons without first taking the Christian Oath of Abjuration. Lionel de Rothschild was elected to parliament five times before, in 1858, a special resolution was passed by the House to enable him to take his rightful seat. Total Jewish eman-cipation was almost a reality; in 1866, the Parliamentary Oaths Act ensured that future Jewish Members of Parliament would face no obstacles, and in 1871 the barrier to graduation from all the British universities was lifted when the necessity to take a specifically Christian oath was removed.

By the end of the nineteenth century, Reform Judaism in England, which had been considered radical upon its emergence sixty years earlier, was viewed as conservative, if not moribund. In response to the 'crisis' in Reform Judaism,[8] Lily Montagu (daughter of Samuel, the Orthodox Jewish banker and Member of Parliament for Whitechapel), together with the intellectual Reform Jew, Claude Montefiore, created a movement which would satisfy those looking for a form of Jewish worship which combined modernity with intellectual and spiritual fulfilment. In 1909, the Jewish Religious Union for the Advancement of Liberal Judaism was founded and in 1911 the first Liberal synagogue was consecrated in central London. It featured mixed seating, increased usage of English and the participation of women in the service. During the inter-war years, support for the movement grew and in 1944 it became the Union of Liberal and Progressive Synagogues.

By the beginning of the twentieth century, the Jewish population of London had expanded to 120,000, swelled by the mass influx of Jews from Eastern Europe fleeing the numerous pogroms and increased economic hardship that followed the assassination of Tsar Alexander II of Russia in 1881. From the Readmission onwards, there had been a constant trickle of Eastern European Jews into the East End of London. The later immigrants settled in and around Whitechapel, joining those who had earlier established the chain of migration. Life for the new arrivals was, in the physical sense, harsh, and a small minority gave up and returned to the Pale.[9] For those who stayed, their priorities were somewhere to live and a place to work. Often these were one and the same, as the 'greeners' slept on the workshop floor, using for bedding the very garments in production.[10] Few skills were taught in the villages and towns of Eastern Europe,[11] and the immigrants found employment in the grim workshops that benefited from the ready supply of greeners who fuelled the 'sweated trades', which included tailoring, cap-making, cabinet-making, boot-, shoe- and slipper-making, cigar- and cigarette-making. 'Only the ruthless few' made it successfully out of the ghetto in pre-First World War London. In conditions which were insanitary, even by Victorian standards, Jewish tailors, machiners and pressers worked 'the longest hours, for the lowest pay, in the worst conditions', the sweatshop master being a co-religionist who, often as not, was also a member of the family. This made protest, and the organisation of exploited workers into trade unions, doubly hard. But, with the aid of Jewish socialists and anarchists and their English counterparts (an interesting example of co-operation between Jew and Gentile, Englishman and alien), more than fifty tailoring trade unions were founded between 1872 and 1915. The majority of these unions were short-lived, weakened, as were their English counterparts, by the structure of local industry which was seasonal and small-scale, by the lack of full-time salaried officials and by the constantly refilling pool of unskilled labour. In spite of this, in 1889 and again in 1912, the Jewish tailors of London staged successful strikes during which more than 10,000 workers fought for improved conditions and increased wages. These strikes took place at the same times as the major strike waves among English workers which heralded the emergence of 'new unions' for the semi-skilled and unskilled.[12]

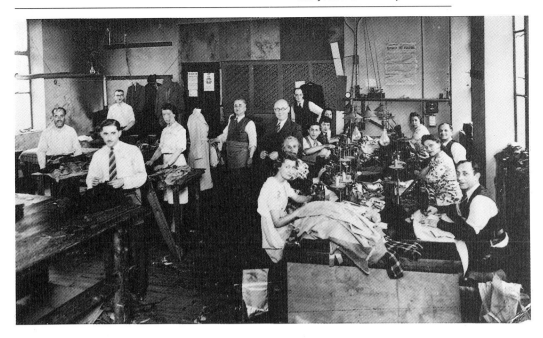

Goldstein's tailoring workshop, Great Eastern Street, 1940

If work was 'hard and bitter', accommodation in the East End for Jew and Gentile was overcrowded and costly and it was not long before the immigrants were being accused of taking both the homes and the jobs of Englishmen. The Anglo-Jewish establishment was concerned and extended the existing network of Jewish charitable organisations to ensure their impoverished co-religionists would be as little burden as possible on the host society. The Jewish Board of Guardians, established in 1859 to help the 'strange poor', was extended to operate a broad range of activities, though six months' residency in London was a prerequisite for relief. As the numbers of immigrants in London increased, further provisions were made. In 1885 The Poor Jews' Temporary Shelter was opened as a refuge for those newly arrived. In the shelter's premises in Leman Street lodging, food, prayer facilities and a labour exchange were provided for up to two weeks. Some 95 per cent of immigrant arrivals passed through the shelter's doors in the years between 1895 and 1914. As a further response to the problems of overcrowding, the Rothschild family oversaw the building of Rothschild Buildings in Flower and Dean Street.[13] This was designed to provide improved housing for Jewish and non-Jewish families in the East End. Attempts were made to stem the flow of immigrants at source and advertisements were placed in Jewish papers in Eastern Europe explaining that the streets of East London were not paved with gold and that intending emigrants would be better advised to remain where they were.

In spite of these attempts, and the sending back to Tsarist Russia of new arrivals unable to fend for themselves, anti-Semitism, or anti-alienism as it was labelled at the time, increased. It was strongest in the peripheral areas of Jewish settlement around Bethnal Green and in essentially non-Jewish areas such as Poplar and Hoxton. It was in these areas that, in the 1930s, the Fascists found their strongest support; they still remain strongholds of racism today. The alien presence and the hostility this aroused among English workers at the end of the nineteenth century led to the passing of a resolution at the 1895 Trades Union Congress Conference calling for controls on the admission of pauper aliens. The British Brothers' League (BBL) was established in 1901. Its membership was drawn largely from the East End and had the support of a number of East London MPs, including Major William Eden Evans Gordon, MP for Stepney. The League was one of the main agitators for controls on Jewish immigration.[14] Pressure was such that, in 1903, a government commission was set up to investigate the effects of the alien presence and, in 1905, following on the commission's recommendations, the Aliens Act was passed. The Act was less restrictive than some had anticipated, and others (particularly members of the BBL) had hoped for, directed, as it was, at Jews who were aliens rather than at 'Jews as Jews'.[15]

The mass immigration of Jews into the East End at the latter end of the nineteenth century is in many ways analogous with the wanderings of the Children in the Desert in biblical times. The early arrivals faced extreme hardship, poverty, and anti-alienism, but they had vision and hope for their children. This gave them the confidence to invest for the future and a forest of Jewish Friendly Societies sprang up in London during the last years of the nineteenth century. By 1900, there were 186 bearing the words 'Hebrew' or 'Jewish' in the title. The immigrants ensured that their children were regular and healthy school-attenders. The Jews' Free School, established in the East End in 1817, had over 3000 pupils by the year 1900.

The Pavilion Theatre, Whitechapel, *c.* 1895. Yiddish Theatre flourished for decades in theatres such as this

One of the school's best-remembered pupils, and subsequent teacher, was Israel Zangwill, the writer who immortalised the tragedy and comedy of immigrant life in the East End in his book, *Children of the Ghetto*. Another successful immigrant schoolchild was the renowned mathematician Selig Brodetsky. The East End of London also produced a number of respected literary and artistic figures including Bernard Kops, William Goldman, Harold Pinter, Arnold Wesker, Isaac Rosenberg, Mark Gertler and David Bomberg.

In what little leisure time they had, East End Jewry eagerly and excitedly support-ed the Yiddish Theatre, an importation of Jewish culture which provided a bridge, in the Hebrew/Germanic language of the *stetl*, between Eastern and Western Europe. Shakespeare's *Merchant of Venice* – featuring Meir Zelniker as a memorable Shylock – and the works of Ibsen and Strindberg were great favourites. The most popular and best-remembered Yiddish play is *The King of Lampedusa*, which was performed during the Second World War and ran for over 200 performances, attracting Jewish and non-Jewish audiences from all over London. Unlike his English counterpart, the East End Jew was known for his temperance, the Jewish weakness being gambling. A late nineteenth-century report revealed how, on receipt of his week's wages, the exploited tailor would frequently lose all of it on the horses.

The cathedral synagogues of Anglo-Jewry, with their dog-collared ministers, were not to the liking of the immigrants who, on their arrival in Whitechapel and Spitalfields opened small synagogues: *chevras*. These sprang up all over the East End, in back rooms, gardens, even in former chapels. In 1887, Samuel Montagu, later the first Lord Swaythling, founded the Federation of Synagogues, which incorporated the majority of the *chevras*. By 1900, the federation's membership exceeded that of the Anglo-Jewish establishment's United Synagogue. The latter was established by Act of Parliament in 1870 to unite the metropolitan synagogues of the Ashkenazi community. The United Synagogue became the mainstay of religious affiliation and at the time of writing retains the support of 64 per cent of London Jewry.

During the inter-war years, as the suburbs around London blossomed, the Jews of the East End moved north, north-east and north-west, to areas such as Golders Green, Hendon, Edgware and Ilford. They were drawn by the development of the underground railway system, the explosion of speculative building and the expan-sion of the building societies. They were also pushed by the policies of the London County Council (LCC), which were discriminatory in matters of housing, employ-ment and education. They were influenced by the Aliens Act of 1919 which was fuelled by the remnants of wartime xenophobia and the, unfounded, fear engen-dered by the Bolshevik Revolution of 1917 that all Jews were 'Bolshies'.[16]

The move to the suburbs was a manifestation of upward socio-economic mobility which frequently encouraged a change in lifestyle. When possible, suburban Jewry sent their children to public and grammar schools, where they were educated to become doctors, dentists, solicitors, accountants and company directors. For those who remained in the East End, choice of employment when, in the depressed years of the late 1920s and early 1930s, there was any available, now included taxi-driving,

A procession of 30,000 Jews marching through Stepney in July 1933 to attend a demonstration protesting against the Nazi treatment of Jews in Germany

the field of light entertainment, which produced such well-known names as Joe Loss and Bud Flanagan and, in the footsteps of Mendoza, boxing champions such as Ted 'Kid' Lewis and Jack 'Kid' Berg. The clothing industry remained a major source of employment. The manufacture of women's wholesale clothing expanded rapidly as women increased their share of the consumer market. Trade names such as Harella, Windsmoor, Dereta and Alexon were born in the small-scale workshops that were so much a part of the Jewish East End.

The clouds of the 1930s carried Fascism. Oswald Mosley, founder of the British Union of Fascists, attempted – but failed – to march his blackshirts through the streets of the East End in the famous Battle of Cable Street in October 1936. It was a climate ripe for the resurgence of anti-Semitism, and Jews at every level of society became the targets, accused of being 'financial sharks', 'Christ-murderers' and the 'Alien Menace'. There were some vicious attempts to stir up racist hatred; the Fascists had some support, but there were also those willing to demonstrate their opposition to anti-Semitic deeds and words. Fascism in London was subdued during the Second World War, but there was a resurgence when peace came. However, the purely anti-Semitic bias changed in the 1950s when the focus became centred mainly on the New Commonwealth arrivals.

For Central Europeans fleeing the rise of Fascism and Nazism in the years between 1933 and 1939, London was regarded as a place of refuge despite the Fascist activity. Departure from Hitler's Germany was difficult and not made easier by the restrictions and controls imposed by the British government and various professional bodies. In all, some 50,000 Jewish refugees from Nazism were admitted to England, the majority settling in London, mostly in the north-west and west of the capital. Among those fortunate enough to gain entry were a number of rabbis, who covered the spectrum from Orthodox, such as Emmanuel Jakobovits who became Chief Rabbi, to Progressive. They brought with them fresh spiritual and theological direction which would be influential in the post-war years. Peace brought further changes in the socio-economic and religious composition of London Jewry. The tight-knit Chasidic Lubavitch community, which originated in late-eighteenth-century Eastern Europe, made its home in north London.

In conclusion, the Jewish community of late-twentieth-century London has been fashioned as much by socio-geographic roots as by ideology and theology. The centre of gravity has moved from the edges of the City of London to the suburbs. In recent years, the expansionary trend has been reversed by the combined effects of a falling birthrate and drift and defection. London Jewry has experienced both tolerance and intolerance. The periodic outbursts of anti-Jewishness and anti-Semitism demonstrate ignorance and fear, and have been particularly virulent at times of economic and social hardship, as for example in the 1880s, 1930s and early post-war years. Interaction can encourage understanding and tolerance, and a recent report revealed that Jews in Britain enjoy more tolerance and suffer less anti-Semitism than in any other country in Europe.[17] It is to be hoped that during the next century London Jewry, together with the other ethnic minorities who have made their homes in the capital, will experience a society free from intolerance and racial attack.[18]

Endnotes

For full details of publications, see Bibliography.

1　The Board of Deputies of British Jews provides figures for the estimated number of Jews in Britain based on synagogue membership and synagogue records of births, deaths and marriages. Thus, those of Jewish birth who are not affiliated to a synagogue are not included in the statistics.

2　Sephardi Jews are so called because they had made their way to, and subsequently settled in, the Iberian peninsula in the years following the fall of the Second Temple.

3　Hyamson, 1959, p209.

4　According to current law there is no 'provision which would prevent a practising Jew from becoming Prime Minister', though there remains an anomaly over the Prime Minister's advisory functions with regard to Crown benefices. According to a written reply from the House of Commons to the author (November 1992) it is 'inconceivable that any barrier could today be placed in the way of adherents of any particular religion or otherwise fitted for the office of Prime Minister'. In other words, should the situation arise 'a commonsense solution will normally offer'.

5　The Ashkenazim are Jews descended from those who, following the fall of the Second Temple, were part of the revived community in Palestine which subsequently migrated to Central and Eastern Europe.

6　For details of the events surrounding the presentation and defeat of the 'Jew Bill' in 1753, see Roth, 1941, pp215–23 in 1978 reprint.

7　For the history of the foundation and growth of Reform Judaism in Britain see Kershen (ed.), 1990 and Kershen and Romain, forthcoming.

8　Kershen and Romain, chapter four, forthcoming.

9　The Pale of Settlement was a restricted area in Western Russia and Poland in which Jews were forced to reside.

10　'Grinners' or 'greeners' were unskilled workers who could be exploited in the harsh conditions that prevailed. Little encouragement was given to raise levels of skill because this would be accompanied by demands for higher wages.

11　For details of the structure of industry, exploitation and class division in the Pale of Settlement see E. Mendelsohn, *Class Struggle in the Pale*, Cambridge University Press, Cambridge, 1970.

12　For details of the structure of the Jewish tailoring trade in London see Kershen, 1988 a; Kershen (ed.), 1988 b; and for the strikes in 1889 and 1912, see Kershen, 'All Out', *Jewish Chronicle*, 18 August 1989, p26; and Fishman, 1975.

13　For the story behind Rothschild Buildings, see White, 1980.

14　For the history of the British Brothers' League, see Holmes, 1979, pp89–97.

15　The Act still retained the right to asylum for those escaping political persecution and was a 'watered-down version' of the 1904 Bill. For details of the Act, see ibid, pp93, 101.

16　Ibid, p219.

17　In their *Anti-semitism World Report* 1992, published in June 1992, the Institute of Jewish Affairs reported that the Jews of the United Kingdom were 'not subject to the anti-semitism which affects other Jewish communities'.

18　Further information on the Jewish community in London can be found in Alderman, 1987, 1992; Bermant, 1971; Black, 1992; Booth, 1889; Cesarani, 1990; Endelman, 1979, 1991; Fishman, 1975; Gainer, 1972; Gartner, 1960; Holmes, 1979; Kadish, 1992; Kushner, 1992; Lipman, 1950, 1991; Newman, 1976; Pollins, 1982.

Houses with weavers' lofts,
Fournier Street

Tapestry panel by Danthon, a family of
Huguenot weavers in Spitalfields, *c.* 1725-50

Silk waistcoat probably manufactured by Maze
and Steer whose address was in Spitalfields,
heart of the Huguenot silk-weaving community

Right: Gold watch by the Huguenot
watchmaker James Tregent, 1767

A Black trumpeter at a tournament in Westminster, 1511, from the Westminster Tournament Roll

Portrait of Olaudah Equiano after Sir Joshua Reynolds. Equiano was a leading spokesman for the Black community in 18th-century London

Spirit of Carnival, Tam Joseph, 1986. The Notting Hill street carnival is Europe's largest. It has in the past had a reputation for unrest, but for most people is a happy bank holiday street party

plate 10

Praying at the Central Mosque, Regent's Park

Central Mosque, Regent's Park

Arabs in Hyde Park, Clare Jarrett, 1988

plate 11

Chinese New Year celebrations, 1993

Early 19th-century paint jar from Berger & Sons, a company founded by the German Louis Steigenberger in 1766

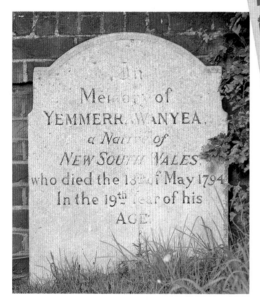

The Eltham gravestone of Yemmerrawanyea, one of two Australian Aborigines brought to London in 1792

Southern Cross 'The Newspaper for Australians Abroad'

plate 12

Constructing St Katharine's Dock, W. Ranwell, 1827. Many of the labourers were Irish

Early 19th-century pewter tankard with harp, inscribed 'FULLWOODS RENTS', an Irish area in Holborn

Irish builders on a construction site in Southwark, 1989

plate 13

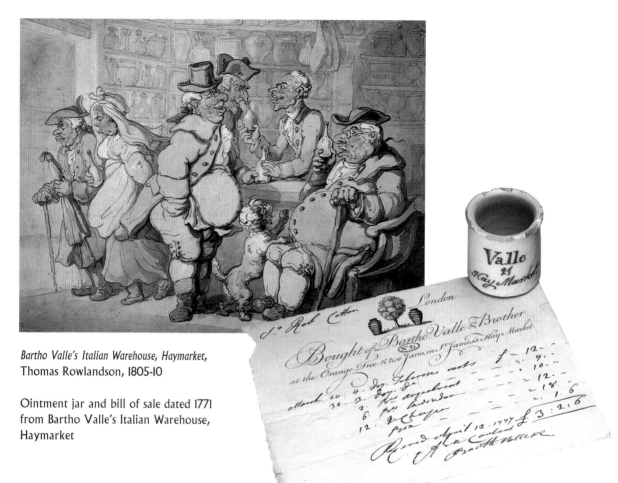

Bartho Valle's Italian Warehouse, Haymarket,
Thomas Rowlandson, 1805-10

Ointment jar and bill of sale dated 1771
from Bartho Valle's Italian Warehouse,
Haymarket

Interior of the Ashkenazi synagogue, Dukes Place, 1809. The artist has caricatured
the congregation, reflecting a long practice of Jewish stereotyping in the English
visual arts

Ætatis suæ 21. Aº. 1616.

Matoaks als Rebecka daughter to the mighty Prince
Powhatan Emperour of Attanoughkomouck als Virginia
converted and baptized in the Christian faith, and
Wife to the worll Mr Tho: Rolff.

Portrait of Pocahontas, 1616. She was a Native American princess who married John Rolfe, an English settler in Jamestown. She came to London in 1616, the first American to set foot in England

plate 15

Edward VI giving John à Lasco and his Congregation a Charter, early 17th century. John à Lasco (Jan Laski) was a Polish clergyman who received a charter in 1548 to found the Strangers' Church in London

plate 16

Latin Americans in London

An Introduction[1]

Apart from a few political exiles such as Simón Bolívar (1783–1830), Latin Americans first began to arrive in London in significant numbers in the 1970s, many of them driven by political and/or economic pressures. In Chile a military coup in 1973 overthrew the popularly elected Marxist leader, Salvador Allende. The political repression and persecution that followed forced many Chileans – members of the intelligentsia, trade unionists and artists, as well as farmworkers and soldiers – to seek asylum in Britain.

Demonstration in 1983 by Chilean exiles in London on the tenth anniversary of the coup in Chile

Voices of experience

Patricia Pons, a Chilean living in London, describes events after the coup in Chile:

> In Santiago we used to meet, go to cinema together, go to parties together, me and Pedro, my sister and another friend, doing everything together. After the coup, we came back to university and I knew Pedro was in the air force but I didn't know what had happened to him or if he was all right. In December a friend rang me and said he was in prison and I went to visit him. I went to do my industrial training in Salvador and when I was coming home in March I heard that Pedro had been released. He was working with a group of people and he collected pig remains and processed it.
>
> In June I got pregnant and he just went, I didn't see him any more. When Lillian was two months old Pedro rang and said, 'Will you have me in your family?' We married when Lillian was one year old. Pedro was offered a grant to study at Hatfield Polytechnic. So, the three of us came to England. The first thought was to come for four years. Maybe Pedro had a better idea. I didn't know what to expect, I had little English except, 'How do you do'. Everything happened very quickly. We brought the iron, we brought towels, we brought sheets, plates, cups, clothes, not terribly many, the guitar of course. Suitcases and suitcases. That was 14th February 1978.[2]

Colombian working in an industrial canteen, North London, 1993

The plight of Nelson Tordecilla and Leonard Sozza exemplifies the story of many other Chileans living in London. Tordecilla, a member of the TUC in Chile, was sentenced to forty years' imprisonment by General Pinochet. In 1976, after three years in prison, he was expelled from the country and came to London, where he has earned his living by working as a cleaner or as a painter and decorator. In 1980, together with other Chilean former refugees, he founded the *Liga Latino Americana de Fútbol*.[3] Leonard Sozza, Allende's public-relations representative, was sent to a concentration camp, then deprived of his citizenship and forced to leave. Settled in Britain, he campaigned for fourteen years against Pinochet's regime. He now works as a translator and legal adviser to the Latin Americans arriving in London.[4]

Political exiles from Argentina also moved to London in the mid-1970s. Other Latin Americans initially came as students. A much larger community of Latin Americans are from Colombia and Bolivia, many recruited as migrant workers in the mid-1970s. First to arrive were young women in their twenties, who came to work as au pairs. Others were recruited by the hotel and catering industries, which faced acute staffing problems. Colombians and other Latin Americans were employed in hotel kitchens or as cleaners, jobs which did not attract British workers. However, to many Latin Americans even low wages gave them the chance to support their families by sending money back home. The 1971 Immigration Act granted employers work permits enabling them to recruit workers from abroad and some employment agencies in Colombia and London, realising that this was a lucrative business, were not averse to exploiting the market:

> They offered credit facilities for air fares and a job – which most of the time did not exist. But to achieve profits they had to get these people past the immigration officials as tourists. In 1977, it was not uncommon for three planes a week to land in Europe packed with 'Colombian tourists'.[5]

Migrant workers play an important part in London's catering trade, but for the workers there is a high degree of insecurity. They are recruited to work for a specific employer in a specific job, and employers are thus able to wield a great deal of power over them because they control the issue of work permits. Workers cannot easily change employers and are not in a position to complain:

> It made it very difficult for the migrant worker to join a union or negotiate better working conditions. After forty-eight working months he had the right to apply for a residence visa which could only be granted if the employer was willing to continue employing the worker.[6]

Many Colombians, uneducated and from poor rural backgrounds, have borrowed heavily to pay for the fare to Britain and they become trapped in a world of low wages, insecure jobs and unemployment. The unsocial hours of work and lack of opportunity to learn English mean they find it very hard to move up the employment ladder. Leonard Sozza confirms this: ' … it's very hard for them to move up here in the employment ranks. I speak five languages, I'm a translator, and even for me it's not that easy.'[7] Self-employment has given some Colombians social mobility. One such self-made 'success' is Lionel Sarmiento, who has his own car-valeting company.[8] He came to London with his parents at the age of twelve, and within two years could speak English fluently. Setting up their own shops is often seen as a way to independence, although the hours may still be long and hard. Fabio Osorio had a job in a sandwich bar, but he left that to start his own refreshment stall in the shopping centre at Elephant and Castle, a popular area for Latin American-owned businesses. In the same area, Inara Silbers from Venezuela has a travel agency, where she also runs the Centro Latino.[9]

All together about 17,500 Latin Americans live in London, mainly concentrated in the boroughs of Lambeth and Kensington and Chelsea. The Latin American Cultural Centre in Kensington provides a social and cultural focus.[10] Another social outlet is the *Liga Latino Americana de Fútbol*. On their one day off – Sunday – Latin Americans from all over London gather on Clapham Common to watch a series of matches which take place between the various Latin American football teams including Collo Collo, the Chilean team, Perfect Colombia, Cultural Bolivia and DTVO Ecuador. This is not just a sports function: the football matches have become a sociable meeting point to exchange news and to get help and advice, especially for new-comers. Flights from Latin America arrive at a weekend and many go straight to Clapham Common from the airport.[11]

Spectators at a soccer match, 1988. Latin American League football has turned Clapham Common into a meeting place on Sundays for Latin Americans in London

Endnotes

For full details of publications, see Bibliography.

1 This introductory background was compiled by Rozina Visram

2 From the Museum of London Oral History Archive

3 *Independent*, 4 December 1991, p14.

4 Ibid.

5 Santiago Castrillon, 'Latin Americans in London', *Ten 8*, no. 16, 1984, p38.

6 Ibid, p39.

7 *Independent*, 4 December 1991, p14.

8 Ibid.

9 *Observer Magazine*, 13 December 1992, p18.

10 'Problems of the Latin American and Spanish Communities in Kensington and Chelsea', Royal Borough of Kensington and Chelsea, 1983.

11 *Independent*, 4 December 1991, p14.

The Poles in London · Keith Sword

Opposite: Juda and Metka
Fiszer were Polish Jews who
came to London at the
beginning of this century.
They opened their umbrella
shop in Hackney in 1907
using the English spelling
of Fisher

Passport and nationality
certificate belonging to
Mrs Fiszer

'Polish London' is not a separate district within the capital. There is no geographically defined settlement of Poles, although it is true that in the 1950s large concentrations of Poles could be found in certain areas of London. Cromwell Road, for
example, passing through Earl's Court and South Kensington, two areas of dense
Polish settlement, was at one time popularly known as the 'Polish corridor'. Today,
though, Poles are dispersed throughout the London boroughs. The physical evidence of their presence can be found in the Polish-owned churches and community
centres, cultural centres, travel bureaux and delicatessens, galleries, boutiques and
pharmacies and, inevitably, the increasing number of plots in London cemeteries
marked by headstones with Polish inscriptions.

Polish travellers, in the form of traders and diplomats or royal emissaries, began
arriving in England as early as the late Middle Ages. The first official ambassador of
the King of Poland, Jan Dantyszek, arrived at the court of Henry VIII in 1522.[1]
Subsequently, from the mid-sixteenth century onwards, Polish visitors included a
number of Protestant scholars who came to England to study the doctrine and
tactics of the post-Reformation churches. The best-known of these was Jan Laski
('à Lasco' in Latin) who was invited to England by Archbishop Cranmer in 1548 and
lived in London intermittently until 1553. In 1550 he became superintendent of the
Strangers' Church at Austin Friars (see colour plate 16).

In the eighteenth century, after the Counter-Reformation in Poland, small
numbers of Polish Protestants arrived, this time in search of refuge. With the third
and final partition of Poland in 1795, religious persecution was replaced by political
repression as the main force driving Poles from their native soil. The new arrivals
to Britain included both the politically compromised and soldiers seeking refuge.
The trickle of political émigrés continued throughout the nineteenth century,
largely as a result of the harsh policies of two of the three partitioning powers,
Prussia and Russia. Several hundred Polish soldiers entered Britain as refugees
after the collapse of the 1831 Rising in Poland. The following year, the Literary
Association of Friends of Poland was founded; it helped refugees from Poland to
find employment, and continued in existence until 1924. By the end of 1852 there
were 250 Polish exiles in England. Many worked as tailors, shoemakers and
tobacconists, or as apprentices to printers, lithographers and engravers. Poles
also worked as music-teachers, private tutors and translators.

From the 1830s onwards many of the Poles arriving in this country held radical
views. Their politics were at variance with those of the more conservative émigré
circles in Paris.[2] The weekly *Demokrata Polski* (*Polish Democrat*), established in
the aftermath of the 1848 revolutions, gave voice to their views and provided a
platform for exiles of other nationalities, for example, Herzen and Kossuth. This
tradition continued for several decades. The first edition of *Robotnik* (the *Worker*),
the organ of the Polish Socialist Party, was published in Mile End Road in 1893 by a
group of such exiles. Among the visitors to the group were Józef Piłsudski, who was
to become the dominant figure in inter-war Polish politics, and Ignacy Mościcki, the
last president of Poland before the Second World War.

While earlier settlers had left Poland for political reasons, from the 1880s
onwards increasing numbers of economic migrants arrived from both Russian and
Prussian areas of Poland. Although predominantly from rural backgrounds, most
settled in urban centres, many in London's East End. They found work in the furni-
ture trade and in slipper or cigarette workshops. The chief centres of settlement
were Whitechapel and Silvertown; smaller groups settled in Poplar, Leytonstone
and Bethnal Green. The most famous Pole to settle during this period, however,
had little to do with these communities. He was the writer Joseph Conrad
(Korzeniowski), who arrived in London in 1878 at the age of twenty and promptly
began a career as a merchant seaman.[3]

In the last decades of the nineteenth century the majority of the settlers arriving
from the Polish lands were of the Jewish faith. However, there were sufficient
Polish Roman Catholics to justify the creation of a Polish Catholic Mission in 1894.
At first the mission was based in Cambridge Road, moving to Mercer Street in 1905
and in 1928 to its present location in Devonia Road, Islington.

During the First World War, Polish prisoners of war from the German army
were brought to Britain. In London Polish POW camps were established at
Alexandra Palace and Feltham. After the War, many stayed on in Britain. A different
group entirely were those politically active in the cause of Polish independence,
who strove to influence the Foreign Office in the period prior to the Versailles
peace conference. These included the leading Polish nationalist, Roman Dmowski,
and August Zaleski, later to become foreign minister of Poland.[4]

Relatively few Poles arrived in Britain between the Wars. The next influx of any
size followed the outbreak of the Second World War, when Polish naval and air-
force units were encouraged to regroup in Britain. In May 1940, following the fall
of France, the exiled Polish president, the prime minister (General Sikorski), the
government and administration transferred to London, accompanied by some
20,000 Polish troops. Thereafter, for as long as the War lasted, offices in such
central-London locations as Knightsbridge, Kensington, Piccadilly and Mayfair
became the focus of Polish hopes for liberation and independence. They became
the nerve-centres for Polish diplomatic activity, the co-ordination of military effort
abroad and the resistance struggle in Poland itself. The Polish military headquarters
were based at the Rubens Hotel, near Victoria Station.[5]

In 1945, when the War ended, émigré Poles who had fought and campaigned for the liberation of their homeland were dealt a shattering blow. With British and American acquiescence, half the territory of pre-War Poland was absorbed by the Soviet Union. A Communist government was installed in Warsaw, and was recognised by Poland's wartime allies, Britain and the United States. As a result, many Poles in the West decided not to return to their homeland. They included people whose pre-War homes had formerly been in eastern Poland, and they were familiar with conditions under Communism, having been a small minority among the waves of Poles deported en masse to Soviet territory during 1940.

The Polish troops were demobilised and eventually resettled in Britain and elsewhere by means of a Polish Resettlement Corps, created in 1946. During the late 1940s they were joined by some 33,000 dependants and by other civilian Poles, the largest group of which were the 14,000 European volunteer workers recruited from refugee camps on the Continent to jobs in British industry.[6] The settlement population included many educated people, some with professional qualifications: lawyers, judges, journalists, engineers and army officers. However, with the exception of doctors and pharmacists, whose qualifications were recognised, most had to enter the British labour market at a much lower level; they became 'declassed'. The occupations 'approved' by the Ministry of Labour, into which large numbers of Poles moved from the Resettlement Corps, were building and construction, agriculture, coalmining, the hotel and restaurant trade, brickmaking, weaving and cotton-spinning, iron and steel manufacture and the railways.[7]

However, eager to remain independent, thousands of Poles set up their own businesses, such as clock and watch or shoe repairs. A number of Polish-owned businesses sprang up, which were more than ready to employ Polish workers. (Among them were numerous 'parcel' firms, which conveyed foodstuffs, medicines and clothes to relatives at home in Poland.) In many British factories and workshops, Polish work-gangs were formed where communication was not a problem. Few Poles at this time progressed to the 'office' – to white-collar employment – since they lacked both the linguistic ability and familiarity with British methods of bookkeeping.[8]

With the removal of employment restrictions, many Poles in heavy manual or 'dirty' jobs opted for lighter or more rewarding work, often by means of the Polish 'bush telegraph'. Although in 1947 most Poles were dispersed in service camps, a process of inter-regional migration quickly developed. As they were released into civilian life, the Poles were drawn to areas where employment and accommodation prospects were more promising. As early as 1951 almost a quarter of all Poles in Britain (some 33,000 out of a total of 140,000) were living in the London area. They settled initially in cheaper areas of the capital, such as Earl's Court, Brixton, Lewisham and Clapham.[9]

The small number of Polish females (the gender imbalance was as high as four to one in the immediate post-War years) led to many mixed marriages in the period up to the end of the 1950s. Many Poles, though, chose to wait, and from the late

1950s onwards, as travel restrictions to and from Poland were relaxed, a steady trickle of new settlers arrived, 75 per cent of them women.[10] In subsequent years, London was a magnet to smaller waves of refugees from Poland, notably in 1968 and in the early 1980s, following the suppression of the Solidarity trade union.

London quickly achieved a central role in Polish political and cultural life. Although the Western allies had withdrawn recognition from the 'London' Polish government in 1945, exiled Poles continued to insist upon its legality and it remained in existence as a government of national protest. Its headquarters for the next four and a half decades were in Eaton Place, a centre popularly known as the *Zamek* (castle). Although some Polish organisations and institutions ceased to exist, others survived and new ones came into being. The Polish University College, founded in 1947 with British sponsorship, functioned into the 1950s and provided some hundreds of Poles with a higher education and qualifications they would not otherwise have received.[11] The Polish Clinic in Weymouth Street, founded in the same year, still exists, and has enabled thousands of Poles who feel uncertain of their command of English to seek medical advice in their own language. Mention must also be made of the unit organisations which helped Poles to retain contact with their former comrades-in-arms; the cultural associations, professional associations and charitable bodies; and the Polish YMCA and the Polish scouting movement. One of the most important and influential Polish institutions in the post-War period has been the Polish Ex-Combatants' Association (SPK), founded in 1946. In recent years, to counteract a declining membership due to natural loss, the association has admitted the sons and daughters of former combatants as members.

Polish soldiers and civilians dining at the White Eagle Club in London, around 1940. A large Polish presence was established during the Second World War

Wherever Poles went, they were accompanied by their priests. The military chaplains who had remained with their units in resettlement camps soon followed the 'demobbed' soldiers into civilian life. The overwhelming majority of Poles who settled in this country were Roman Catholics (although even today there remains a small Polish Evangelical parish in London). The Polish Catholic Mission in Devonia Road, Islington, had, during the War years, become a 'Polish Cathedral in exile', and the Polish president and other notables worshipped there regularly. Other churches also became centres of Polish life, notably Brompton Oratory in Kensington, where Masses in Polish were heard each Sunday.[12]

Inevitably, however, as large numbers of Poles moved into London in the late 1940s, something had to be done for the thousands of Poles scattered throughout the capital. Under an agreement between the Polish Catholic hierarchy and the English and Scottish hierarchies, Polish priests were allowed to settle and minister to the spiritual needs of their compatriots. The first 'parish' established by a Polish priest was in Brockley-Lewisham in 1951. Today there are ten Polish parishes in London, six of which have their own churches and three of which have chapels alongside their parish centres. Balham and Ealing are two of the most vibrant centres. Even those Poles who do not attend church regularly will generally turn up for *pasterka* (midnight mass on Christmas Eve), *święcone* (the ritual blessing of food at Easter) or the procession at *Boże Ciało* (Corpus Christi).[13]

One of the great achievements of the Polish community during the post-War years has been the financing and construction of a large Polish Social and Cultural Centre (POSK) in King Street, Hammersmith. Attempts to collect funds for a centre began as early as the 1960s, although it was not until the end of 1974 that construction was completed and Polish organisations began to move in. In 1976 the Polish Library moved to the centre, and by the end of the 1980s it contained over 100,000 books, several hundred manuscripts, 40,000 photographs and more than 5000 periodical titles. As a resource built up by a minority community to inform both its own members and the host community about the homeland and the Polish diaspora, the Polish Library has no equal in Britain. POSK is now home to a host of other institutions, including the Polish University Abroad (PUNO), the Federation of Poles in Great Britain, the Polish Ex-Combatants' Association, the Polish Home Army Association (veterans of the underground resistance movement during the Second World War), the Piłsudski Institute and the Polish Educational Society (PMS). The PMS provides textbooks and other course materials for more than seventy Polish Saturday schools throughout the country, eleven of them in London. The POSK building is also a focus of Polish social and cultural life, containing an art gallery, bookshop, café, restaurant, bar, conference room, theatre and bridge and billiard rooms. It also has great value as a cultural symbol in its own right and is looked on with pride by all Poles, including the many thousands in the provinces who contributed to its building fund, but are only rarely able to make use of its facilities.

In the nearby districts of Earl's Court and South Kensington, a concentration of Polish institutions serves as a reminder of the original wartime settlement patterns. There is Orbis, the Polish-owned bookshop in Earl's Court and, in neighbouring South Kensington, the Polish Airmen's Club and two of London's best-known Polish restaurants: Daquise and the Polish Hearth Club (*Ognisko*). At 20 Princes Gate is one of the oldest and most impressive monuments to the wartime Polish settlement in London, the Polish Institute and Sikorski Museum. It has a particularly strong collection of military memorabilia and archive material from the Second World War period.

A visit to one of London's Polish bookshops provides evidence of the wealth of publications produced by Poles. The *Dziennik Polski* (*Polish Daily*) is the only Polish-language daily newspaper published in Europe outside Poland, and has been published continuously in Britain for more than half a century. Inevitably, however, the readership has declined: in the late 1940s some 35,000 copies of the *Dziennik* were printed, but today the figure is 7000. Most second-generation Poles feel more at home with English-language reading materials than with Polish.

Polish Girl Guides in Ealing, 1991

The second generation born outside Poland were brought up to think of themselves as Poles. They were expected to speak Polish at home, and were sent to Saturday schools to learn about their homeland. They observed Polish customs and traditions within the home, and wherever possible attended Polish mass and became involved in Polish parish activities. Assimilation was frowned on, although a degree of integration was recognised to be inevitable; for example children were expected to do well in the British educational system. However, the restrictions and pressures which they experienced in early life alienated many youngsters. They found the stress on tradition stifling, while in the wider community the eternal historical debates and political-military nature of the clubs and institutions held little relevance for them. In the past decade, though, there has been a discernible revival of Polish ethnic feeling among the young, due no doubt to the fact that Poland has been so often in the headlines and at different times 'fashionable'. The Polish Pope, the Solidarity trade union, martial law and the collapse of Communism have all contributed to this.

During the period of Communist rule in Poland, political émigrés were proud of their uncompromising stand, refusing to travel to Poland or to have any contact with 'Warsaw' representatives in the embassy and consulate. Events such as the annual service at the Katyn memorial in Gunnersbury cemetery (to commemorate the 14,000 captive Polish officers murdered by the Soviets in 1940) drew a large attendance, and protest demonstrations were organised outside the Polish embassy. The émigrés believed that one day – when Communism was defeated – they would return to Poland. In the meantime, many refused to accept British citizenship. In the end, relatively few of the original settlement community lived to witness the downfall of Communism in Poland in 1989. Those who did have made nostalgic return journeys to their homeland, but in the main have shown little inclination to pull up roots and move back there permanently after so many decades in their adoptive country. The Poland of the 1990s, although a sovereign democratic state once again, is not the country remembered in idealised terms from their youth, and Britain is the country where their children and grand-children live.

When the changes in Poland came, the leading political institutions – the presidency and government in exile – had survived for almost half a century. Once democratic government was restored to Poland, their *raison d'être* ceased. In December 1990, the presidential insignia of office, which had remained in London since the Second World War, were handed to Lech Wałęsa, the freely elected president, in Warsaw. The government in exile was dissolved in 1991, and from that moment the Federation of Poles in Great Britain became the over-arching representative body of Poles in Britain. The political energies of the community, instead of being channelled into demonstrations, were henceforth directed to acting in partnership with the new regime. 'London Poles' see themselves as ideally placed to mediate between the homeland and British institutions, even to the extent of becoming a political lobby on behalf of Warsaw.

But new directions call for new leadership. The generational changes taking place within the Polish community have led to forceful calls for the younger element to be allowed a greater role in community institutions. This is already happening to some degree, although many of the 'younger' or second generation are now in their forties. Recent initiatives by some younger 'Anglo-Poles' have focused on fostering business contacts with the new Poland. It is possible that this new scope for employing knowledge of Poland, its language, history and institutions may provide job opportunities for younger generations of 'British Poles', and therefore provide fresh incentives to retain their ethnic culture.

Endnotes

For full details of publications, see Bibliography.

1 Swiderska, 1962.
2 Brock, 1953 and 1961.
3 Baines, 1971; Najder, 1983.
4 Davies, 1972.
5 Raczyński, 1962.
6 Tannahill, 1958; Kay & Miles, 1992.
7 Zubrzycki, 1956.
8 Sword, 1989.
9 Patterson, 1964 and 1968.
10 Zubrzycki, 1956.
11 Patterson, 1977.
12 Polish University College, 1953; *Education in Exile*, 1956, pp37–42.
13 Gula, forthcoming.

Somalis in London · Shamis Hussein

Somali settlement in London generally falls into two phases: a sailor community that traces its presence in London's East End to the second half of the nineteenth century; and more recently, political refugees fleeing from Siad Barre's regime and the resulting civil war in Somalia since the 1980s.

As with the lascar seamen from India, and the Chinese sailors, the Somalis, who came from what was then British Somaliland, were employed by the British merchant navy to work in the engine rooms of the steam-powered liners bound for England. Many of them were formerly nomadic herdsmen.[1] They were mainly unskilled men, *tacabir* (the intrepid migrants who ventured abroad), whose fundamental aim was to seek better employment, to accumulate wealth and eventually retire back to Somaliland. Like other colonial seamen, Somali crews were part of the trading pattern linking Britain, eastern Africa, India and the Far East. They began to come to Europe after the opening of the Suez Canal in 1869.

The Somalis have a long tradition of seafaring. This is confirmed by Mohamed Yusuf Salad, born in Aden in 1907, a retired Somali sailor: '... and all the Somalis go to sea. Everybody get a ship at that time, nobody work on the land, they worked on the ships.'[2] There have even been ships carrying the name 'Somali', such as HMS *Somali*, a 'tribal' class destroyer, and a P&O liner.[3]

While ships were docked in London, the Somalis stayed in sailor lodging-houses like the Queen Victoria Seamen's Rest in Poplar. They may also have lodged in the Strangers' Home in Limehouse. In time a small transient community of Somali sailors grew up in the East End of London. Small communities like this also appeared in Britain's other ports: Cardiff, Liverpool, South Shields. Unlike the Chinese in East End's Chinatown, or Yemeni sailors, the Somali sailors generally did not take local British wives; instead they maintained families in Somalia and Aden, making periodic trips to see them.[4]

However, there is evidence of some intermarriage, especially in the early days. This is borne out by Marian Abdillahi, whose great-grandmother was Welsh. The history of the early sailor community remains hazy. There are occasional references

Musa Jama Ali was born in Somaliland in 1919 and served in the British forces during the Second World War. He is one of the oldest members of the Somali community in London

163

Somali Restaurant and
Boarding House, Leman St,
1950s

in literature which give us some glimpses of their lives. But Somalis, like the early Asian settlers, tended to be subsumed in the wider 'lascar' or 'coloured' community.[5] However, there is evidence in London's East End of lodging-houses and cafés owned or patronised by Somali sailors in Cable Street and in Leman Street during the inter-war period.[6] For instance, Ali Mirreh and Ali Noor opened boarding-houses and restaurants which catered to Black American soldiers stationed in England during the Second World War.[7] In common with other 'coloured' seamen, Somalis were affected by the race riots which occurred across the country in 1919.[8]

The Second World War saw an increase in the number of Somalis employed in the British merchant navy. From this date to the early 1970s the Somalis remained dependent on this source of employment. A few Somali restaurants and nightclubs operated in Tower Hamlets during this period, patronised largely by the Somali sailors, but by 1978 these had closed. This reflected the decline of British merchant shipping in the mid-1970s and the end of seafaring opportunities for the Somali sailors. Many then looked for shore-based employment in London, but age and lack of marketable skills made them dependent on social welfare.[9]

The 1960s and 1970s saw the arrival of Somali wives in Britain. According to Ali Mohamed Elmi: 'In those days there were not many Somali families, they were all men in the beginning. Somali women came later, my wife was the third woman to come over here in April 1962.'[10] Many of the Somali wives who joined their sailor husbands in London came from Aden, where some of them had jobs. Following the independence of Aden in 1967 some Somalis who were British subjects arrived in

England. In London some Somali women work as hospital cleaners and shop assistants. For many of the Somali sailors and their wives the hope of returning to Somalia has receded because of the civil war.

The 1980s saw the second phase of Somali settlement in Britain. Members of this phase comprise refugees, particularly from the Issaq clans from northern Somalia (once part of British Somaliland), who had fled political reprisals under Siad Barre's regime. Many have ended up in refugee camps in Ethiopia. Others managed to escape to Britain: some are British citizens (having held on to their British passports, even after Somalia became independent in 1960); some have managed to join relatives already settled in Tower Hamlets; some are political asylum-seekers. Mrs Anab Ali Mohammed, who worked as a clerk for the Somali Academy of Science and Arts in Somalia, escaped to London with her five children by bribing the police at the airport in January 1986, while her husband, who was a policeman, went to Ethiopia:

> I think I was the first or second person in Tower Hamlets to come for political asylum. After one month I'd finished all my money [Anab had come with US $1000]. I buy some clothes for the children, because it is winter so when I have left they bring me to the homeless section of Tower Hamlets and they sent me to a bed and breakfast hotel in Edgware Road where I lived for seven months. It was very difficult for me because there's no other Somalis living there. I only knew a little bit of English so it was very difficult because when I lived in Somalia I lived in a large house ... Then they gave me this flat. I started my life again ... Now I go to Tower Hamlets College in Poplar High Street. The course I finish now is Women in Technology ... I take computer studies, word-processing, database, maths and English.[11]

The refugees who came in the 1980s were generally from the wealthier classes, such as Hassan Ismail, a Somali doctor who works for the Somali community in Bethnal Green:

> I did my studies in Somali National University, then in Sweden and later in the United Kingdom. I was working in Somalia as a medical doctor for a long time. I was forced to leave my country because of Siad Barre's atrocities. Now I work in the community – an entirely different experience. I would not say I am happy about my situation, yet I could be amongst the luckiest since I am working and own my own house. Nevertheless, I am looking forward to returning.[12]

Many Somali youths have come to London in recent years from the Gulf States, where their parents have residence rights, but these rights are not transferred to the children once they come of age. Faisal Mohammed, a Somali Liaison Officer in London, deals with education and is the son of a seaman:

I was born in Newport in 1967. My father was a seaman and he married my mother from Aden in 1966. Even though I was very keen to have a higher education it was not easy for me because of the ethnic minority problems. Unlike my father's generation, however, I feel I have a right to the country I was born in and would like to receive what I deserve. Nevertheless, I would like to move to Somaliland should the situation improve.[13]

The ousting of Siad Barre in 1991 has not eased the Somali crisis; civil war has continued.

Ninety per cent of Britain's Somali population live in Greater London. There are small communities in Ealing, Brent and south-east London, but the majority of Somalis live in Tower Hamlets where, at 10,000 strong, they form one of the largest ethnic minority groups.

Two Somalis learn word processing skills at a community centre in Bethnal Green, 1990

A study in Tower Hamlets has shown that the Somali population is a young one, with 90 per cent aged under forty-five, and 40 per cent under sixteen.[14] While the majority of the Somali refugees are unemployed, many of the older ones have chosen to return to the hazardous situation in Somalia rather than not engage in work. Ostensibly, 90 per cent of the Somali community intend to return once the situation improves in the homeland. Perhaps because of this, Somalis, and their British sympathisers, have tended to concentrate their efforts in campaigning for improvements in the homeland rather than focusing on the wide range of problems facing the refugees in London. Despite this, Somalis have established a unique cultural presence at centres such as Oxford House in Bethnal Green, where their strong oral tradition is maintained through songs and stories. Islam is an important feature of Somali life, and the mosque functions as a place of worship, of learning, and a meeting place. The Somali broadcasting service of the BBC's World Service keeps them in touch with developments at home. Time will tell whether the majority of Somalis really will return, or whether they will remain to form a more permanent community in London.

Somali festival
at Oxford
House, Bethnal
Green, 1992.
There has
been a Somali
presence in
East London
for over a
century

Endnotes

For full details of publications, see Bibliography.

1 Not all Somalis in Britain have come directly
   from Somalia. There is a long tradition
   among Somalis of emigrating and working at
   sea. Many went to work in Aden, a British
   colony until 1967 and an important centre
   for shipping.

2 *The Somali Sailors*, Ethnic Communities Oral
   History Project, Borough of Hammersmith
   and Fulham, 1992.

3 *Journal of the Anglo Somali Society*, Summer
   1992, p22.

4 Fawzi El-Solh, 1991, pp539–40.

5 Banton, 1955; Collins, 1957.

6 *Lodging-House Applications*, Tower Hamlets
   Archives.

7 Charles L Geshekatar, 'Anti-Colonialism and
   Class Formation: The Eastern Horn of
   Africa before 1950', *International Journal of
   African History Studies*, 18, 1985, p20.

8 Jacqueline Jenkinson, 'The 1919 Race Riots
   in Britain: a Survey', in Lotz & Pegg, 1986,
   pp182–207.

9 Fawzi El-Solh, 1991, pp540-41.

10 *The Somali Sailors*, Ethnic Communities Oral
   History Project, Borough of Hammersmith
   and Fulham, 1992.

11 Ibid.

12 Interview conducted by the author,
   November 1992.

13 Interview conducted by the author,
   November 1992.

14 Ian Lewis, *The Somali Community of Tower
   Hamlets: A Demographic Survey*, University
   of London, London, 1991.

South Asians in London[1] · Rozina Visram

South Asians began to appear in London's history at least as early as the seventeenth century. Their presence is part of the long history of contact between Britain and the Indian subcontinent, dating back to the establishment of the East India Company in 1600. Although recorded in parish burial and baptism notices, in petitions to the East India Company, official reports, newspapers and paintings, the history of the early community, as opposed to that of individuals, remains obscure. Records are scattered and fragmentary, and the problem is further compounded by terminology. Contemporaries used terms like 'Coloured' and 'Black' to describe Asians as well as Africans, West Indians and Arabs.[2]

For the long period before the First World War, there is no definite pattern of migration. Some Asians, such as servants and ayahs (nannies), were brought to Britain to serve the personal needs and whims of their masters and mistresses. Many were sent back to India when no longer required,[3] but others remained to serve in the households of wealthy India-returned *nabobs*. Like African servants, Indians were fashionable in the eighteenth century as a status symbol. Some servants were sold or given away, some ran away to escape maltreatment.

The Ayahs' Home, Hackney, around 1900. The home provided temporary accommodation for South Asian nannies

Another, more common, practice was to employ Indian servants and ayahs for the duration of the voyage to England. Although return passages were meant to be provided, more often they were not and, once in London, the Indians were discharged and left to find their own passage home with India-bound families. Unable to find a return engagement, some were forced to remain permanently in London.[4]

A lodging-house, which came to be known as the Ayahs' Home, was opened in Jewry Street, Aldgate, in the 1870s. In 1900, when the London City Mission took it over, the home was moved to Hackney. Until the Second World War, the home served as a lodging-house for ayahs and a recruiting centre for families travelling to India. Ayahs were sent to the home by families who had brought them to Britain. The return ticket, if one was provided, served as a source of revenue for the home; it was bought by the next India-bound family, and the ayah was enabled to work her passage back.[5] However, since no law compelled families to provide a return passage, even after 1900 cases of ayahs being stranded in London were not uncommon.[6]

Indian sailors (lascars) were employed in response to the demands of the labour market. Recruited in Bengal, the Punjab and the west coast of India, they were employed in small numbers by the East India Company from the eighteenth century. In the nineteenth century there was an increase in the demand for lascars. There were several reasons for this. During the Napoleonic Wars, when crews were needed for the Royal Navy, lascars replaced them in the merchant fleet. They were cheap, being paid only one-seventh the European rate. When ships began to be built more cheaply in the shipyards of India, shipping companies employed lascars to crew ships to London. Later, with the coming of steam-powered liners, stokers were required. Europeans were reluctant to take such employment, but Indians were considered to be docile, cheap and plentiful, and also able to withstand the heat. As the volume of shipping increased with the opening of the Suez Canal in 1869, more lascars were employed.

The British government considered lascar desertion a major problem. To combat it, successive Merchant Shipping Acts (eg in 1823, 1855 and 1894) tightened regulations to prevent lascars remaining behind in Britain. However, like many seamen, lascars jumped ship, some to escape maltreatment, others in the hope of earning more money on shore to repay debts back home. A few lost their ships when they fell ill. In time, a small community of Indian seamen grew up around the London Docks in Stepney, extending later into Poplar, near the West and East India Docks, and Canning Town.

Unable to obtain regular shore employment, these early migrants took up a variety of occupations. Some worked as peripatetic street entertainers, others as hawkers and small-time traders selling scarves, spices and herbs on market stalls in Wentworth Street and Petticoat Lane in Aldgate. The most famous was the street herbalist, Dr Bokanky depicted by the social investigator Henry Mayhew in 1861. Others became crossing-sweepers or sold Christian tracts, and some were beggars.

THE CITY TOLLS.

Indian crossing sweeper, St Paul's churchyard 1848. *Punch* complained that he demanded a toll for crossing

As most Asians in London were male, many married white women. This was generally frowned upon and was the subject of much negative comment, as lascars were viewed with contempt. In 1817, for example, a London magistrate informed a parliamentary committee that 'in Shadwell ... the population consists entirely of foreign sailors, Lascars, Chinese, Greeks, and other filthy, dirty people of that description'.[7]

The First World War led to an increase in the Asian population in the East End. Sailors were recruited in large numbers into the merchant marine. Some jumped ship to work in factories in and around London, where wages were higher;[8] some were actually encouraged to do so. After the war, the community faced troubled times when attacks on the 'Coloured' population took place, notably during the riots in Canning Town in 1919, which was one aspect of a nationwide outbreak of racial violence that year.

Several institutions catered for the lascars, both the residents and those passing through. The Strangers' Home for Asiatics, Africans and South Sea Islanders was founded in Limehouse in 1857. The Lascar Mission, founded by St Luke's church, was set up in 1887 and Reverend E. Bhose, a Bengali, was appointed chaplain. In 1921 the Wesleyan Methodist Church appointed Kamal Chunchie as a pastor to the 'Coloured' population in the Port of London. Chunchie, who came from Ceylon (Sri Lanka), had fought on the western front during the First World War.

Discrimination suffered by the 'Coloured' population in the East End (he himself had experienced indignities and discrimination as a 'nigger') led him, in 1926, to set up the Coloured Men's Institute in Tidal Basin Road, Canning Town. Its governing body included such impressive figures from the Black community as Dr Harold Moody, Professor J. A. Barbour-James, Professor R. K. Sorabji and Shoran S. Singha.[9]

Princess Sophia Duleep Singh, one of the daughters of the Maharajah Duleep Singh, selling the *Suffragette* outside Hampton Court Palace, 1913

From the mid-nineteenth century onwards, Asian professionals began to arrive in London: lawyers and doctors, academics and retired civil servants, merchants (Cama and Company in 1856 were the first) and traders. Students came in search of qualifications, and some stayed on. Many became involved in the campaign for India's freedom from British rule. They were joined by nationalist politicians and London, as the centre of imperial power, became an important platform for nationalist agitation. Dadabhai Naoroji, Shapurji Saklatvala, Shyamaji Krishnavarma and Krishna Menon, to mention a few, lived in London. There were also women campaigners, such as Madame Cama, and Sophia Duleep Singh, who was active in London in the suffragette movement. Campaigners for India's freedom formed associations such as the India League and published pamphlets and newspapers. They forged alliances with British sympathisers and parliamentarians, especially on the radical Left, and even stood for parliament themselves. In the late nineteenth and early twentieth centuries three Asians – Naoroji (Liberal), Bhownaggree (Conservative) and Saklatvala (Communist) – were elected to represent London constituencies in parliament.

The 1920s saw another distinct phase of migration from the subcontinent. Single males, mainly Sikhs, began to arrive from the Punjab. They came to seek adventure or work, and stayed a few years, perhaps returning later for another spell of employment. On arrival, they headed for the East End, around Aldgate, to look for friends or kinsmen. Those fluent in English were absorbed in factories in London, but many more became pedlars. With a vendor's licence and a suitcase full of clothes obtained from a supplier, they set out on weekly rounds, hawking their goods from door to door. In many areas of London, Sikh pedlars were a familiar sight in the 1920s and 1930s.

In the 1920s teashops and restaurants began to appear, catering for single men. Their proprietors were usually Sylheti sailors. One of the earliest Indian restaurants in the West End was established in 1920 in Leicester Square, and drew its clientele largely from British Army officers and families who had resided in India,[10] although 'curry' had been added to the menu of the Norris Street Coffee House, in Haymarket, as early as 1773.[11] Such restaurants formed the basis of the expansion of the Indian restaurant trade in the 1950s.

Lodging-houses for sailors was another enterprise. Some Asians, for example S. T. Ally, ran several in the East End.[12] Doctors, too, set up practices, for example,

Dr Boomla in Plumstead, South London and Dr Katial (who became the first Asian mayor of Finsbury in 1938) in Canning Town. By the 1930s, a small community of sailors and Sikh pedlars was established in Spitalfields and Poplar. A local paper reported their presence at what had become an annual event:

> Several hundred dusky-skinned natives from all parts of India who are now living in East London attended a tea-party held in celebration of the Indian New Year, at Poplar Town Hall, E. They were the guests of the Indian Social Club, the members of which are mostly wealthy merchants and doctors.[13]

A house in Aldgate East was used as a *Gurdwara*, or Sikh temple. In 1941 the East London Mosque was established on Commercial Road. As more Asians were recruited for the war effort the population grew, but it is difficult to estimate its size as there are no official statistics and censuses merely record the place of birth. Figures for the Asian population would therefore include Whites born in India.[14]

The 1950s and 1960s were a crucial period for the settlement of South Asians from India and Pakistan in London. Post-war reconstruction, coupled with a booming economy, created an acute labour shortage. This coincided with upheavals on the Indian subcontinent, following partition in 1947. Men were encouraged to take the risk of coming to Britain. Migration, in any case, for many Asians was not new and needs to be seen within the framework of longer historical and colonial

A Sikh family sheltering from a German bombing raid in the crypt of Christ Church, Spitalfields, November 1940

relationships, rather than merely in 'push-and-pull' terms. First to arrive were ex-non-commissioned army officers, doctors and teachers, followed by those from rural backgrounds. Asians came from the Punjab, Gujarat, Sylhet and Kashmir.

Once in Britain, the needs of the British economy largely determined their destination, since Asians acted as industrial replacement labour. They went to areas of rapid economic growth, or to areas of industrial decline and outwards-migration, where industries had no capital to invest in new technology. In west London, expanding new industries in food-processing, plastics, man-made textiles and rubber all needed labour. Firms advertised in newspapers in India. Many Punjabi Sikhs came to fill this gap; in 1951 there were 350 Asians in Southall, and by the mid-1960s they constituted 12 per cent of Southall's population. At one factory alone, Woolf's rubber plant, 90 per cent of all unskilled labour was Punjabi.[15] Initially, men commuted to Southall from Aldgate, but travel was costly and time-consuming, so they moved to Southall. In Tower Hamlets, on the other hand, Bangladeshis came to work in the local factories and then moved into jobs in the 'rag trade' where demand for labour was high but did not attract White workers.[16]

Within this settlement pattern, several common features are discernible. Early migrants were men. They lived in all-male lodging-houses, originally White-owned, later with Asian landlords. In inner-city areas, large Victorian houses were cheaper and suitable for multi-occupancy. The work Asians did was not classified by craft; usually it was unskilled work rejected by Whites.

In the late 1960s and the 1970s, as families were reunited, the pattern of accommodation changed. The male lodging-houses gave way to rented properties and later to owner-occupied housing. Indian women went out to work. For women, this was a novel but unpleasant experience:

> For a long time I never realised how badly paid and overworked I was, but what made me feel bad in those days was the rudeness and lack of respect with which I and other Asian women were treated by the supervisors. Now I have begun to understand, bad pay, rotten conditions and this insufferable contempt shown to us, it is part of the same picture.[17]

Concentration in inner-city residences encouraged many Asians to set up businesses. This enabled them to escape the rut of dead-end factory work and to cater for the needs of the Asian population. Streets in many boroughs were transformed as sari shops, grocers, travel agencies and electronics shops appeared. Indian restaurants, a trade dominated by the Bangladeshis, became a feature of many London streets, attracting a cosmopolitan clientele. Asian cinemas, newspapers, social and cultural centres (for example, the *Bharatiya Vidya Bhavan* in Kensington) and places of worship have provided a community focus. In 1957 the Indian Workers' Association was formed, followed by the Pakistani Workers' Association in 1961. The 1960s and onwards also saw Asians mobilising against racism.[18] The career of the late Vishnu Sharma is a good illustration of this.

Family eating
out at an
Indian
restaurant,
Brick Lane,
1978

Arriving in Britain in 1957, he first worked in a factory in Southall, later as a bus conductor, and then in 1967 became an immigration adviser. He organised several strikes and anti-racialist campaigns, notably against the bussing of Asian school-children, racist violence and immigration laws. He was a founding member of the Campaign Against Racial Discrimination (CARD) and the Joint Council for the Welfare of Immigrants (JCWI), and was elected general secretary, and later president, of the Indian Workers' Association.[19] Many young Asians have added their own voice to this struggle, for example, the Southall Black Sisters, the Newham Monitoring Project and the Federation of Bangladeshi Youth Organisations, although factionalism has sometimes fragmented such movements.[20]

In the 1960s, groups from the subcontinent were joined by Asians from the diaspora: the Caribbean, Fiji, Mauritius and east and central Africa. Numerically, the 'East African Asians' were the most significant. East African Asians, unlike South Asians from the subcontinent, came primarily as refugees. Indian merchants had settled in East Africa as early as the thirteenth century. Colonial rule encouraged further settlement as Asians were recruited to fill the labour gap or were attracted by economic opportunities. They came to occupy the role of middlemen: as traders and in the lower ranks of the bureaucracy. Urbanised, educated and socially mobile, Asians in East Africa formed a successful commercial and professional group.[21] In the past many had come to Britain for higher education and returned, but after independence the policy of Africanisation affected Asians. In Kenya, in 1967, Asians holding British passports were removed from government administration and licensing laws displaced them from businesses. As British subjects, they came to settle in Greater London and elsewhere in Britain, but even their British passports did not guarantee them entry. A new Immigration Act, passed in 1968, restricted the right of free entry to patrials only (those having a parent or grandparent born in Britain), and British Asians from Kenya had to wait for vouchers. In 1972, when Idi Amin expelled Asians from Uganda, those with British passports were reluctantly allowed in. The hostile reaction from many sections of the population of Britain and the government's dispersal policy are well documented.

Today there are 1,476,900 South Asians in Britain. Of these 521,900 are in London, living in every borough. Some, for example, Hounslow, Tower Hamlets and Newham, have visible communities. Asians are represented in all areas of economic life. There are industrialists, such as Swaraj Paul of the Caparo Group Ltd, millionaire entrepreneurs like K.D. Patel, as well as small, family-run businesses which often provide Londoners with a vital service outside normal shopping hours. (The Asian 'corner shop' is, however, now likely to be affected by Sunday supermarket trading.) Asians are employed in manufacturing and service industries, and in the professions. They are not passive members of society; many are active in the trade-union movement, in politics, at local and national level, as well as in com-munity campaigns. Examples include Sibghat Kadri QC, Tariq Ali, Lord Meghnad Desai of St Clement Danes, the Labour peer, and Piara Khabra, MP for Southall.

The Asian community is not static, nor is it a homogenous community. The lack of homogeneity is seen not only in religious and linguistic terms, but also in social class. Asians in Britain have different national, regional, urban and rural origins, with different traditions and expectations. Those born in Britain have different perceptions and responses. For all its diversity, it is a dynamic community that has enriched British society at all levels, economically, socially and culturally.

Yet life has not been easy. For many Britons, images of India are still coloured by the colonial past, influencing their responses to Asians. Some Asians have managed to insulate themselves from racism and discriminatory practices by setting up their own enterprises, and by the complex networks of family relationships and social cohesiveness. Others have joined in the collective Black struggle for social justice, for example, the Campaign Against Racial Discrimination in the 1960s and the Anti-Racist Alliance of today. There are pressures in some quarters to set up separate institutions, such as schools.

Jayabehn Desai, spokesperson of the Grunwick strike committee, 1977. The year-long strike by young Asians won widespread support from trade unionists

Historically, much writing on Asians tends to depict them in stereotypical terms as a community frozen in time: traditional, conservative and clannish. Today, in some circles, a new stereotype of the Asian community is emerging: that of an enter-prise culture. Asian children are perceived as the most successful in schools, outperforming their White peers. Young and not-so-young Asians are depicted as successful entrepreneurs in industry, the arts and the media. This picture, too, is a stereotype. The reality is complex.[22] The Asian community does not exist in isolation. It is part of British society and has to operate within the dominant culture, a culture which has tended to exclude and marginalise visible minorities.[23]

Endnotes

For full details of publications, see Bibliography.

1 The term South Asians refers to people originating from India, Pakistan, Bangladesh and Sri Lanka. Geographically this is more accurate than the commonly used term 'Asian', which will nevertheless be used in the text as a form of shorthand.

2 As did many of the early researchers. See: K. Little, 1948; M. Banton, 1955.

3 India Office Records: E/1/55, Misc. Letters Received, 1771.

4 See *Morning Post & Daily Advertiser*, 31 January 1777; *Morning Chronicle*, 8 June 1797; *Public Advertiser*, 2 December 1786.

5 Evidence given by Mrs S. Dunn, matron of the Ayahs' Home, to the Committee on Distressed Colonial and Indian Subjects, 1910.

6 *Stri-Dharma* (Journal of the Women's Indian Association), vol. xi, no.10, August 1928, p199.

7 *First Report from the Committee on the State of the Police of the Metropolis*, 1917, p195.

8 India Office Records: L/P & J/6/1462 ff 4505.

9 Kamal A. Chunchie, *Twenty-five Years Among Coloured People in London Dockland*, report for the year 1945–6.

10 See advertisements in *London Guide*, an annual publication in the 1920s, Ward Lock.

11 See *Public Advertiser*, 6 December, 1773, quoted in J. M. Holzman: *The Nabobs in England: A Study of the Returned Anglo-Indian*, 1760–1785, New York, 1926, p90.

12 Lodging-House Applications, Tower Hamlets Archives.

13 *East London Advertiser*, 20 October 1933; see also letter from M. L. Bhargava, secretary of the Indian Social Club, to Poplar Borough Council, 22 November 1938.

14 For the pre-1947 history of south Asians in Britain, see Visram, 1986, 1987.

15 Race Today Collective, 1983, p8.

16 Seán Carey & Abdus Shukur: 'A Profile of the Bangladeshi Community in East London', in *New Community*, vol. xii, no. 3, Winter 1985, p409.

17 A. R. Wilson, 1978, pp50–5.

18 See *The Fight Against Racism: A Pictorial History of Asians and Afro-Caribbeans in Britain*, Institute of Race Relations, London, 1986.

19 *Guardian*, 4 May 1992.

20 See *Southall: The Birth of a Black Community*, Institute of Race Relations/Southall Rights, 1981; *Forging a Black Community: Asian and Afro-Caribbean Struggles in Newham*, Newham Monitoring Project, Campaign Against Racism and Fascism, 1991.

21 Robinson, 1986, pp39–42.

22 A recent report by the Policy Studies Institute has shown that although many East African Asians and Indians were doing well, the Pakistanis and Bangladeshis remained a disadvantaged group. See Trevor Jones, *Britain's Ethnic Minorities*, Policy Studies Institute, Poole, Dorset, 1993.

23 Further sources on the South Asian community in London include Adams, 1987; Ballard & Ballard, 1977; Copley & Visram, 1989; Eade, 1990; Hiro, 1991; Robinson, 1986 and 1990; and Vadgama, 1984. First-hand testimony of Asian experiences in London can be found in Gifford, 1990; A. R. Wilson, 1978; and in *Asian Voices: Life Stories from the Indian Subcontinent* (1993), produced by the Ethnic Communities Oral History Project run by the Borough of Hammersmith and Fulham. An overview of Bangladeshis in Britain is available in the report *Bangladeshis in Britain, 1986–87* produced by the House of Commons Home Affairs Committee, HMSO, London, 1987.

The Spanish in London • Javier Pes

Spaniards have come to London for many centuries, despite the turbulent history of Anglo-Spanish relations. Roman London's cosmopolitan population probably included Iberian-born citizens, and in the Middle Ages Anglo-Spanish trade in leather and wine brought Spanish seamen and merchants to London.

Perhaps London's most famous Spaniard, Princess Catherine of Aragon, arrived in the capital in the winter of 1501. She was fifteen years old, the daughter of Ferdinand and Isabella, the Catholic monarchs of Spain, and the bride of Prince Arthur. After his early death, she married the young Henry VIII. A blue plaque at 49 Bankside, Southwark, commemorates where she first stayed. Catherine of Aragon brought with her an entourage of Spanish courtiers, maids-in-waiting and servants, as well as a large dowry. She later introduced a note of Spanish learning into the Tudor court when in 1523 she appointed the distinguished humanist scholar, Juan Luis Vives, as tutor to her daughter Princess Mary.[1]

With Queen Mary's accession to the throne in 1553, and her subsequent marriage to Philip II of Spain, there occurred another brief period of royal Spanish 'immigration'. Philip II and his large entourage of aristocrats, guards, priests and servants arrived in the spring of 1554. The streets of London were said to have been full of Spaniards.[2] Initially they were greeted enthusiastically by Londoners, but this Anglo-Spanish honeymoon quickly soured and within only a year Philip had gladly left London. 'The English like us Spaniards as much as they like the devil, and treat us accordingly,' complained one of his courtiers.[3] Twenty-three years after Philip II's initial visit to London, some of the survivors of his great Armada arrived. Ordinary seamen remained prisoners of war until a £10 ransom was paid, but an aristocrat such as Don Pedro de Valdés, commander of the *Nuestro Señora Rosario*, had to wait three years before Philip II paid his £3000 ransom. Valdés was kept in comfortable captivity at the London home of Sir Francis Drake's relative, Richard Drake, as something of a trophy and curiosity, regularly displayed to distinguished visitors. In between these appearances he edited the first Spanish–English dictionary, published in 1591.[4]

A number of Sephardic Jews from Spain had arrived in London as early as 1494, fleeing the persecution of the Spanish Inquisition.[5] Approximately 150 years later more Spanish-born *Marranos* (forcibly converted Jews) arrived via Amsterdam after the Cromwellian Readmission of 1656. Among their number was the merchant

Somers Town in the 1830s. At this time there was a colony of Spanish political exiles in the area

David Abarbanes Dormido, born in Córdoba in 1632, and his family, who were former victims of the Inquisitors. In London Dormido became a leading member of the Spanish and Portuguese Jewish community.[6]

Many penniless Spanish political exiles arrived in London in 1823.[7] They were liberals and constitutionalists opposed to the reactionary absolutist monarchy of Ferdinand VII (1814–33). This community of exiles consisted of soldiers, writers, priests and professionals, together with their wives and families or their widows. They included Agustin Arguelles, a former Minister of Justice, who settled in elegant Bloomsbury, but most of the exiles lodged in the grey, narrow and less salubrious streets of Somers Town. The number of Spanish as well as Italian and French exiles lodging in Somers Town in the 1820s meant that the area acquired a 'foreign' reputation.[8]

One exile, Antonio Puigblanch, a Catalan priest, remembered always feeling cold, homesick and hungry in London. He busied himself translating Jeremy Bentham's *Constitutional Code* because Bentham's legal and political works were greatly admired by Spanish liberals. Bentham, in turn, was instrumental in securing small pensions for the exiles of £36 a year from the British government.[9] Another exile who succeeded in finding employment other than the poorly-paid teaching and translating which was the lot of most of the exiles was Juan Alcalá Galiano, formerly a member of the Spanish *Cortes* (parliament). He was appointed the first professor of Spanish, at the newly founded University College, London, in 1828.[10]

A coffee house in Somers Town called the Paragon became the favourite meeting place for the exiles. Here they exchanged information, books and newspapers, some of which had been printed in London. Their political discussions made Somers Town both a 'miniature constitutional Spain' and a dissident intellectual centre of the Spanish-speaking world.[11]

Many thousands of Spaniards were made refugees and exiles by the tragic events of the Spanish Civil War (1936–9). Among those who were allowed to enter Britain were 3826 Basque children.[12] The British National Joint Committee for Spanish Relief organised their evacuation by sea from the besieged and bombarded city of Bilbao in the spring of 1937. Sailing on the small ship, the *Habana*, was fifteen-year-old Jesús Martínez and his brother, leaving behind their parents and two sisters:

We saw people who were dying or who were leaving, to other parts of the Basque country, in the mountains away from the bombing, or to France. And we were taken to Bilbao to be examined by the English doctor, Dr Ellis, and two or three days later we were bundled [on to the *Habana*]. My mother said we were 'going now' as if we were going anywhere. […] We knew we were coming to England.

I remember in the morning, everyone scrambling to the side of the ship to see the quay, which was all with banners and bunting, and it looked pretty and lovely after the turmoil in Spain, and we might have thought it was for us but of course it was one week after the coronation of King George VI.[13]

Top: Jesús and Feliciana Martínez

Identification card and tag issued to Jesús Martínez, a refugee from the Spanish Civil War

Jesús Martínez and his young fellow refugees were first accommodated in a camp near Southampton. From there the children went to foster families throughout Britain or to Basque children's hostels, for example in Cambridge and Carshalton. Many never saw their parents again; others saw them only after the end of the Second World War.[14]

After the victory of the Francoist forces in 1939, many political exiles were granted asylum in Britain. They included Dr Juan Negrín, a scientist and member of the Republican government, who set up the Republican government in exile in London, which existed until 1945.[15] Also among the exiles were writers, academics, musicians and doctors: men such as the Catalan surgeon Josep Trueta who had developed new surgical methods for treating the casualties of modern warfare in Barcelona. He was invited to London in the spring of 1939 to advise on the city's defence and went on to practise in Oxford and to teach at the university.[16]

The community of Republican exiles in London created *El Hogar Español* (The Spanish House), which was situated at Inverness Terrace, Bayswater. The social, cultural and above all political life of the exiles in London revolved around this building. For instance it was at *El Hogar Español* that many anti-Franco meetings at such venues as Caxton Hall or demonstrations in Trafalgar Square were organised.[17]

By the end of the Second World War a new *barrio español* (Spanish quarter) began to form in North Kensington, specifically around Ladbroke Grove. Jesús Martínez and another Basque refugee, Feliciana Sanchez, were living there when they married in 1952, and have lived in the area ever since. It was here and also in Victoria that the Spaniards who began coming to London in the early 1960s found accommodation. These were some of the millions of working-class Spaniards who were forced to find work abroad because of the country's post-war economic problems.[18] Many emigrated to Latin America (Argentina, Mexico and Venezuela were the traditional destinations of Spanish economic emigrants) as well as to Australia and Canada; others went to work on the farms and in the factories of 'rich' Europe, especially France and Germany.

Spaniards who came to London did so with a 'green card' work permit for a restricted range of jobs in service industries.[19] Women worked principally as domestic servants for wealthy families, as office cleaners or as chambermaids in hotels. Many Spanish men worked as waiters or chefs in hotels and restaurants or as porters and cooks in hospitals. Their experience of London was largely of exhausting work, long, anti-social hours, and poor pay and conditions.[20] Despite the difficulties of organising themselves under such conditions, Spaniards created a number of clubs and institutions which formalised some of the informal self-help of the early 1960s. Among these were the *Federación de Asociaciónes de Emigrantes Españoles en el Reino Unido*, which opened in 1975 to help workers vulnerable to exploitation.[21]

The increased Spanish population in London led to the creation of a small 'London-Spanish economy'. This consisted of a few Spanish restaurants, travel agents that specialised in selling tickets to workers coming and going from Spain, and food shops, the largest of which is the Garcia & Sons *supermercado* which

Demonstration outside the Spanish Embassy in the mid-1960s protesting against the regime of General Franco

has traded in the Portobello Road since 1957. Spanish nursery schools and two secondary schools were also established by the 1970s, the two secondary schools merging in 1982 to form the *Colegio Español* in Portobello Road.[22]

An interesting phenomenon has been the retention of regional identities. Most Spaniards came from the depressed areas of Galicia in the north west or of Andalusia in the south. *El Centro Gallego de Londres* was created in 1967 by Galicians, and *El Peña Nuestra Andalucía* was founded in 1977.[23] Both of these regional community centres provide a place for members to meet and chat, read the Spanish newspapers, watch Spanish satellite television and organise cultural and sporting events.

The number of economic migrants fell dramatically in the mid-1970s as Spain's economy improved. The turning point was in 1973 when the number of work permits granted was 4358. By 1975 the number had fallen to 2100.[24] Most Spaniards returned to Spain, sometimes to a house or flat they had bought with their saved earnings. However, some have stayed on in London; many are now reaching retirement age and prefer to stay settled in their new British home and to visit Spain regularly as holiday-makers rather than emigrate a second time back to Spain.

Just as the flow of working-class Spaniards coming to London to work fell, the number of young middle-class Spaniards coming to London began to rise dramatically. In 1985 18,000 Spanish students came to London as opposed to only eighty work-permit holders.[25] Since Spain's entry into the EEC in 1989, restrictions on Spaniards entering the UK have gradually been lifted, until in the last two years there has been almost complete freedom of movement and employment between the two countries. Young Spaniards now come as au pairs, to study English or to follow tertiary education, and they are, in part, attracted by the excitements and freedoms of London's metropolitan life. To supplement parental allowances or to support themselves independently, some young Spaniards give private Spanish lessons or work in the numerous Spanish restaurants and *tapas* bars that have become a fashionable part of contemporary London. Together with young Latin Americans, they have created a vibrant Hispanic sub-culture in the capital reflected in their own Spanish language version of *Time Out* called *Tiempo Libre*.

In 1991 the census counted 19,047 London residents who were born in Spain.[26] In addition, there are an uncounted number of Londoners born in the UK, of Spanish parents. This generation of Spanish-Londoners includes the actor Alfred Molina, who grew up in the Portobello Road, and the politician Michael Portillo, whose father was a Civil War exile. Over time, many Spaniards have settled in London. Dynastic politics, religious persecution and war have compelled some to emigrate; work, education, business and pleasure have motivated others. As new generations of Spaniards come, and Londoners with Spanish backgrounds grow up, they add in their way to the city's long and never static history of cultural and ethnic diversity.

Endnotes

For full details of publications, see Bibliography.

1   Loades, 1986, p118.
2   Walter Besant, *East London*, Chatto and Windus, London, 1903, p187.
3   Rodriguez-Salgado, 1988, p6; Muñoz, 1887.
4   Martin & Parker, 1988, p247.
5   Schischa, 1974, p214–15.
6   Diamond, 1974, p24–5.
7   Gobbi, 1978, p6.
8   Ibid, p7.
9   Ibid.
10 Hale Bellot, 1929, p105.
11 Gobbi, 1978, p8.
12 Luis Botín, 1988, p105.
13 Oral evidence, Museum of London Oral History Archive.
14 Botín, op. cit., p108.
15 Ibid, p85.
16 Ibid, p89.
17 Oral evidence, Museum of London Oral History Archive.
18 Carr, 1982, p724.
19 Spanish economic migrants came to the UK in order to do a specific job usually in the service industries, as outlined in the work permit. They had to renew this permit and register with the police every year for four years. They were also obliged to carry green police registration cards. After four years they could apply to the Home Office for indefinite leave to remain in the UK. If this was granted employment restrictions were lifted, and right to abode in the UK was granted, as long as the person was not out of the country for a prolonged period.
20 Ruz *et al.*, 1984, p1.
21 Botín, op. cit., p145.
22 Ibid, p155.
23 Ibid, p184.
24 Ibid, p145.
25 Ibid, p146.
26 *1991 Census, County Report: Inner London* (part 1), vol. 1, OPCS/HMSO, 1993, p113; *1991 Census, County Report: Outer London* (part 1), vol. 1, OPCS/HMSO, 1993, p130.

The Vietnamese in London

An Introduction[1]

In terms of London's history, the Vietnamese are recent arrivals. They came as refugees, first in small numbers, in the aftermath of the withdrawal of US troops from Saigon in 1975.[2] In the mid-1970s many fled from Vietnam to Hong Kong and the countries bordering the South China Seas, where they were placed in refugee camps. As the exodus of the 'Boat People' continued through the late 1970s, resources were overstretched and life in the camps became intolerable. Following an appeal from the United Nations High Commissioner for Refugees and the Governor of Hong Kong, the British government agreed to admit a quota of 1000 refugees from Hong Kong, and another 500 from camps in Malaysia and Thailand. Because of Britain's jurisdiction over Hong Kong and indirect responsibility for the refugees, the British government called for international negotiations on the crisis. This resulted in the international conference in Geneva in 1979, at which Britain pledged to take a second quota of 10,000 Vietnamese from Hong Kong.

In all, up to 1990 about 22,000 Vietnamese refugees were given asylum in Britain. Of these, 11,500 were admitted under the two quotas, and the rest were ship rescues and family reunion cases. The great majority of the refugees came between the years 1979 and 1981, but from then until 1990 only family reunion cases were admitted.

Unlike some earlier generations of refugees in Britain, the Vietnamese could not turn to an already established community for help. The British government also instituted a policy of dispersed clusters when settling the Vietnamese, as they had done with the Asians from Uganda. Dispersal was meant to minimise the formation of Vietnamese ghettoes in areas of existing heavy 'ethnic' settlement, to avoid over-burdening local authority housing and to maximise the integration of the refugees within the community.

For the Vietnamese, dispersal was a disaster. It split up families and relatives and had the effect of isolating the Vietnamese from their compatriots. It also led to secondary migration within two or three years; many Vietnamese who had been settled in rural areas and small towns in England, Scotland, Wales and Northern Ireland moved to urban areas with large Chinese communities. Above all, London was the preferred location.[3]

Today about 14,000 former Vietnamese refugees, 54 per cent of the total Vietnamese population in the United Kingdom, live in London. Six London

boroughs contain the most significant populations: Hackney and Tower Hamlets
in the north, and Greenwich, Lambeth, Lewisham and Southwark in the south.
The Vietnamese have also settled in many other London boroughs, including
Camden, Croydon, Hammersmith and Fulham, Haringey, Islington, Newham
and Wandsworth.

A Vietnamese wedding in
London

The Vietnamese in London are not
a homogeneous community, culturally,
geographically or linguistically. They
come from both Vietnamese and
Chinese cultural backgrounds, mainly
from North and South Vietnam;
others are from Cambodia and Laos.
The majority are ethnic Chinese from
North Vietnam, where their families
had been settled for several generations. Linguistically, many of the
Vietnamese from Chinese cultural
backgrounds speak both Cantonese
and Vietnamese. Regardless of cultural
background, most Vietnamese are
Buddhists or Catholics. Within the
Vietnamese community in London
there is a slight preponderance of males over females. It is also a young community:
at the end of 1983 (the last year for which comprehensive figures are available)
about 60 per cent were judged to be under the age of twenty-five. They came originally mostly from non-urban areas, many being farmers or fishermen. A few were
doctors, teachers, clerks, accountants, traders and journalists.[4]

For many Vietnamese, the experience of life in London has been rather bleak.
The scars inflicted by the long years of war in Indo-China/Vietnam[5] and the traumas
of escape and refugee status have been exacerbated by dislocation and social and
cultural isolation. Racism or racial harassment has been another painful experience,
and unemployment and poor housing are two major problems. A high proportion
of Vietnamese in the middle age group are unemployed, and transferring their skills
to an industrialised urban economy has proved difficult. Even Vietnamese professionals, such as doctors and teachers, have found it difficult to get their qualifications recognised or to obtain grants for requalification, which could help them find
suitable employment. Many have to rely on their children to act as communicators
and translators with the outside world. The men suffer from a lack of self-esteem
and loss of status as heads of household and family providers, which often results in
family tensions and conflict. As a result, many Vietnamese families encourage their
children to work hard at school, as they desire to see them succeed.

Despite these disadvantages, some Vietnamese, especially those in the thirty to
forty age group, have managed to find unskilled or semi-skilled employment in

factories and bakeries, as waiters and cooks in restaurants (mostly
in Soho) and as cleaners. Vietnamese youngsters who have gone
through their schooling in Britain have sometimes continued to
higher education, qualifying in accountancy, electronics, medicine,
engineering, mathematics and computer science. Others have set
up their own businesses, such as Vietnamese restaurants.

Self-help groups and community organisations providing advice,
services and cultural and social activities are another example of
community enterprise. Over forty such groups have been set up
across London since the early 1980s, including two Vietnamese housing associations, *An Viet* and New World. Many of the community groups have gained ethnic
minority grant funding from government for employment projects. They also give
a sense of self-help and community solidarity. Vietnamese luncheon clubs bring the
elderly together, at the same time providing social services, and in Southwark there
is an active women's group, *Dien Dan Phu Nu – Viet*. Saturday schools for mother-
tongue teaching encourage in the young a sense of their Vietnamese cultural
heritage. There are also student organisations, youth clubs and community news-
letters. Communities in the different boroughs regularly celebrate Vietnamese/
Chinese New Year and the Autumn Moon Festival, when families come together
to enjoy Vietnamese music and such traditional activities as dragon-dancing.

Elderly Vietnamese
refugees at a luncheon club
in Lambeth, 1988

Young Vietnamese men
practising a dance for the
Chinese New Year at the
Chinese Community
School, South London, 1987

187

Voices of experience

Mr Duc Cung, born in 1939, served with nationalist forces in Vietnam, was imprisoned in a re-education camp between 1975 and 1980, then escaped by boat with his son and came to London in 1981.

The organiser wanted profit, big profit. First of all I was taken in a van with about twenty people to the Mekong Delta where we joined many cars and trucks. The taxi took us to the big boat, we called the 'big fish' and took us to the open sea. Two hundred and four people in a big boat, not big with that amount of people. The boat broke, water got in and after two days we could not get to Thailand. In the end we were lucky and an American aircraft found us on the sea. The third day we were rescued by a British oil tanker. When we were in Thailand we learnt that the aircraft tried to get many ships to rescue us, but not anyone wanted to do that job. That one, the tanker, refused as well but the pilot said, 'If you refuse, that boat will die this evening and you will be responsible for it.'

I have a lot of chances to build a life. If I am good enough I can find a way to live. I forget everything behind and start from the beginning. Very few people can get the same thing. They must accept a new job.

Most of the people who accept the new life quick, build life quicker. Most of the people who look at the back, they sit down and dream, so in the end they stay behind the other people. That is my lesson from London. I forgot I was an army captain, I forgot I was a shop-owner, I forgot I got a big house in my country, a good life.[6]

Endnotes

For full details of publications, see Bibliography.

1 This introductory background was compiled by Rozina Visram with the help of Richard Allen and Jack Shieh (Director) of Refugee Action.

2 In 1975 only thirty-two Vietnamese were admitted and three in 1976. See P. R. Jones, 1982.

3 Bell & Clinton, 1992; see also Robinson & Hale, 1989. They suggest that although Vietnamese mobility is higher than that of the white population, other ethnic groups, like the Bangladeshis, have also experienced great mobility.

4 P. R. Jones, 1983, pp450–51; Tran Duc Quan, *Research into the Employment, Training and Education Needs of Refugees from Vietnam in Islington and Hackney*, Islington Council, 1990.

5 First against the French, the then colonical power in Indo-China, until their defeat in 1954. Following partition of Vietnam, the USA military assisted South Vietnam against the Communist Viet Minh from North Vietnam. The Vietnam War ended with USA withdrawal from Saigon in 1975.

6 From the Museum of London Oral History Archive.

PART III

Finding Out More About London's Overseas Communities

This is an introduction to some of the sources available for researching the history of communities in London from overseas. It does not pretend to be comprehensive, but indicates where material relevant to *The Peopling of London* project was located, and where more may yet be found.

Getting Started

Before visiting any of the sources listed below, anyone conducting research on particular communities, or on immigration in general, would be advised to consult some of the books and articles listed in the endnotes to the individual chapters in this volume and in the bibliography at the end. If you do not want to conduct primary research of your own, these may provide answers to many of your basic questions. You will be able to find some of them in local libraries, and many in the larger open-access libraries such as the Guildhall Library.

If you cannot find what you want from the published literature, you may wish to explore some of the libraries, archives and museums listed below. Before you do so, however, it is important that you are clear about the areas of research you are interested in, and have some specific questions in mind.

Archives and museums have to cope with very large numbers of enquiries, often with relatively few members of staff and scarce resources to do so. So the more specific you can be with your enquiries, the more effectively they will be able to respond. Opening hours vary from place to place, and some institutions see researchers only by appointment, or upon issue of a reader's ticket. It usually pays to ring in advance of a visit to ascertain questions of access. Many libraries, archives and museums issue leaflets detailing how to use their resources, and study of these always saves a great deal of time in directing your enquiries to the correct areas. Some of the larger libraries and museums publish catalogues of their holdings, which are invaluable for getting the most out of your research, and others have developed materials specifically geared to the needs of the National Curriculum.

Libraries, Archives and Record Offices

London's libraries, archives and record offices are a rich source for the study of London's overseas communities. They have printed books, periodicals, magazines

Page from the baptisms register of the parish of St George-in-the-East showing the baptism of two Black people in 1785. From the Greater London Record Office

and pamphlets, together with maps, photographs, prints, and miscellaneous printed ephemera, ranging from theatre and music-hall programmes and posters to handbills and notices issued by community organisations.

Newspapers are often stored on microfilm, going back to the last century, and in some archives in the form of files of press cuttings. They are a varied and indispensable source, often giving glimpses into the lives of ethnic groups; they are also useful for tracing local events and people's responses to immigration. While researching in newspapers can often be like looking for a needle in a haystack, a number of local history libraries have begun to make the task easier by compiling indices covering the last twenty or thirty years, classified by ethnic groups, local events and famous people.

Another useful source is the official administrative records of central and local government, which stretch back many centuries. Central government records, housed at the Public Record Office (see below) include census returns. These are also often available at local libraries and archives, where records include parish registers, rate books, vestry minutes, Poor Law records, electoral registers and the annual reports of the Medical Officers of Health. Council Committee minutes, reports, research papers and statistical surveys also give information on local ethnic communities, as do specialist directories, provided one has some initial information on the people concerned.

Local organisations, businesses, societies and sometimes families deposit their records with the local archives. Increasingly, libraries are building collections of people's reminiscences on video and tape. Other sources are directories and lists of community organisations and societies.

Much time, patience and perseverance are required to tap the rich resources contained in libraries, archives and record offices. Catalogue indices do not necessarily carry headings or entries for London's individual communities, although increasingly many are beginning to organise this. Much also depends on the interests of generations of individual librarians and archivists, and the emphasis may vary from institution to institution. As interest in the history of London's 'ethnic communities' has grown, so librarians and archivists are responding and this is being reflected in their collections and indices, particularly those developed since the Second World War. Most important, the staff themselves are a major resource, invariably willing to give their time and to offer advice and guidance.

The following list of London's libraries, archives and record offices gives a brief description of the relatively easily accessible visual and documentary material on particular communities in each collection, as relevant to *The Peopling of London* project. The information given here does not list details of all material in their collections, or of published sources on these communities. Addresses and telephone numbers are given at the end of the list.

National and London-wide resources

Bishopsgate Library

Contains printed books and documents relevant to the Huguenots, Jews and to other immigrant groups in the area around Spitalfields. There is also a copy of the privately-printed history of the Goldstein family, nineteenth-century Jewish settlers.

Black Cultural Archives

This is a specialist archive for the study of Black people in Britain and the diaspora. Although still in the early stages of development, it has a growing amount of material. There are collections of photographs, documents, slavery and indenture papers, biographical texts on many personalities and artefacts.

British Library

A copyright library, open only to specialist researchers with a reader's ticket. It has extensive collections of printed books and periodicals, manuscripts, maps and sheet music and broadsheets. Parliamentary Reports on immigrant communities are also held here. There is a specialist Newspaper Library in Colindale, which includes collections of newspapers produced for London's overseas communities from the nineteenth century onwards. The National Sound Archive in South Kensington has a collection of oral history recordings of members of ethnic minority communities.

Corporation of London Records Office

The Records Office holds a great deal of relevant material from the medieval period onwards. The range of documents include records of alien lodging-house keepers in the late thirteenth century, of alien merchants involved in foreign exchange in the late fourteenth century, a large amount of material relating to the relief of Huguenot refugees, and, at the other extreme, photographs of the Latvian revolutionaries thought to have been involved in the Siege of Sidney Street in 1911.

Greater London Record Office

The GLRO houses records dating back to the mid-sixteenth century, and has a range of material relevant to the study of the immigrant population of London outside the City. Many references to immigrants in the GLRO records are contained in 'authority' or local-government-related documents: reports of quarter sessions, justices of the peace and magistrates, as well as reports of the administrators of the Poor Law and charities. It is the main source in London of parish records, and also holds church records, wills, inventories, school records and family papers. The records are complex and would necessitate a good deal of patient searching. There is a general index and the GLRO also has a very useful consultation service.

Some of the GLRO records relevant to *The Peopling of London* project include records of the United Synagogue and its constituent synagogues; Huguenot family papers, in particular for the Gascherie, and Hanrott families, who came to England between 1685 and 1690; the baptism register of the German Evangelical Church; records from the German School in Devonia Road, Islington and documents relating to Christopher Muller, a bookkeeper who was a commissioning agent for the fur trade before the First World War. For the Irish community, there are Poor Law records. For the Black communities, Ghazala Faizi has provided a very useful survey of GLRO collections relevant to the study of Black history in *A History of the Black Presence in London* (GLC, 1987), which accompanied the GLC exhibition of that name. The GLRO also has separate sections for its extensive collections of printed books, prints and photographs. The latter two collections form a valuable source of visual material.

Guildhall Library

The collections of reference books and pamphlets, both on the open shelves and in the stack, are open to all enquirers, and there is an index by community. The Department of Prints and Maps has a good collection of prints including a series of Hogarths depicting Huguenots and Blacks, and illustrations of overseas communities' places of worship. The collections are partly indexed by community, as are those of the Department of Manuscripts, which holds some relevant material, ranging from an indenture of agreement between alien cobblers and the Cordwainers Company dating to 1395, and a printed proclamation for the relief of French refugees, issued by James II in 1687.

India Office Library and Records

This holds all records on the British involvement with India and the surrounding Asian countries for the period 1600–1947. The archives of the East India Company (1600–1858), the Board of Control (set up in 1784 to supervise the affairs of the company) and the India Office (1858–1947) are all located here, providing a vast range of material for researching South Asians in Britain. The library also contains printed books, prints, photographs, drawings and maps. A useful starting point is *A Brief Guide for Teachers* (Steve Ashton and Penelope Tuson, British Library, 1985). Also useful is the article 'Archives and Education: the India Office Library and Records' (*Teaching History*, 47, February 1987).

Polish Social and Cultural Centre (POSK)

Houses the Polish Library, with over 100,000 books, 40,000 photographs and more than 5000 periodical titles. The majority of the material is about Poland itself, although there is a small amount of material relating to Poles in Britain and other countries.

Port of London Authority Library

This library and archive, administered on behalf of the Port of London Authority by the Museum of London, contains books, maps, prints, photographs and manuscript records. There is some material relating to 'lascar' sailors, the Strangers' Home, and Irish dock labour.

Public Record Office

The PRO is the national repository for the records of the UK government and the law courts of England and Wales. The records are divided into two sites. Chancery Lane holds law court records to the present day, and government records up to 1800. Kew holds post-1800 government records. It publishes a number of guides to the collections, including leaflet 70, 'Immigrants: Documents in the Public Record Office' and leaflet 9, 'Tracing an Ancestor Who was an Immigrant'. Named individuals can sometimes be traced, and there is a wealth of avenues of research, from medieval records of taxes on foreigners, to lists of passengers arriving by ship in the nineteenth century. Census data and aliens registration certificates are also available.

Local Resources

Camden

Camden Local Studies Library and Archives

A reorganised common comprehensive index catalogue serves both Holborn and Swiss Cottage. The area around Holborn and Finsbury in Islington formed the centre of nineteenth-century Italian settlement in London. Holborn has documents (a few dating back to the nineteenth century), photographs and a full set of *Back Hill* journal for the Italian community. There are also reports on the Irish and poor Blacks for the St Giles and Seven Dials area. Swiss Cottage has visual and documentary sources for the Irish, Cypriot and South Asian communities (in particular, Krishna Menon, Labour councillor for St Pancras in the 1930s). Both centres have material on their present-day communities for the last two decades.

City of Westminster

City of Westminster Archives and Local Studies Library

There are two separate archives, at Victoria and Marylebone. Victoria has listed deposits of records connected with Italian businesses, for example, the Caprice restaurant (1900–65) and the Fabricotti Milliner business (1905–9). Marylebone has articles and pamphlets on the Huguenots for the period 1700–1800. For the Irish, there are nineteenth-century reports relating to the dwellings of the industrial classes such as Gray's Buildings. The Greeks are mainly represented by photographs (especially of the Cathedral of St Sophia) and pamphlets dating back to the 1870s. Sources for the Black community include material on the Cato Street conspiracy. There is also material on the Chinese Legation.

Ealing

Ealing Local History Library

Much of the relevant original material relating to post-war immigration, especially of the Afro-Caribbean and South Asian communities, is contained in local newspapers, available on microfilm. There is a useful index for the last two decades. There is also a large collection of photographs, arranged mainly topographically. Within the collection researchers would be able to find photographs of various communities including the South Asian, Black and Polish.

Italian barrel organ player, Greenwich, 1884. From Woodlands Local History Library

Greenwich
Woodlands Local History Library
This has eighteenth-century material on the Huguenots, including the Papillon family tree. Material on the Black population includes documents, papers and photographs of the Black American, Dr George Rice, and the manuscript and photographs of the life of Elizabeth Knight, a suffragette, and her Black husband, Donald Knight, who worked at Woolwich Arsenal. Woodlands also has illustrations and entries from the Dreadnought Seaman's Hospital, which show records of Black and Asian sailors. For the Australasian community, there is material connected with the burial place in Eltham churchyard of one of the first two native Australians to come to London. For the Italians, there are nineteenth-century photographs. There is also material for the last twenty years on most other communities living in Greenwich.

Hackney
Hackney Archives Department
Material on the German community includes a newspaper cuttings file and oral history reports on the anti-German agitation during the First World War; visual and documentary material on the German Hospital in Dalston; and the records of the Loddiges and Berger families. There are miscellaneous documents on the Huguenots and the French Hospital. There are photographs of Jewish synagogues and correspondence from Jewish servicemen, and some material on the Ayahs' Home. There is also material for the last twenty years on most of Hackney's communities.

Hammersmith and Fulham
Ethnic Communities Oral History Project
An archive of oral history recordings, with accompanying publications.

Haringey

Haringey Archive Service

These contain many reports for the last two decades on most of the local communities, particularly the Irish, Cypriot and Black communities. There is also a collection of specially commissioned photographs of the Black community.

Hounslow

Hounslow Local Studies Department

There are two separate archives, at Chiswick and Hounslow. Much of the material relevant to *The Peopling of London* project is in the form of reports and articles in local newspapers. These are available on microfilm, and there is a comprehensive subject index, especially for the last decade. Chiswick has material on the Black, Chinese, Irish and Polish communities; Hounslow has material for the South Asian communities.

Islington

Finsbury Local History Library

For the South Asian communities, Finsbury has documents and photographs, especially for Dadabhai Naoroji, MP for Finsbury in the 1890s, and Chuni Lal Katial, Mayor of Finsbury in the 1930s. For the Italian community, there are reports, press cuttings and photographs, including material from the library's 'Little Italy' exhibition, and copies of *Back Hill*. For the Black communities, there are various entries from the parish registers, newspaper clippings and prints, for example, by Hogarth and Cruikshank. For the Irish, there are a few medical and public health inspectors' reports. 'Immigrants into Islington', a series of articles on the history of Islington's communities published in the *Illustrated Islington Journal* spring 1988 to autumn 1990, provides a useful starting point for tracing records in the archives. The Central Library has boxes of newspaper cuttings, reports and ephemera, on all the major communities in Islington, especially for the last two decades.

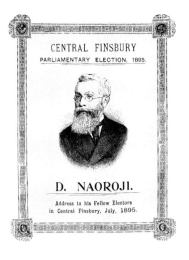

Election address by Dadabhai Naoroji, Britain's first South Asian MP, in 1895. From Finsbury Local History Library

Lambeth

Lambeth Archives Department

For the Huguenot community, there are papers of the Minet family. For the Black communities, there are entries from the parish registers, advertisements for performers in the music hall and theatre posters dating back to the nineteenth century; there is also a collection of material on SS *Empire Windrush*, which arrived in 1948 with the first post-war Caribbean settlers, and of 1960s photographs. All the other communities of Lambeth are represented in borough surveys and ward profiles for the last twenty years.

Lewisham

Lewisham Local History Centre

The Black presence is evident in newspaper items, especially for the post-war period, relating to the housing of settlers from the Caribbean at Carrington House, and the reaction of the local community; there are also photographs of a Black nurse from before the Second World War. For the German community in the Forest Hill area, there are documents connected with the German Evangelical Church. For the French Huguenots, there is a copy of the Papillon family tree, the original of which is at Woodlands, Greenwich. Documentation for the other major communities in the borough relates to the last twenty years.

Newham
Newham Local Studies Library
As the docks expanded many different groups of people moved into Newham, and this is reflected in the library's collections. For the Germans, there are documents relating to anti-German sentiment during the First World War, the German firm of Ohlendorff and a German school admission register. For the Jews from Eastern Europe and Lithuanians (definition is difficult since 'Pole', 'Russian Pole' and 'Lithuanian' are used indiscriminately), there are reports from newspapers and the Medical Officer of Health. For the Irish and Italians, there are photographs and reports. Newham also has material for the Black and Asian communities, including Nancy Sharpe's *Report on the Negro Population in London and Cardiff* (1930); newspaper cuttings for the 1919 riots; cuttings, photographs and reports on the Coloured Men's Institute and on Pastor Kamal Chunchie. There is also material for the last twenty years on most of Newham's present-day communities. *People Who Moved to Newham*, an education pack designed for schools, is a useful starting point for research.

Weaver's staff belonging to George Dorée, a Bethnal Green silk-weaver of Huguenot descent. From Tower Hamlets Local Studies Library

Southwark
Southwark Local Studies Library
This has reports, cuttings and photographs for the Irish community, including the material from a display on 'The Irish in Southwark'. For the Black and South Asian communities, there are entries from the parish registers, posters and newspaper cuttings, especially for such individuals as Harold Moody and Frederick Akbar Mahomed.

Tower Hamlets
Tower Hamlets Local Studies Library and Archive
Because of its location, over the centuries the borough has been settled by different groups of immigrants from different countries. A comprehensive catalogue index makes the task of the researcher easier. Collections of photographs, files of newspaper cuttings, official reports and contemporary accounts are available for many communities, notably the Chinese in Limehouse and Pennyfields, the Huguenot silk-weavers in Spitalfields and the Jews in Whitechapel. There are reports and photographs of synagogues, churches and schools, and societies connected with these communities. There are also files of material, both documentary and visual, on the

Irish, the Germans and the South Asians. A file on lodging-house applications and inspectors' reports gives interesting insights into lodging-houses and their proprietors. There is also material on other communities in Tower Hamlets, especially for the last two decades.

Wandsworth

Wandsworth Local History Library
This has secondary material on the Huguenots. For the South Asian communities, there is a large collection of newspaper cuttings and documents on Shapurji Saklatvala, MP for Battersea in the 1920s. For the Black communities, there is material on John Archer, elected Mayor of Battersea in 1913.

Museums

Museums, with a few notable exceptions, have only recently become aware of the importance of reflecting the long history of London's cultural diversity in their collections and displays. Only in the last few years has historical material been consciously collected in order to represent the histories of different communities. Supplementing this material, many museums are now pursuing vigorous programmes of contemporary collecting and recording. These result in collections of photographs, oral history recordings on tape, and ephemera such as letters, papers and packaging, that will in time become valuable historical resources themselves.
A good deal of relevant material has already been collected in the past, without its potential being recognised at the time. For example, many late-eighteenth- and early-nineteenth-century paintings and prints depict Black people, often in the background of the scene as servants or as members of the crowd. Their potential as a source of evidence for Black history has only recently been recognised, by, for example, David Dabydean in his book *Hogarth's Blacks* (Manchester University Press, Manchester, 1987). Other material may be relevant because of common association. For example, it may not have been recorded whether a particular hurdy-gurdy or barrel organ in a collection was actually used by an itinerant Italian musician. However, the fact that Italians are frequently depicted playing them allows the object to be used as an example of one similar to those used by Italian street musicians.

Few museums index their collections by community. Researchers interested in material relevant to particular communities will therefore probably find it easiest to explain their particular field of enquiry to the curator, who can then guide them to relevant collections. Material held in museums that is relevant to the history of overseas communities can be divided into two sorts. The first is material that depicts or records members of such groups, the second consists of objects and images made or used by them.

In the first category of material, paintings, prints, drawings and photographs are always a good place to start. While much useful material is held in the collections described above, there is a great deal in museums that still remains to be explored. Trade cards, advertisements, tickets, bills of sale and other ephemera can provide valuable evidence about foreign businesses and community organisations. Passports, diaries and letters give insights into particular individuals' lives. Busts and ceramic figurines depict both eminent people of the time and working-class individuals such as boxers, street sellers and entertainers. Other possible sources include commemorative mugs, medals, handkerchiefs, woven pictures and wax figures.

The second category of material is as varied as the makers themselves. Again, images such as prints and paintings are a good place to start as indexes of foreign-born artists who practised in London are readily available. For other material it may be best to begin by narrowing down the search to material by certain individuals, such as scientific instrument-makers or watchmakers or -sellers whose name appears on their products. The majority of overseas workers, however, did not leave distinctive signatures on their work, and only a combination of historical detective work and statistical probability will allow you to infer that a specific object stands a good chance of having been made or used by a particular group.

The relevance of much of the material in London's museums to this subject is only just being realised, as new questions are asked about it. The more one delves into museum collections, the more one finds, and interesting material is always being discovered.

The following list of museums with material relating to London's overseas communities does not claim to be comprehensive, but rather indicates the possibilities that exist. Most individual museums will have some material of relevance.

Museums with a National or London-wide Remit
Museum of London
The museum holds relevant material from prehistoric times to the present. This includes archaeological material, paintings, prints, drawings, photographs, trade cards and other ephemera, costume and textiles, and other social history material. It is building up its oral history collections, and now houses some elements of the former London History Workshop archive. Knowledge of the potential of the collections has increased greatly during *The Peopling of London* project, and a database of all the material used is available. The large research archive compiled during the project is also available to researchers, and is housed in the library, with other relevant publications.

British Museum
The Departments of Prehistoric and Romano-British Antiquities, of Medieval and Later Antiquities and of Coins and Medals have some material relating to London's overseas populations in their broadest sense. Extensive material of potential relevance is held in the Department of Prints and Drawings, but is not indexed by community. The staff can, however, direct you to useful catalogues, and prints by most artists can be found. The printed *User's Guide* by Anthony Griffiths and Reginald Williams (British Museum Publications, London, 1987) is a good place to begin a

Seal matrix of Pauteronius de Podio, an Italian merchant in medieval London. From the Museum of London

Banner from the Jews' Orphan Asylum, Norwood. From the London Museum of Jewish Life

search. For London, the collection of drawings and watercolours by George Scharf, which includes depictions of many different 'foreigners', is a particularly useful source. The Heal collection of trade cards, in the Department of Prints and Drawings, is an excellent source for foreign businesses, particularly those of Huguenots, Jews and Italians.

Imperial War Museum

The museum houses archives, particularly consisting of photographs and oral history recordings, relating to the Commonwealth contribution to the First and Second World Wars.

Jewish Museum

This covers the history of Judaism and the Jewish presence in Britain from medieval times. There are good collections of plate, paintings, prints, marriage scrolls and trade cards. Notable objects include a Rembrandt etching of Menasseh ben Israel and a jug depicting the eighteenth-century Jewish boxer, Daniel Mendoza.

London Museum of Jewish Life

The museum covers the history of London's Jewish community, with particular emphasis on the nineteenth and twentieth centuries. The collection is strong on material relating to settlement, self-help, entertainment, tailoring and other businesses. There is an extensive collection of photographs of East End Jewish life, and some reconstructed room settings.

London Transport Museum

The holdings include a small amount of material relating to the employment of New Commonwealth settlers by London Transport.

National Maritime Museum

Among much relevant material, the museum has scientific instruments made by Dutch craftsmen.

Admiral Fitzroy's storm barometer, around 1880, by the London Italian makers Negretti and Zambra. From the Science Museum

National Portrait Gallery

The primary collection and the archive contain paintings, prints and photographs of many individuals of overseas birth or extraction who have made an impact on British life. There is a published *Concise Illustrated Catalogue* of the collection.

Science Museum

In particular the museum has scientific instruments by Dutch, Huguenot and Italian makers as well as material relating to the Spitalfields weaving industry and engineering firms founded by overseas settlers.

Victoria and Albert Museum

Most collections have some material of relevance. The Indian and South East Asian Collection has developed collaborative ventures with South Asian communities in Britain. The Textiles and Dress Collection has material relating to Huguenot weavers, amongst others. The Prints, Drawings and Paintings Collection and the National Art Library are good general sources.

Local Museums

Bruce Castle Museum

The museum has collections reflecting the history of the borough of Haringey, including some material relating to the Greek-Cypriot and Black communities.

Croydon Museums Service

Collections are strong on cultural diversity, and there is an emphasis on collaboration with local communities. The building is due to open in 1994.

Forty Hall Museum

The museum has some material relating to the Greek-Cypriot community in the borough of Enfield.

Freud Museum

There is an extensive collection of material relating to Sigmund Freud and his family, including their flight from Nazi Germany and subsequent settlement in London.

Geffrye Museum

This museum has made particular efforts to address itself to local communities in Hackney through a re-examination of its collections, and a series of special exhibitions.

Grange Museum of Community History

The collections comprise principally material relating to the borough of Brent. Relevant material is principally photographic, covering mainly the Irish and Black communities in the post-War period.

Greenwich Borough Museum

There is a small amount of material relating to the South Asian community in the collections.

Gunnersbury Park Museum

Itself housed in the former home of members of the Rothschild family, the museum is building up its collections relating to overseas communities in the boroughs of Ealing and Hounslow.

Hackney Museum

The museum places a particular emphasis on recording the diversity of the borough. Communities represented in the collections include the Chinese, South Asian, African-Caribbean, Greek-Cypriot, Turkish-Cypriot, Jewish and Irish.

Heritage Centre, Spitalfields

Housed in a former synagogue, the centre is currently attempting to raise funds for displays on the rich heritage of Spitalfields, including that of the Huguenot, Jewish and Bengali communities.

Islington Museum Service

A relatively new venture, the service is undertaking a number of collaborative ventures with local communities, including the Kurdish.

Passmore Edwards Museum

The museum service is currently building up its holdings relating to the diverse populations of Newham and the surrounding area.

Wandsworth Museum

The museum is currently working on collaborative ventures with local communites.

Addresses

Libraries, Archives and Record Offices

National and London-wide

Bishopsgate Library
230 Bishopsgate
London EC2M 4QH
071-247 6844

Black Cultural Archives
378 Coldharbour Lane
London SW9 8LF
071-738 4591

British Library
Great Russell Street
London WC1B 3DG
071-636 1544

Corporation of London
  Records Office
PO Box 270
Guildhall
London EC2P 2EJ
071-260 1251

Greater London Record
  Office and History Library
40 Northampton Road
London EC1R 0HB
071-633 6851

Guildhall Library
Aldermanbury
London EC2P 2EJ
071-606 3030

India Office Library
  and Records
Orbit House
197 Blackfriars Road
London SE1 8NG
071-928 9531

National Sound Archive
29 Exhibition Road
London SW7 2AS
071-589 6603

Newspaper Library
Colindale Avenue
London NW9 5HE
081-200 5515

Polish Social and Cultural
  Centre (POSK)
238–46 King Street
Hammersmith
London W6 0RF
071-741 1940

Port of London Authority
  Library and Archive
Unit C14
Poplar Business Park
10 Preston's Road
London E14 9RL
071-515 1162

Public Record Office
Ruskin Avenue
Kew
Surrey TW9 4DU
081-876 3444
and
Chancery Lane
London WC2A 1LR
081-876 3444

Document by which
Bonevie the Jew transferred
a house in West Cheap to
Alexander de Dorset,
1217–21. From the Public
Record Office

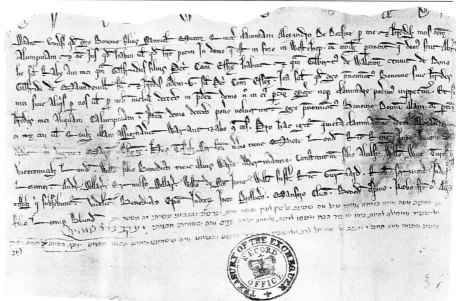

Local

Camden

Camden Local Studies
 Library and Archives
Swiss Cottage Library
88 Avenue Road
London NW3 3HA
071-413 6522

Local Studies Library
Holborn Library
32–8 Theobalds Road
London WC1X 8PA
071-413 6342

City of Westminster

Archives and Local Studies
Victoria Library
160 Buckingham Palace
 Road
London SW1W 9UD
071-798 2180

Archives and Local History
Marylebone Library
Marylebone Road
London NW1 5PS
071-798 1030

Ealing

Local History Library
Central Library
103 Ealing Broadway
 Centre
London W5 5JY
081-567 3656

Greenwich

Local History Library
'Woodlands'
90 Mycenae Road
London SE3 7SE
081-858 4631

Hackney

Hackney Archives
 Department
Rose Lipman Library
De Beauvoir Road
London N1 5SQ
071-241 2886

Hammersmith and Fulham

Ethnic Communities Oral
 History Project
Shepherds Bush Library
7 Uxbridge Road
London W12 8LJ
081-749 0982

Haringey

Haringey Archive Service
Bruce Castle Museum
Lordship Lane
London N17 8NU
081-808 8772

Hounslow

Local Studies Department
Library Centre
24 Treaty Centre
High Street
Hounslow TW3 1ES
081-570 0622

Chiswick Reference Library

Chiswick Library
Reference Division
Dukes Avenue
London W4 2AB
081-994 5295

Islington

Finsbury Local History
Finsbury Library
245 St John Street
London EC1V 4NB
071-278 7343

Local History Section
Central Library
2 Fieldway Crescent
London N5 1PF
071-609 3051

Lambeth

Lambeth Archives
 Department
Minet Library
52 Knatchbull Road
London SE5 9QQ
071-733 3279

Lewisham

Local History Centre
The Manor House
Old Road
Lee
London SE13 5SY
081-852 5050/7087

Newham
Local Studies Library
Stratford Reference Library
Water Lane
London E15 4NJ
081-519 6346

Southwark
Local Studies Library
211 Borough High Street
London SE1 1JA
071-403 3507

Tower Hamlets
Tower Hamlets Local
History Library and
Archive
Bancroft Library
277 Bancroft Road
London E1 4DQ
081-980 4366

Wandsworth
Wandsworth Local History
Library
Battersea Library
256 Lavender Hill
London SW11 1JB
081-871 7467

Museums

National and
London-wide

British Museum
Great Russell Street
London WC1B 3DG
071-636 1555

Imperial War Museum
Lambeth Road
London SE1 6HZ
071-416 5000

Jewish Museum
Woburn House
Tavistock Square
London WC1H 0EP
071-388 4525

London Museum of
Jewish Life
The Sternberg Centre
80 East End Road
Finchley
London N3 2SY
081-349 1143

London Transport Museum
Covent Garden
London WC2E 7BB
071-379 6344

Museum of London
London Wall
London EC2Y 5HN
071-600 3699

National Maritime Museum
Romney Road
Greenwich
London SE10 9NF
081-858 4422

National Portrait Gallery
St Martin's Place
London WC2H 0HE
071-306 0055

Science Museum
Exhibition Road
London SW7 2DD
071-938 8000

Victoria and Albert Museum
Cromwell Road
London SW7 2RL
071-938 8500

Local

Bruce Castle Museum
Lordship Lane
London N17 8NU
081-808 8772

Croydon Museums Service
Central Library
Katharine Street
Croydon CR9 1ET
081-760 5632

Forty Hall Museum
Forty Hill
Enfield EN2 9HA
081-363 8196

Freud Museum
20 Maresfield Gardens
Hampstead
London NW3 5SX
071-435 2002

Geffrye Museum
Kingsland Road
London E2 8EA
071-739 9893

Grange Museum of
Community History
Neasden Roundabout
Neasden Lane
London NW10 1QB
081-452 8311

Greenwich Borough Museum
232 Plumstead High Street
London SE18 1JT
081-855 3240

Gunnersbury Park Museum
Gunnersbury Park
London W3 8LQ
081-992 1612

Hackney Museum
Central Hall
Mare Street
London E8 1HE
081-986 6914

Heritage Centre
Spitalfields
19 Princelet Street
London E1 6QH
071-377 6901

Islington Museum Service
Recreation Department
345 Holloway Road
London N1 0RS
071-607 7331

Passmore Edwards Museum
The Old Dispensary
30 Romford Road
London E15 4BZ
081-534 0276

Wandsworth Museum
Disraeli Road
Putney
London SW15 2DR
081-871 7074

Appendices

Appendix 1

Principal Events in
The Peopling of London

500,000 BC	EARLIEST human presence in Britain. Population comes and goes over time depending on the severity of the Ice Age
25,000 BC	BRITAIN deserted, but connected to the Continent by land exposed by low sea levels
15,000 BC	PEOPLE begin to repopulate southern Britain
6000 BC	BRITAIN becomes an island as sea levels rise. Settlers now come from overseas by boat
4000 BC	FARMING introduced in Lower Thames valley. People from overseas may have brought new crops and animals
2000 BC	POSSIBLE Bronze Age merchants and traders in Lower Thames valley
150 BC	POSSIBLE settlement of Celtic-speaking peoples from across the Channel
AD 43	ROMAN conquest of Britain begins
50	LONDON founded by the Romans. The earliest Londoners come from all over Europe and even North Africa
410	WITHDRAWAL of Roman administration and beginning of invasions of Angles, Saxons, Jutes and Frisians. They settle in the countryside around London
604	ITALIAN bishop Mellitus comes to preach in London. Founds the first church of St Paul
871–2	AFTER a series of earlier attacks, a viking 'Great Army' spends the winter in London. More attacks until 886 when a territory for the Danes is established in eastern England
994	RENEWED Danish attacks on London
1016	DANISH leader Cnut accepted as King of England. Danish dynasty rules in London
1066	WILLIAM, Duke of Normandy, with an army that includes Flemings and Bretons, conquers England
1089	CLUNIAC monks from Charité-sur-Loire arrive to take possession of Bermondsey Abbey
1128	FIRST recorded mention of 'the street of Jews' in London. A community had been established shortly after the Norman conquest. Numerous 'alien' merchants also present by this period
1130	'MEN OF COLOGNE' gained the right to reside in London
1281	RIVAL German merchants form a single federation, The Hanse
1288	IRISH tailor victim of first recorded murder in Fleet Street

1290	JEWS expelled from England
1337	FLEMISH weavers invited to settle to develop England's weaving industry
1440	A TAX is introduced on all aliens. Figures show the majority are from the Low Countries and Germany
1507	BLACK trumpeter recorded at the court of Henry VII
1509	HENRY VIII becomes King. His reign sees the presence of large numbers of overseas artists and craftworkers in London
1517	EVIL May Day: attacks against 'aliens' in the city
1547	RECORD of first known Polish resident of London, John à Lasco
1550	STRANGERS' Church founded at Austin Friars, with intially a Dutch, German and French congregation
1554	QUEEN Mary marries Philip II of Spain, resulting in a Spanish presence in London
1555	JOHN Lok brings 'certaine black slaves' from Africa. Beginning of continous Black presence in London
1567	PERSECUTION of Protestants in Spanish Netherlands. Dutch settlers seek refuge in London
1581	ITALIAN Church has congregation of sixty-six
1600	EAST India Company granted charter
1616	THE first American visitor, the Virginian princess Pocahontas, arrives in London
1630s	BEGINNING of the presence of South Asians in London, brought as servants
1656	JEWS readmitted to England by Cromwell. Synagogue established in Creechurch Lane
1677	GREEK Orthodox Church built in St Giles
1685	WIDESPREAD persecution of Huguenots in France brings around 20,000 refugees to London
1688	DUTCH King William of Orange and wife Mary jointly rule England. Strong Dutch influence on London's arts, crafts and financial organisation
1700s	SIGNIFICANT presence of Black and South Asian slave-servants and seamen
1708–9	UP TO 15,000 refugees from the Palatinate (Germany) find a temporary haven in London

1750s	LONDON is by now home to significant communities of Sephardi and Ashkenazi Jews, Irish, Blacks and Huguenots, as well as smaller populations of Germans and South Asians
1772	MANSFIELD judgement gives impetus to the decline of slavery in England
1775	AMERICAN War of Independence brings American refugees to London
1780s	FIRST records of Chinese sailors in the dock area
1783	BRITISH withdrawal from America brings thousands of 'Empire Loyalist' troops to London, including many Blacks
1789	FRENCH Revolution brings refugees to London
1792	BENNELONG and Yemmerawanyea, Aborigines, become the first Australians to visit the city
1814–15	PARLIAMENTARY report published on 'Lascars and other Asiatic seamen'
1823	SPANISH political exiles establish a community in Somers Town
1837	VICTORIA becomes Queen. Marries Prince Albert of Saxe-Coburg-Gotha in 1840
1848–9	REVOLUTIONS in Europe bring political exiles to London, including Karl Marx
1845–50	THE 'Great Famine' in Ireland sees a climax of Irish immigration
1850s	LONDON is now a cosmopolitan capital with a population that includes Jews, Chinese, Germans, Greeks, Spaniards, Irish, Blacks, South Asians, Turks, Italians, French and North Americans
1857	OPENING of 'The Strangers Home' for Asiatics, Africans, South Sea Islanders and Others in the West India Dock Road
1880s	SMALL Chinese community comes into existence in Limehouse, as well as a small Somali community around the docks
1881	ASSASSINATION of Tsar Alexander II leads to persecution of Jews in Eastern Europe, and great expansion of Jewish population in London
1905	ALIENS Act, introduced to reduce Jewish settlement, marks the end of liberal policies on immigration
1914	BEGINNING of First World War, which sees many colonial troops and workers contributing to the war effort. Aliens Restriction Act of 1914 leads to confiscation of German businesses and internment of some Germans. British Nationality and Status of Aliens Act makes all inhabitants of the British Empire British subjects
1915	RIOTS against London's German community following the sinking of the *Lusitania*
1919	ALIENS Act brings further restrictions against immigration. The summer sees race riots across the country, including Canning Town and Poplar in London
1920s	GREEK-Cypriot settlement in London begins. PUNJABI pedlars begin to arrive
1933	ADOLF Hitler becomes Chancellor in Germany. Many Jews flee persecution up until the outbreak of war and settle in London
1936	SPANISH Civil War brings refugees to London
1939	BEGINNING of Second World War. War sees foreign governments in exile in London and the internment of Germans and Italians. Soldiers and workers from all over the British Empire are stationed in London, as well as large numbers of American troops
1945	END of Second World War and many exiles, especially Poles, choose not to return to the new regimes in their countries
1946	BEGINNING of European Volunteer Workers scheme, which brings people from all over Europe to help in post-war reconstruction
1948	BRITISH Nationality Act confirms people of the Commonwealth countries as British citizens. The *Empire Windrush* arrives, bringing first post-war Caribbean settlers
1950s	CONTINUED efforts to rebuild London's industry and infrastructure lead to the encouragement of settlers from Ireland, the Caribbean, South Asia, Italy and Cyprus. Chinese community develops in Soho
1956	REFUGEES from Russian invasion of Hungary arrive in London
1962	COMMONWEALTH Immigrants Act is introduced, reducing immigration from the 'New Commonwealth'
1960s	'SWINGING London' attracts visitors from all over the world, especially Australia, New Zealand, South Africa and North America. Migrant workers from Spain, Portugal, Latin America, Morocco and Egypt also arrive
1967	ASIANS are expelled from Kenya and many, as British passport holders, settle in London
1970s	POLITICAL refugees arrive from Chile, Argentina and other countries
1972	ASIANS are expelled from Uganda and many also settle in London
1973	OIL crisis sees financial boom in Gulf states which results in Arab investment, and Arab presence, in London
1974	TURKISH invasion of part of Cyprus brings refugees to London
1979	VIETNAMESE refugees begin to arrive
1980s	SOMALIS, Kurds, Tamils arrive in London as refugees
1993	SINGLE European Market created

211

Appendix 2

Statistics

Table 1: London Residents Born Overseas, 1991	
South Asia	278,835
Ireland	256,276
Africa	183,341
Caribbean	150,745
South East Asia	106,213
Cyprus	50,684
North America	44,293
Australia and New Zealand	41,694
Germany	32,027
Italy	30,052
Poland	21,823
Spain	19,047

Figures derived from the 1991 census survey, Office of Population and Census Surveys.

Table 2: Ethnic Affiliation of London Residents, 1991	
Black	534,300
South Asian	521,900
Chinese/other Asian	288,900

Figures derived from the 1991 census survey, Office of Population and Census Surveys.

Contributors

Colin Holmes graduated from the University of Nottingham and was a Revis post-graduate scholar. He has taught at the University of Sheffield since 1963 and was appointed to a personal chair in History in 1989. His current research interests are the history of immigration and the study of racism. He has written several works on these subjects and he is joint editor of the journal Immigrants and Minorities.

Nick Merriman was born in Birmingham. He studied Archaeology at Cambridge University and Museology at Leicester University. He has published several books and articles and is particularly interested in making museums more widely accessible to the public. He is currently Head of the Department of Early London History and Collections at the Museum of London.

Rozina Visram is of Tanzanian origin. She studied at Makerere University College, Uganda, at Edinburgh University and also at London University. Formerly a teacher in history and politics, she has published several books on Indians in Britain. She was the researcher for The Peopling of London exhibition at the Museum of London, 1993/4. She is currently a freelance researcher and writer.

Peter Fraser was born in Guyana. As well as being a published editor he teaches at Goldsmiths' College, London in the Department of Historical and Cultural Studies. His current field of research covers Caribbean social and intellectual history of the nineteenth and twentieth centuries and the history of Black people in Britain.

Camillia Fawzi El-Solh is of Egyptian/Irish parentage. She is a freelance UN consultant on socio-economic development in the Arab region. She now lives in Oxford where she is Research Associate at the Centre for Cross Cultural Research on Women at Oxford University as well as researching Arab immigrant communities in Britain.

Rick Bouwman was born in Australia and now lives in London. He was formerly Research Curator at the Australian Gallery of Sport. He is also a published author and editor of numerous books and articles.

Anthony Shang was born in Singapore. He was educated at the London School of Economics and the University of Sussex. He is a freelance writer and television producer, specialising in

Far Eastern affairs. He has written two books about Chinese communities and numerous articles for both academic and journalistic publications.

Panikos Panayi was formerly Alexander von Humboldt Research Fellow at the University of Osnabrück when his field of research included Germans in British history and minorities in wartime, together with racial violence in Britain. He is a published author and at present is lecturer in History at De Montfort University in Leicester.

Sav Kyriacou was born in London and is of Greek-Cypriot origin. He holds a degree in History and Education from Digby Stuart College. For the past five years he has been working for the Ethnic Communities Oral History Project in Hammersmith & Fulham.

Zena Theodorou was born in Cyprus. She has a doctorate in Classics and her current field of research is emotional expression in Greek language and literature. She is also a development worker for ethnic minorities in Haringey.

Seán Hutton was born in Dublin and educated at University College Dublin and Hull University. Formerly a teacher of history at Bridlington School, North Humberside, he became Executive Director of the British Association for Irish Studies and is now Vice Chairman. He is also a freelance lecturer and writer and a published poet.

Lucio Sponza was born in Venice where he studied economics. He came to London to study Social & Economic History and completed a PhD at Birkbeck College. He now teaches Italian at the University of Westminster. His current field of research is the Italians in Britain during the Second World War.

Anne Kershen was born in London and was a curator at the London Museum of Jewish Life. She is presently Barnet Shine Senior Research Fellow at Queen Mary and Westfield College, where she is completing an official history of Reform Judaism in Britain. She has published numerous other works on aspects of Judaism and is currently researching immigrant migration from ghetto to suburb in London.

Richard Tames lives in London. Born in Essex, he studied History at Cambridge University and then completed a post-graduate degree in Politics with Sociology at Birkbeck College,

London. He teaches British History at both the Syracuse University and the American University and has written books on London's history. He is also a qualified 'Blue Badge' London guide and City of London guide.

Keith Sword was born in Southampton. He is a widely published author and is currently Research Fellow at the School of Slavonic and East European Studies, University of London. His areas of research are modern Polish history, the migrations of Poles in recent times, Poles abroad and Polish ethnic identity.

Shamis Hussein comes from Somalia. She holds an MA in International Relations. She regularly contributes to academic journals, newspapers and radio. At present she is a consultant on projects for women and development in Somalia for the United Nations.

Javier Pes is a London-born Spaniard. He holds degrees in History from Cambridge University and Museum Studies from Leicester University. He is now Assistant Curator in the Department of Later London History and Collections at the Museum of London.

Bibliography

ADAMS, 1987
Caroline Adams (ed.), *Across Seven Seas and Thirteen Rivers: Life Stories of Pioneer Sylhetti Settlers in Britain*, T.H.A.P. Books, London, 1987

ALDERMAN, 1987
G. Alderman, *The Federation of Synagogues*, The Federation of Synagogues, London, 1987

ALDERMAN, 1992
G. Alderman, *Modern British Jewry*, Oxford University Press, Oxford, 1992

ALLEN, 1959
H. C. Allen, *The Anglo-American Relationship since 1783*, A. & C. Black, London, 1959

ALOMES, 1988
Stephen Alomes, *A Nation at Last? The Changing Character of Australian Nationalism*, Angus & Robertson, Sydney, 1988

ALONEFTIS, 1984
Vicky Aloneftis, 'A Cypriot identity', *Ten 8*, issue 16, 1984

AL-RASHID, 1992
Madawi Al-Rashid, 'Political migration and downward socio-economic mobility: the Iraqi community in London', *New Community*, vol. 18, no. 4, July 1992

ANDERSON, 1980
Gregory Anderson, 'German clerks in England, 1870–1914: another aspect of the great depression debate', in *Hosts, Immigrants and Minorities: Historical Responses to Newcomers in British Society 1870–1914*, Kenneth Lunn (ed.), Dawson, Folkestone, 1980, pp201–21

ANGLO-GERMAN PUBLISHING CO. 1913
Die Deutsche Colonie in England, London, 1913

ARNOLD, n.d.
Matthew Arnold, *On the Study of Celtic Literature and Other Essays*, J. M. Dent & Sons, London and E. P. Dutton & Co., New York, n.d.

ARONSFELD, 1985
C. C. Aronsfeld, 'The Germans', *History Today*, August 1985, pp8–15

ASHTON, 1986
Rosemary Ashton, *Little Germany: Exile and Asylum in Victorian England*, Oxford University Press, Oxford, 1986

BAILYN & MORGAN, 1991
Bernard Bailyn and Philip D. Morgan, *Strangers within the Realm: Cultural Margins of the First British Empire*, University of North Carolina Press, Chapel Hill, 1991

BAINES, D., 1991
Dudley Baines, *Emigration from Europe 1815–1930*, Macmillan, London, 1991

BAINES, J., 1971
J. Baines, *Joseph Conrad: A Critical Biography*, Penguin, Harmondsworth, 1971

BALLARD & BALLARD, 1977
Roger Ballard and Catherine Ballard, 'The Sikhs: the development of South Asian settlement in Britain', in *Between Two Cultures: Migrants and Minorities in Britain*, James L. Watson (ed.), Basil Blackwell, Oxford, 1977

BANTON, 1955
M. Banton, *The Coloured Quarter: Negro Immigrants in an English City*, Jonathan Cape, London, 1955

BELL & CLINTON, 1992
John Bell and Lola Clinton, *The Unheard Community: A Report on the Housing Conditions and Needs of Refugees from Vietnam Living in London*, for Refugee Action, Community Development Foundation, London, 1992

BELLOT, 1929
H. Hale Bellot, *University College London*, University of London Press, London, 1929

BENNETT, 1991
Christopher Bennett, *The Housing of the Irish in London: A Literature Review*, PNL Irish Studies Centre Occasional Papers Series, Polytechnic of North London Press, London, 1991

BERGHAHN, 1987
Marion Berghahn, *Continental Britons: German Jewish Refugees from Nazi Germany*, Berg, Leamington Spa, 1987

BERMANT, 1971
Chaim Bermant, *The Cousinhood: The Anglo-Jewish Gentry*, Eyre & Spottiswoode, London, 1971

BERRIDGE, 1978
Virginia Berridge, 'East London opium dens and narcotic use in Britain', *The London Journal*, vol. 4, no. 1, 1978

BESANT, 1903
Walter Besant, *East London*, Chatto & Windus, London, 1903

BLACK, 1992
G. Black, *Lender to the Lords, Giver to the Poor*, Valentine Mitchell, Macmillan, London, 1992

BOOTH, 1889
Charles Booth, *Life and Labour of the People in London* (vol. 1), Macmillan, London, 1889

BOTÍN, 1988
M. de Luis Botín, *Españoles en el Reino Unido*, Ministero de Trabajo y Seguridad Social, Madrid, 1988

BRAND, 1902
William F. Brand, *London Life Seen with German Eyes*, A. Siegle, London, 1902

BREITENSTEIN & HOMMERICH, 1976
Rolf Breitenstein and Angelika Hommerich (eds), *German Sites in London*, Oswald Wolff, London, 1976

BRETT, 1992
Judith Brett, *Robert Menzies' Forgotten People*, Macmillan Australia, Melbourne, 1992

BROCK, 1953
P. Brock, 'Polish Democrats and English Radicals', *Journal of Modern History*, vol. 25, 1953, pp139–56

BROCK, 1961
P. Brock, 'Polish Socialists in Early Victorian England', *Polish Review*, vol. 6, 1961, pp33–53

BROOKE & KEIR, 1975
Christopher Brooke and Gillian Keir, *London 800–1216: The Shaping of a City*, Secker and Warburg, London, 1975

BURCKHARDT, 1798
Johann Gottlieb Burckhardt, *Kirchen-Geschichte der Deutschen Gemeinden in London*, Ludwig Friedrich Fues, Tübingen, 1798

CARR, 1982
Raymond Carr, *Spain 1808–1975*, Oxford University Press, Oxford, 1982

CASTRILLON, 1984
Santiago Castrillon, 'Latin Americans in London', *Ten 8*, issue 16, 1984

CENSUS OF ENGLAND AND WALES, 1861
Census of England and Wales, 1861, vol. 2, Her Majesty's Stationery Office, London, 1863

CENSUS OF ENGLAND AND WALES, 1911
Census of England and Wales, 1911, Birthplaces, His Majesty's Stationery Office, London, 1913

CESARANI, 1990
David Cesarani (ed.), *The Making of Modern Anglo-Jewry*, Blackwell, Oxford, 1990

CHAPMAN, 1980
Stanley D. Chapman, 'The migration of merchant enterprise: German merchant houses in England in the eighteenth and nineteenth centuries', *Bankhistorisches Archiv*, vol. 6, 1980, pp20–41

CLANCY et al, 1991
Mary Clancy, John F. Cunningham and Alf MacLochlainn (eds), *The Emigrant Experience: Papers Presented at the Second Annual Mary Murray Weekend Seminar, Galway, 30 March– 1 April 1990*, Galway Labour History Group, Galway, 1991

COLEMAN, D. C., 1977
D. C. Coleman, *The Economy of England 1450– 1750*, OUP, Oxford, 1977

COLEMAN, P., 1991
Peter Coleman, *The Real Barry Humphries*, Coronet, London, 1991

COLLINGWOOD & WRIGHT, 1991
R. G. Collingwood and R. P. Wright, *The Roman Inscriptions of Britian. Volume 2, Fascicule 3*, Alan Sutton Publishing, Stroud, 1991

COLLINS, 1957
S. Collins, *Coloured Minorities in Britain*, Lutterworth Press, London, 1957

COLPI, 1991 (a)
Terri Colpi, *The Italian Factor: The Italian Community in Great Britain*, Mainstream, Edinburgh, 1991

COLPI, 1991 (b)
Terri Colpi, *Italians Forward: A Visual History of the Italian Community in Great Britain*, Mainstream, Edinburgh, 1991

COMMAGER, 1974
Henry Steele Commager, *Britain Through American Eyes*, McGraw-Hill, Maidenhead, 1974

CONNOR, 1987
Tom Connor, *The London Irish*, London Strategic Policy Unit, London, 1987

CONSTANTINIDES, 1977
Pamela Constantinides, 'The Greek-Cypriots: factors in the maintenance of ethnic identity', in *Between Two Cultures: Migrants and Minorities in Britain*, James L. Watson (ed.), Basil Blackwell, Oxford, 1977

COPLEY & VISRAM, 1989
Anthony Copley and Rozina Visram (eds), 'Indians in Britain – past and present', *Indo-British Review. A Journal of History*, vol. 16, no. 2, June 1989, pp1–199

COWIE, 1956
Leonard W. Cowie, *Henry Newman: An American in London 1708–43*, S.P.C.K., London, 1956

CUNNINGHAM, 1897
W. Cunningham, *Alien Immigrants to England*, 1897, reprinted Frank Cass & Co., London and Augustus M. Kelley, New York, 1969

CURTIS, L., 1984
Liz Curtis, *Nothing but the Same Old Story: The Roots of Anglo–Irish Racism*, Information on Ireland, London, 1984

CURTIS, L. P., 1971
Lewis P. Curtis, Jr, *Apes and Angels: The Irishman in Victorian Caricature*, David & Charles, Newton Abbot, 1971

DABYDEEN, 1987
David Dabydeen, *Hogarth's Blacks: Images of Blacks in Eighteenth Century English Art*, Manchester University Press, Manchester, 1987

DAVIES, 1972
N. Davies, 'The Poles in Great Britain, 1914–1919', *Slavonic and East European Review*, vol. 50, 1972, pp63–9

DAVIS, 1991
Graham Davis, *The Irish in Britain 1815–1914*, Gill & Macmillan, Dublin, 1991

DIAMOND, 1974
A. S. Diamond, 'The community of resettlement 1656–1684', *The Jewish Historical Society of England*, vol. 24, 1974

DIMBLEBY & REYNOLDS, 1988
David Dimbleby and David Reynolds, *An Ocean Apart: The Relationship Between Britain and America in the Twentieth Century*, BBC Hodder & Stoughton, London 1988

DIRECTORY OF AMERICANS, 1901
Directory of Americans Resident in London, American Firms and Agencies, Eden Fisher, London, 1901

DOLLINGER, 1970
Philippe Dollinger, *The German Hansa*, Macmillan, London, 1970

DORGEEL, 1881
Heinrich Dorgeel, *Die Deutsche Colonie in London*, A. Siegle, London, 1881

DUTHIE, 1987
Ruth Duthie, 'Introduction of plants to Britain in the 16th and 17th centuries by strangers and refugees', *Proceedings of the Huguenot Society*, vol. 24, no. 5, 1987, pp403–20

EADE, 1990
John Eade, 'Bangladeshi community organisation and leadership in Tower Hamlets, East London', in *South Asians Overseas: Migration and Ethnicity*, Colin Clarke, Ceri Peach and Steven Vertovec (eds), CUP, Cambridge, 1990

ECONOMU & HALLIDAY, 1988
Marianna Economu and Paul Halliday, *Here and There: The Greek Cypriot Community in London*, Interprinter, Salonica, 1988

EDUCATION IN EXILE, 1956
Education in Exile: A History of the Committee for the Education of Poles in Great Britain, Her Majesty's Stationery Office, London, 1956

EDWARDS & WALVIN, 1983
Paul Edwards and James Walvin, *Black Personalities in the Era of the Slave Trade*, Macmillan, London, 1983

ENDELMAN, 1979
Todd M. Endelman, *The Jews of Georgian England: Tradition and Change in a Liberal Society, 1714–1830*, Jewish Publication Society of America, Philadelphia, 1979

ENDELMAN, 1991
Todd M. Endelman, *Radical Assimilation in English Jewish History*, Indiana University Press, Indianapolis, 1991

ENGELSING, 1961
Rolf Engelsing, *Bremen als Auswandererhafen 1683–1880*, Bremener Staatsarchiv, Bremen, 1961

ETHNIC COMMUNITIES ORAL HISTORY PROJECT, 1988
Polish Reminiscence Group, *Passport to Exile: The Polish Way to London*, Ethnic Communities Oral History Project, London, 1988

ETHNIC COMMUNITIES ORAL HISTORY PROJECT, 1989
Polish Reminiscence Group, *Travelling Light: Poles on Foreign Soil*, Ethnic Communities Oral History Project, London, 1989

FAHEY, 1991
Paddy Fahey, *The Irish in London: Photographs and Memories*, Centerprise, London, 1991

FARRELL, 1990
Jerome Farrell, 'The German community in 19th century East London', *East London Record*, no. 13, 1990, pp2–8

FAWZI EL-SOLH, 1991
Camillia Fawzi El-Solh, 'Somalis in London's East End: a community striving for recognition', *New Community*, vol. 17, no. 4, July 1991

FAWZI EL-SOLH, 1992
Camillia Fawzi El-Solh, 'Arab communities in Britain: cleavages and commonalities', *Islam & Christian–Muslim Relations Journal*, vol. 3, no. 2, December 1992

FILE & POWER, 1981
Nigel File and Chris Power, *Black Settlers in Britain 1555–1958*, Heinemann Educational Books, London, 1981

FINESTEIN, 1957
Israel Finestein, *A Short History of Anglo-Jewry*, Lincoln & Prager, London, 1957

FISHMAN, 1975
William J. Fishman, *East End Jewish Radicals*, Duckworth, London, 1975

FLETCHER JONES, 1990
Pamela Fletcher Jones, *The Jews of Britain. A Thousand Years of History*, The Windrush Press, Gloucestershire, 1990

FRAME, 1992
Janet Frame, *You are About to Enter the Human Heart*, Women's Press, London, 1992

FRYER, 1984
Peter Fryer, *Staying Power: The History of Black People in Britain*, Pluto Press, London, 1984

GAINER, 1972
B. Gainer, *The Alien Invasion*, Heinemann, London, 1972

GARRATT, 1853
Samuel Garratt, *Motives for Missions*, Constable, London, 1853

GARTNER, 1960
L. Gartner, *The Jewish Immigrant in England 1870–1915*, George Allen & Unwin, London, 1960

GEORGE, 1925
M. Dorothy George, *London Life in the Eighteenth Century*, 1925, reprinted Penguin, Harmondsworth, 1966

GIFFORD, 1990
Zerbanoo Gifford, *The Golden Thread. Asian Experiences of Post-Raj Britain*, Pandora, London, 1990

GILLEY, 1969
Sheridan Gilley, 'The Roman Catholic mission to the Irish in London', *Recusant History*, vol. 10, no. 3, 1969, pp123–45

GILLEY 1971
Sheridan Gilley, 'Heretic London, holy poverty and the Irish poor', *Downside Review*, 89, no. 294, 1971, pp64–89

GILLEY, 1973
Sheridan Gilley, 'The Garibaldi riots of 1862', *Historical Journal*, vol. 16, no. 4, 1973, pp697–732

GILLEY, 1985
Sheridan Gilley, 'The Irish', *History Today*, June 1985, pp 17–23

GILLMAN & GILLMAN, 1980
Peter and Leni Gilman, *Collar the Lot!*, Quartet Books, London, 1980

GOBBI, 1978
Claire Gobbi, 'The Spanish quarter of Somers Town: an immigrant community 1820–30', *Camden History Review*, no. 6, 1978

GOODWAY, 1982
David Goodway, *London Chartism 1838–1848*, Cambridge University Press, Cambridge, 1982

GREATER LONDON COUNCIL, 1986
Greater London Council, *A History of the Black Presence in London*, GLC, London, 1986

GREEN, D. R., 1988
David R. Green, 'Little Italy in Victorian London: Holborn's Italian Community', *Camden History Review*, no. 15, 1988

GREEN, J., 1990
Jonathon Green, *Them. Voices from the Immigrant Community in Contemporary Britain*, Secker & Warburg, London, 1990

GREENWOOD, 1874
James Greenwood, *The Wilds of London*, Chatto & Windus, London, 1874

GREER, 1990
Germaine Greer, *Daddy, We Hardly Knew You*, Picador, London, 1990

GULA (forthcoming)
J. Gula, *The Roman Catholic Church in the History of the Polish Exiled Community in Britain, 1939–1950*, School of Slavonic and East European Studies, London, (forthcoming)

GUNDARA & DUFFIELD, 1992
Jagdish S. Gundara and Ian Duffield (eds), *Essays on the History of Blacks in Britain from Roman Times to the Mid-twentieth Century*, Avebury, Aldershot, 1992

GWYNN, 1985
Robin D. Gwynn, *Huguenot Heritage: The History and Contribution of the Huguenots in Britain*, Routledge & Kegan Paul, London, 1985

HACKMANN, 1991
Willem Hackmann, 'Nicolaus Kratzer: the King's Astronomer and Renaissance instrument-maker', in *Henry VIII: A European Court in England*, D. Starkey (ed.), Collins & Brown, London, 1991

HALLIDAY, 1992
Fred Halliday, *Arabs in Exile: Yemeni Migrants in Urban Britain*, I. B. Tauris, London, 1992

HAZELKORN, 1990
Ellen Hazelkorn, *Irish Immigrants Today: A Socio-Economic Profile of Contemporary Irish Emigrants and Immigrants in the UK*, PNL Irish Studies Centre Occasional Papers Series, Polytechnic of North London Press, London, 1990

HAZELTON, 1991
Fran Hazelton, *London's American Past: A Guided Tour*, Papermac, London, 1991

HENIG, 1984
Martin Henig, 'A cache of Roman intaglios from Eastcheap, City of London', *Transactions of the London and Middlesex Archaeological Society*, vol. 35, 1984, pp11–15

HIRO, 1991
Dilip Hiro, *Black British, White British: A History of Race Relations in Britain* (rev. edn), Grafton Books, London, 1991

HIRSCHFELD, 1984
Gerhard Hirschfeld (ed.), *Exile in Great Britain: Refugees from Hitler's Germany*, Berg, Leamington Spa, 1984

HITCHENS, 1990
Christopher Hitchens, *Blood, Class and Nostalgia: Anglo-American Ironies*, Chatto & Windus, London, 1990

HOLMES, C., 1979
Colin Holmes, *Anti-Semitism in British Society 1876–1939*, Edward Arnold, London, 1979
HOLMES, C., 1988
Colin Holmes, *John Bull's Island: Immigration and British Society, 1871-1971*, Macmillan Education, Basingstoke, 1988
HOLMES, M., 1965
Martin Holmes, 'Evil May Day 1517: the story of a riot', *History Today*, vol. 15, 1965, pp642–50
HONEYBOURNE, 1961
Marjorie Honeybourne, 'The pre-Expulsion cemetery of the Jews in London', *Transactions of the Jewish Historical Society of England*, vol. 20, 1961, pp145-59
HUGHES, 1987
Robert Hughes, *The Fatal Shore*, Collins Harvill, London, 1987
HUMPHRIES, 1992
Barry Humphries, *More Please*, Vintage, London, 1992
HUMPHRIES & TAYLOR, 1986
Steve Humphries and John Taylor, *The Making of Modern London 1945–1985*, Sidgwick & Jackson, London, 1986
HYAMSON, 1950
A. Hyamson, *The Sephardim of England*, Methuen, London, 1950
JACKSON, 1963
John Archer Jackson, *The Irish in Britain*, Routledge & Kegan Paul, London and The Press of Western Reserve University, Cleveland, 1963
JAMES, 1985
Clive James, *Falling Towards England*, Jonathan Cape, London, 1985
JAMES, 1990
Clive James, *May Week was in June: Unreliable Memoirs III*, Jonathan Cape, London, 1990
JONES, D., 1979
Douglas Jones, 'The Chinese in Britain: origins and development of a community', *New Community*, vol. 7, no. 3, 1979
JONES, E. A., 1924
Edward Alfred Jones, *American Members of the Inns of Court*, Saint Catherine Press, London 1924
JONES, P.R., 1982
Peter R. Jones, *Vietnamese Refugees: A Study of Their Reception and Resettlement in the United Kingdom*, Research and Planning Unit, Paper no. 13, Home Office, London, 1982
JONES, P.R., 1983
Peter R. Jones, 'Vietnamese refugees in the UK: the reception programme', *New Community*, vol. 10, no. 3, Spring 1983
KADISH, 1992
S. Kadish, *Bolsheviks and British Jews*, Valentine Mitchell, London, 1992

KATSCHER, 1887
Leopold Katscher, 'German life in London', *Nineteenth Century*, vol. 21, 1887, pp726–41
KAY & MILES, 1992
D. Kay and R. Miles, *Refugees or Migrant Workers? European Volunteer Workers in Britain, 1946–1951*, Routledge, London and New York, 1992
KELLENBENZ, 1978
Hermann Kellenbenz, 'German immigrants in England', in *Immigrants and Minorities in British Society*, Colin Holmes (ed.), George Allen & Unwin, London, 1978, pp63–80
KENIN, 1979
Richard Metz Kenin, *Return to Albion: Americans in England 1760–1940*, National Portrait Gallery, and Smithsonian Institution, Holt, Rinehart and Winston, New York, 1979
KENT, 1950
William Kent, *London for Americans*, Staples Press, St Albans, 1950
KERSHEN, 1988 (a)
A. J. Kershen, *Trade Unionism Amongst the Tailoring Workers of London 1872–1915*, London Museum of Jewish Life, London, 1988
KERSHEN, 1988 (b)
A. J. Kershen, *The Women's Wholesale Clothing Industry*, London Museum of Jewish Life, London, 1988
KERSHEN, 1990
A. J. Kershen, *150 Years of Progressive Judaism*, London Museum of Jewish Life, London, 1990
KERSHEN & ROMAIN (forthcoming)
A. J. Kershen and J. Romain, *A History of Reform Judaism in Britain*, Valentine Mitchell, London, (forthcoming)
KIERNAN, 1978
V. G. Kiernan, 'Britons old and new', in *Immigrants and Minorities in British Society*, Colin Holmes (ed.), George Allen & Unwin, London, 1978, pp23–59
KINROSS, 1991
Felicity Kinross, *Coffee and Ices: The Story of Carlo Gatti in London*, Felicity Kinross, London, 1991
KNITTLE, 1936
Walter Allen Knittle, *Early Eighteenth Century Palatine Emigration*, 1936, reprinted Genealogical Publishing Company, Baltimore, 1979
KUSHNER, 1992
T. Kushner, *The Jewish Heritage in British History*, Valentine Mitchell, London, 1992
LAI, 1986
Annie Lai et al, 'Chinatown Annie: the East End opium trade 1920–1935', *Oral History Journal*, vol. 14, no. 1, 1986
LEES, 1979
Lynn Hollen Lees, *Exiles of Erin: Irish Migrants in Victorian London*, Manchester University Press, Manchester, 1979

LENNON, McADAM & O'BRIEN, 1988
Mary Lennon, Marie McAdam and Joanne
O'Brien, *Across the Water: Irish Women's Lives in
Britain*, Virago Press, London, 1988
LEONI, 1966
Peppino Leoni, *I Shall Die on the Carpet*, Leslie
Frewin, London, 1966
LESLIE, 1963
R. F. Leslie, 'The background of Jewish
immigration', *East London Papers*, vol. 6, no. 2,
December 1963
LIPMAN, 1950
V. D. Lipman, *Social History of the Jews in England
1850–1950*, Watts, London, 1950
LIPMAN, 1991
V. D. Lipman, *History of the Jews in Britain Since
1858*, Leicester University Press, Leicester, 1991
LITTLE, 1948
Kenneth Little, *Negroes in Britain: A Study of Racial
Relations in English Society*, Routledge & Kegan
Paul, London and Boston, 1948 (rev. edn 1972)
LOADES, 1986
David Loades, *The Tudor Court*, Batsford,
London, 1986
LORIMER, 1978
Douglas A. Lorimer, *Colour, Class and the
Victorians: English Attitudes to the Negro in the Mid-
nineteenth Century*, Leicester University Press and
Holmes & Meier, New York 1978
LOTZ & PEGG, 1986
Rainer Lotz and Ian Pegg (eds), *Under the
Imperial Carpet: Essays in Black History
1780–1950*, Rabbit Press, Crawley, 1986
LOVELL, 1977
John Lovell, 'The Irish and the London docks',
*Bulletin of the Society for the Study of Labour
History*, no. 35, 1977, pp16–17
LOYN, 1962
H. R. Loyn, *Anglo-Saxon England and the Norman
Conquest*, Longman, London, 1962
LUNN, 1980
Kenneth Lunn (ed.), *Hosts, Immigrants and Min-
orities: Historical Responses to Newcomers in British
Society 1870–1914*, Dawson, Folkestone, 1980
LUNN, 1993
Kenneth Lunn, 'Irish labour recruitment schemes
1937–1948', *Labour History Reveiw*, vol. 57, pt 3,
1992, pp20–23
MCAULEY 1993
Ian McAuley, *Guide to Ethnic London*, 2nd ed.,
Immel Publishing Ltd, London, 1993
MACCOLL & WALLACE, 1989
Gail MacColl and Carol McD. Wallace, *To Marry
an English Lord: The Victorian and Edwardian
Experience*, Sidgwick & Jackson, London, 1989
MACINTYRE, 1986
Stuart Macintyre, *The Oxford History of Australia:
vol. 4, The Succeeding Age, 1901–1942*, OUP,
Melbourne, 1986

MCKELLAR, 1991
Elizabeth McKellar, *The German Hospital at
Hackney: A Social and Architectural History*,
Hackney Society Publication, London, 1991
MARGOLIOUTH, 1852
Moses Margoliouth, *A History of the Jews of Great
Britain*, vol. 2, Richard Bentley, London 1852
MARKS, 1990
Laura Marks, *Working Wives and Working
Mothers: A Comparative Study of Irish and East
European Jewish Married Women's Work and
Motherhood in East London 1870–1914*, PNL Irish
Studies Centre Occasional Papers Series, PNL
Press, London, 1990
MARR, 1992
David Marr, *Patrick White: A Life*, Vintage,
London, 1992
MARSDEN, 1975
Peter Marsden, 'Excavation of a Roman palace
site in London, 1961–1972', *Transactions of the
London and Middlesex Archaeological Society*, vol.
26, 1975, pp1–102
MARSHALL, 1991
Oliver Marshall, *Ship of Hope*, Ethnic
Communities Oral History Project/The North
Kensington Archive at Nottingdale Urban
Studies Centre, London 1991
MARTIN & PARKER, 1988
C. Martin and G. Parker, *The Spanish Armada*,
Hamish Hamilton, London, 1988
MAY, 1978
J. P. May, 'The Chinese in Britain, 1860–1914', in
Immigrants and Minorities in British Society,
Colin Holmes (ed.), George Allen & Unwin,
London, 1978
MAYHEW, 1861
Henry Mayhew, *London Labour and the London
Poor – a Cyclopedia of Conditions and Earnings*,
Griffin, Bohn and Co., London, 1861
MORTON, 1986
Brian N. Morton, *Americans in London: An
Anecdotal Street Guide to the Homes and Haunts
of Americans from John Adams to Fred Astaire*,
Mac-donald, Queen Anne Press, London, 1986
MOSSE *et al*, 1991
W. E. Mosse *et al* (eds), *Second Chance: Two
Centuries of German-speaking Jews in the United
Kingdom*, J. C. B. Mohr, Tübingen, 1991
MUDIE-SMITH, 1905
Richard Mudie-Smith, *Religious Life of the People
in London*, Hodder & Stoughton, London, 1905
MULVEY, 1983
Christopher Mulvey, *Anglo-American Landscapes:
A Study of Nineteenth-Century Anglo-American
Travel Literature*, CUP, Cambridge, 1983
MUÑOZ, 1887
A. Muñoz, *Sumaria y Verdadera Relación del Buen
Viage que el Principe Philipe hizo en Inglaterra*,
Sociedad de Bibliófilos Españoles 15,
Madrid, 1887

MURDOCH, 1985
Tessa Murdoch (ed.), *The Quiet Conquest: Huguenots in London 1685 to 1985*, Museum of London, London, 1985

NAJDER, 1983
Z. Najder, *Joseph Conrad: A Chronicle*, CUP, Cambridge, 1983

NATIONAL MARITIME MUSEUM, 1976
National Maritime Museum, *1776: The British Story of the American Revolution*, National Maritime Museum, London, 1976

NEVILLE, 1971
Richard Neville, *Play Power*, Paladin, London, 1971

NEWMAN, 1976
A. Newman, *The United Synagogue 1870–1970*, Routledge & Kegan Paul, London, 1976

NEWSON, 1982
Gerald Newson, *American London: People and Places of Popular and Historic Interest*, Q Books Ltd, Edgware, 1982

NG, 1968
Ng Kwee Choo, *The Chinese in London*, OUP for Institute of Race Relations, London, 1968

NICOLSON, 1974
Colin Nicolson, *Strangers to England. Immigration to England 1100–1952*, Wayland Publishers, London, 1974

NORTON, 1973
Mary Beth Norton, 'The fate of some black loyalists of the American Revolution', in *Journal of Negro History*, vol. 57, 1973

NORTON, 1974
Mary Beth Norton, *The British Americans: The Loyalist Exiles in England 1774–1789*, Constable, London, 1974

OAKLEY, 1987 (a)
Robin Oakley, *Changing Patterns of Distribution of Cypriot Settlement*, Research Paper 5, Centre for Research in Ethnic Relations, University of Warwick, Warwick, 1987

OAKLEY, 1987 (b)
Robin Oakley, 'The control of Cypriot migration to Britain between the wars', *Immigrants and Minorities*, vol. 6, no. 1, March 1987

O'CONNELL, 1993
James O'Connell, 'The *Irish Post* survey', *The Irish Post*, 12 December 1992—23 January 1993

ORMROD, 1973
David Ormrod, *The Dutch in London*, Her Majesty's Stationery Office, London, 1973

Ó SÚILLEABHÁIN, 1989
Donncha Ó Súilleabháin, *Conradh na Gaeilge i Londain 1894–1917*, Conradh na Gaeilge, Dublin, 1989

Ó TUATHAIGH, 1991
M. A. G. Ó Tuathaigh, 'The historical pattern of Irish emigration: some labour aspects', in *The Emigrant Experience: Papers Presented at the Second Annual Mary Murray Weekend Seminar, Galway, 30 March—1 April 1990*, Mary Clancy, John F. Cunningham and Alf MacLochlainn (eds), Galway Labour History Group, Galway, 1991, pp9–28

PANAYI, 1989
Panikos Panayi, 'Anti-German riots in London during the First World War', *German History*, vol. 7, no. 2, 1989, pp184–203

PANAYI, 1991
Panikos Panayi, *The Enemy in Our Midst: Germans in Britain During the First World War*, Berg, Oxford, 1991

PATTERSON, 1964
Sheila Patterson, 'Polish London', in *London, Aspects of Change*, R. Glass et al (eds), MacGibbon & Kee, London, 1964

PATTERSON, 1968
Sheila Patterson, *Immigrants in Industry*, OUP, London and New York, 1968

PATTERSON, 1977
Sheila Patterson, 'The Poles: an exile community in Britain', in *Between Two Cultures: Migrants and Minorities in Britain*, James L. Watson (ed.), Basil Blackwell, Oxford, 1977

PELLAPAISIOTIS, n.d.
Haris Pellapaisiotis, *Laying the Foundations*, Theatro Technis Project, Centurion Press, London, n.d.

PETTEGREE, 1987
Andrew Pettegree 'The stranger community in Marian London', *Proceedings of the Huguenot Society*, vol. 24, no. 5, 1987, pp390–402

POLISH UNIVERSITY COLLEGE, 1953
Polish University College. Report of the Principal for the Period 1947–1953, London, 1953

POLLINS, 1982
Harold Pollins, *Economic History of the Jews in Britain*, Litman Library of Jewish Civilisation, London, 1982

POLLINS, 1985
Harold Pollins, 'The Jews', *History Today*, July 1985

QUINLIVAN & ROSE, 1982
Patrick Quinlivan and Paul Rose, *The Fenians in England 1865–1872: A Sense of Insecurity*, John Calder, London and Riverrun Press, New York, 1982

RACZYŃSKI, 1962
E. Raczyński, *In Allied London*, Weidenfeld & Nicolson, London, 1962

RIEGER, 1942
J. Rieger, 'The British Crown and the German churches', in *And Other Pastors of Thy Flock*, F. Hildebrandt (ed.), CUP, Cambridge 1942, pp101–23

ROBINSON, 1986
Vaughan Robinson, *Transients, Settlers and Refugees. Asians in Britain*, Clarendon Press, Oxford, 1986

ROBINSON, 1990
Vaughan Robinson, 'Boom and gloom: the success and failure of South Asians in Britain', in *South Asians Overseas: Migration and Ethnicity*, Colin Clarke, Ceri Peach and Steven Vertovec (eds), CUP, Cambridge, 1990

ROBINSON & HALE, 1989
Vaughan Robinson and Samantha Hale, *The Geography of Vietnamese Secondary Migration in the UK* (Research Paper in Ethnic Relations – no. 10), Centre for Research in Ethnic Relations, University of Warwick, Coventry, 1989

RODRIGUEZ-SALGADO, 1988
Mia Rodriguez-Salgado, *Armada*, National Maritime Museum, London, 1988

ROSSITER, 1991
Ann Rossiter, 'Bringing the margins into the centre: a review of aspects of Irish women's emigration', in *Ireland's Histories: Aspects of State, Society and Ideology*, Seán Hutton and Paul Stewart (eds), Routledge, London and New York, 1991, pp223–42

ROTH, 1941
Cecil Roth, *A History of the Jews in England*, 1941, reprinted Clarendon Press, Oxford, 1978

ROTH, 1950
Cecil Roth, *The Great London Synagogue*, Edward Goldston & Sons, London, 1950

RUZ *et al*, 1984
Fernando Ruz *et al*, *Out of the Shadows: Migrants in Pimlico and Victoria*, Migrants Resource Centre, London, 1984

RYAN, 1894
W. P. Ryan, *The Irish Literary Revival: Its History, Pioneers and Possibilities*, Ward & Downey, London 1894

SAINSBURY, 1987
John Sainsbury, *Disaffected Patriots: London Supporters of the American Revolution 1769–82*, Alan Sutton, Gloucester, 1987

SALVONI, 1990
Elena Salvoni (with Sandy Fawkes), *Elena: A Life in Soho*, Quartet Books, London, 1990

SCHAIBLE, 1885
Karl Heinrich Schaible, *Geschichte der Deutschen in England*, Karl J. Trübner, Strasbourg, 1885

SCHISCHA, 1974
A. Schischa, 'Spanish Jews in London in 1494', *The Jewish Historical Society of England*, vol. 24, 1974

SCHÖLL, 1852
Carl Schöll, *Geschichte der Deutschen Evangelischen Kirchen in England*, Steinkopf, Stuttgart, 1852

SCHÖNBERGER, 1937
Gustav Schönberger, 'Geschichte der Deutschen in England', in *Festschrift zum 70. Geburtstag von Freiherrn Bruno von Schröder*, Gustav Schönberger (ed.), Finsbury Press, London, 1937

SCHWEITZER, 1989
Pam Schweitzer (ed.), *Across the Irish Sea: An Age Exchange Publication Based on Memories of London Irish Pensioners*, Age Exchange Theatre Trust, London 1989

SCOBIE, 1972
Edward Scobie, *Black Britannia: A History of Blacks in Britain*, Johnson Publishing Co., Chicago, 1972

SCOULOUDI, 1987
Irene Scouloudi, 'The stranger community in the metropolis, 1558–1640', in *Huguenots in Britain and their French Background, 1550–1800*, I. Scouloudi (ed.), Macmillan Press, London, 1987

SHANG, 1984 (a)
Anthony Shang, 'Chinatown and beyond', *Ten 8*, issue 16, 1984

SHANG, 1984 (b)
Anthony Shang, *The Chinese in Britain*, Batsford, London, 1984

SHANG, 1991
Anthony Shang, 'Seeds of Chinatown: the Chinese in Britain', in *Race and Social Work, A Guide to Training*, Vivienne Coombe and Alan Little (eds), Tavistock Publications, London, 1991

SHAW, GWYNN & THOMAS, 1985
R. A. Shaw, R. D. Gwynn and P. Thomas, *Huguenots in Wandsworth*, Wandsworth Borough Council, London, 1985

SHYLLON, 1974
Folarin O. Shyllon, *Black Slaves in Britain*, OUP for Institute of Race Relations, London, 1974

SHYLLON, 1977
Folarin O. Shyllon, *Black People in Britain 1555–1833*, OUP for Institute of Race Relations, London, 1977

SINCLAIR, 1980
Keith Sinclair, *A History of New Zealand*, Allen Lane, London, 1980

SMITH, 1874
J. T. Smith, *Vagabondiana or, Anecdotes of Mendicant Wanderers through the Streets of London with portraits of the most remarkable*, Chatto and Windus, London, 1874

SMITH, 1985
Terence P. Smith, *The Medieval Brickmaking Industry in England, 1400–1450*, British Archaeological Reports (British Series), 138, Oxford, 1985

SNOWMAN, 1977
Daniel Snowman, *Britain and America: An Interpretation of British and American Culture 1945 to 1975*, New York University Press, New York, 1977

SOCIETY OF FRIENDS OF FOREIGNERS IN DISTRESS, 1814
Society of Friends of Foreigners in Distress, *Songs, Duets, &c. in the Grand Miscellaneous Concert at King's Theatre, on Friday, June 3rd, 1814, for the Benefit of the Society of Friends of Foreigners in Distress*, D. N. Shury, London, 1814

SOMERSET, 1983
Felicity Somerset, 'Vietnamese refugees in Britain: resettlement experiences', *New Community*, vol. 10, no. 3, Spring 1983

SPECHT, 1989
Maureen Specht, *The German Hospital in London and the Community It Served 1845–1948*, Anglo-German Family History Society, London, 1989

SPILLER, 1926
Robert E. Spiller, *The American in England During the First Half Century of Independence*, Holt, New York, 1926

SPONZA, 1988
Lucio Sponza, *The Italian Immigrants in 19th Century Britain: Realities and Images*, Leicester University Press, Leicester, 1988

STERN, 1954
Walter M. Stern, 'The London sugar refiners around 1800', *Guildhall Miscellany*, no. 3, 1954, pp 25–36

STEWART–MACDONALD & MACDONALD, 1972
John Stewart-MacDonald and Leatrice D. MacDonald, *The Invisible Immigrants*, Runnymede Special Publication, London 1972

STRONG, 1984
Roy Strong, *The English Renaissance Miniature*, Thames & Hudson, London 1984

SWIDERSKA, 1962
H. Swiderska, 'J. Dantyszek: a Polish diplomat in England in 1522' *Oxford Slavonic Papers*, vol. 10, 1962, pp38–45

SWIFT & GILLEY, 1985
Roger Swift and Sheridan Gilley (eds), *The Irish in the Victorian City*, Croom Helm, London, 1985

SWIFT & GILLEY, 1989
Roger Swift and Sheridan Gilley (eds), *The Irish in Britain 1815–1939*, Pinter Publishers, London, 1989

SWORD, 1989
K. Sword (with N. Davies and J. Ciechanowski), *The Formation of the Polish Community in Britain*, School of Slavonic and East European Studies, London, 1989

TANNAHILL, 1958
J. A. Tannahill, *European Volunteer Workers in Britain*, Manchester University Press, Manchester, 1958

THRUPP, 1969
Sylvia L. Thrupp, 'Aliens in and around London in the fifteenth century', in *Studies in London History*, A. E. J. Hollander and W. Kellaway (eds), Hodder and Stoughton Ltd, London, 1969

TIMPE, 1909
Georg Timpe, *Die Deutsche St. Bonifatius Mission in London 1809–1909*, F. Mildner and Co., London, 1909

TOWEY, 1988
Peter Towey, 'German sugar bakers in the East End', *Anglo-German Family History Society Mitteilungsblatt*, vol. 5, 1988

TRUETA, 1980
Josep Trueta, *Trueta: Surgeon on War and Peace*, translated by Meli and Michael Strubell, Gollancz, London, 1980

VADGAMA, 1984
Kusoom Vadgama, *India in Britain: The Indian Contribution to the British Way of Life*, Robert Royce, London, 1984

VINCE, 1990
Alan Vince, *Saxon London. An Archaeological Investigation*, Seaby, London, 1990

VISRAM, 1986
Rozina Visram, *Ayahs, Lascars and Princes: Indians in Britain 1700–1947*, Pluto Press, London, 1986

VISRAM, 1987
Rozina Visram, *Indians in Britain*, Batsford, London, 1987

VON ARCHENHOLTZ, 1797
Johann Wilhelm von Archenholtz, *A Picture of England*, London, 1797

WALKER, 1964
Mack Walker, *Germany and the Emigration 1816–1885*, Harvard University Press, Cambridge, Massachusetts, 1964

WALLER, 1985
P. J. Waller, 'The Chinese', *History Today*, September 1985, pp8–15

WALTER, 1989
Bronwen Walter, *Irish Women in London: The Ealing Dimension*, Ealing Women's Unit, London, 1989

WALVIN, 1973
James Walvin, *Black and White: The Negro and English Society 1555–1945*, Allen Lane, London, 1973

WALVIN, 1984
James Walvin, *Passage to Britain: Immigration in British History and Politics*, Penguin Books/Belitha Press, Harmondsworth, 1984

WARD, 1899
Adolphus William Ward, *Great Britain and Hanover: Some Aspects of the Personal Union*, Clarendon Press, Oxford, 1899

WATSON, 1977
James L. Watson, 'The Chinese: Hong Kong villagers in the British catering trade', in *Between Two Cultures: Migrants and Minorities in Britain*, James L. Watson (ed.), Basil Blackwell, Oxford, 1977

WATTS, 1991
Karen Watts, 'Henry VIII and the founding of the Greenwich Armouries', in *Henry VIII: A European Court in England*, D. Starkey (ed.), Collins & Brown, London, 1991

WEINTRAUB, 1979
Stanley Weintraub, *The London Yankees: Portrait of American Writers and Artists in England 1894–1914*, W. H. Allen, London, 1979

WHITE, 1980
Jerry White, *Rothschild Buildings: Life in an East End Tenement Block, 1887–1920*, Routledge & Kegan Paul, London, 1980

WILLIAMS, 1963
Gwynn A. Williams, *Medieval London. From Commune to Capital*, The Athlone Press, London, 1963

WILLIAMSON, 1956
Geoffrey Williamson, *Star-spangled square. The Saga of Little America in London*, Bles, Barlavington, 1956

WILSON, A. R., 1978
Amrit Rao Wilson, *Finding a Voice: Asian Women in Britain*, Virago Press, London, 1978

WILSON, C., 1969
Charles Wilson, 'New introduction', in *Alien immigrants to England*, W. Cunningham, 1897, reprinted Frank Cass & Co., London and Augustus M. Kelley, New York, 1969

WRENCH, 1948
John Evelyn Wrench, *Transatlantic London: Three Centuries of Association between England and America*, Hutchinson, London, 1948

WRIGHT & TINLING, 1958
Louis B. Wright and Marion Tinling, *William Byrd of Virginia: The London Diary 1717–21*, OUP, Oxford, 1958

ZUBRZYCKI, 1956
Jerzy Zubrzycki, *Polish Immigrants in Britain: A Study in Adjustment*, Martinus Nijhoff, The Hague, 1956

List of Illustrations

The publishers would like to acknowledge the following institutions and individuals who have granted permission to reproduce their material in these pages:

223

List of Colour Plates

Index

Index

Retail trades *see* Shopkeepers;
   Street traders
Rhodesians 84
Riots:
   medieval 20, 35, 39
   eighteenth-century 21, 123
   in 1915 and 1919 22, 115, 164,
   171
   Notting Hill 22, 58–9
Roman London 3, 4, 5, 8, *29–32*,
   51, 111, 179
Rothschild family 9, 11, 14, 141,
   143, 205
Royal Navy 55, 163, 170
   see also Sailors

Sailors:
   accommodation for 11, 55,
   88–9, *163–4*, 171, 172
   Black 15, 26, 51, *52–5*, 198
   Chinese 11, 15, *88–9*, 90, 91,
   171
   Indian *see* Lascars
   Somali 163–5, 166, 168
   Yemeni 73–4
   see also Navy, merchant;
   Royal Navy
St Bartholomew's Hospital and
   Priory 34
St George's Lutheran Church 11,
   112
St Giles 10, 13, *119*
St Patrick's, Soho Square 10
St Paul's Cathedral 8, 32, *33*, 64, 70
St Peter's Church, Clerkenwell 131,
   133, 134, 135
Savoy 44
Savoy Palace 111
Scandinavians 11–12
Scholars *see* Students
Schools:
   American 62, 70
   Asian 177
   Chinese 90, *94*, 95, 96
   German 111, 112, 114, 195
   Greek-Cypriot 100, 104
   Italian 131, 133, 135
   Jewish 112, 139, 144, 145
   Polish 159, 160
   Spanish 182–3
   Vietnamese *187*
   see also Language teaching
Schools, British,
   immigrants in:
   Americans 63
   Asians 177
   Black 60
   Irish 124
   Polish 160
   Vietnamese 186, 187
Science and technology 41, 42, 45,
   130, 204
Scots 20, 39, 41
Second-generation 'immigrants' 25,
   74, 95, 160, 161, 183
Servicemen and -women 51, 82,
   163, 174, 68–70, 164, 155, 157,

158, 159
Shadwell 89, 171
Shoe-making and repairs 36, 44,
   136, 142, 155, 157
Shopkeepers/retailers 15, 17
   Asian 15, 174, 176
   German *113–15*
   Italian 10, 131
   Latin American 152
   Polish *155–6*, 160
   Spanish 182
   see also Businesspeople
Sikhs 12, *172–3*, 174
Silvertown 112, 155
Slaves/slavery 3–6, 13, 24, 26, 27,
   31, *51–5*, 60, 64–6
Socialism 122, 132, 142, 155, 172
Soho ix, 10
   Chinese in 10, 16, 88, 90, 93–4
   Cypriots in 10, *98–9*
   Huguenots in 10, 44, 46
   Italians in 10, 132, 134, 135, 136
   Vietnamese in 187
Somalis 7, 11, *163–8*
Somers Town *180*
Southall 12, 22, 174, 176
South Asians 3, 5, 7, 8, 11, 12, 15,
   17, 21, 23–5, *169–78*, *196–205*
South Kensington 13, 154, 159–60
Southwark 10, 34, 39, 42, 134, 179
   Irish in 10, 13, 119
   Vietnamese in 186, 187
Soviet Union 142–3, 148, 154, 157
Spanish people x, 16, 20, 36, 39,
   179–84
   see also Sephardic Jews
Spitalfields ix, 10–11, 42, 123, *173*,
   201, 204–5
   Huguenots in *10–11*, 44
   Jews in 139, 145
Sport 13, 19–20, 70, 80, 82, 127
   Black people in 19, 57, 59, 60, 65
   see also Boxers; Football
Sri Lanka 18, 171, 178
Stepney ix, 3, 144, *146*, 170
Stoke Newington 13, *106*
Strangers' Home 163, 171
Street traders 7, 129–30, 131, *134*,
   170–73
Suburbs 10–12, 76, 85, 112
   Greek-Cypriots in 100, 102,
   104, 105
   Jews in 12, 141, 145, 147
Sudanese 75
Suffragettes *172*, 198
Synagogues ix, 9, 11, 111, 139, 140,
   141–2, 145, 148
Tailoring *see* Clothing and textile
   industries
Taxation of foreigners 22, 35, 36,
   39
Television/broadcasting 19, 59, 80,
   95, 167
Thais 10, 185
Theatre 19, 66–7, 68, 121, 131
   Black people in 19, 59, 66–7
   Jewish 19, *144–5*

Tower Hamlets 11, 21, 164, 165,
   166, 174
Trade unions 13, 114, 142, 143,
   152, 176–7
Turkish-Cypriots 13, 98, *106–8*,
   205

Uganda *see* East African Asians
Underground railway 17, 67, 145
Unemployment:
   among Arabs 74, 78
   among Black people 55, 60
   among Chinese 95
   among Cypriots 98
   among Irish 123
   among Somalis 164, 166
   among Vietnamese 186
United States of America *see*
   Americans
Unskilled work 60, 73–7, 118–21,
   142, 157, 170
   see also Building work; Industry

Venezuela 152
Victoria, Queen 67, 141
Vietnamese 7, 95, *185–9*
Vikings 4, *32–4*

Walloons 10, 14, 41, 43
Weavers 7, *10–11*, *38–9*, 42, 44,
   201, 204
West Indians *see* Caribbean people
Whitechapel ix, 11, 155
   Germans in 11, 112, 113
   Irish in 13, 119
   Jews in 11, 142, *144*, 145
William I, King 4, *34*, 35
Women:
   Arab 74, 76, 77
   employment of 12, 40, *100*, 108,
   174
   Indian campaigners 172
   Irish 121, 123, 126
   and Judaism 142
   Vietnamese 187
   see also Marriage; Suffragettes
Word-processing 165, *166*
World War, First *21–2*, 23, 68–9,
   82, *114–16*, 134, 155, 163, 171
World War, Second 10, 15, 22,
   69–70, 90, 116, 134–5, 164
   Asians in *173*
   Poles in *155–8*, 160–61
Writers 17–18, 83
   American 18, 66
   Arab 75
   Asian 18
   Black 18, 59, 66
   Irish 18, 121
   Jewish 36, 144
   Polish 155

Yemenis 74–5, 79